PRICING STRATEGIES

PRICING STRATEGIES

ALFRED R. OXENFELDT

A DIVISION OF AMERICAN MANAGEMENT ASSOCIATIONS

Library of Congress Cataloging in Publication Data

Oxenfeldt, Alfred Richard, 1917–
  Pricing strategies.

  Includes bibliographical references and index.
  1. Price policy. I. Title.
HF5417.O94   338.5'26   74-78207
ISBN 0-8144-5368-6

© 1975 AMACOM
A division of American Management Associations, New York.

Second Printing

To My Beloved Martha

PREFACE

THE TITLE OF THIS BOOK suggests the importance of strategy formulation, but, regrettably, no brilliant stratagems are offered. On the contrary, a depressing message emerges from a close examination of almost every issue: Price problems are to be solved, if at all, only by resolving many fairly small questions that could be considered mere details. Brilliant strategies do exist and sometimes produce startling successes, but success is far more usually achieved by handling many matters of moderate importance very carefully, logically, and cleverly. Marketing and pricing executives should pursue several consistent, mutually reinforcing substrategies at any time; the development of effective substrategies is usually the pivotal element in successful price-making.

An analogy favored by management scientists likens an executive to an engineer at a control panel full of toggle switches—the executive's job is to find the right setting for each switch. Presumably the executive takes the interdependence of the switches into account, but such a view of business decisions leaves little room for strategy. Instead, it simply requires knowledge of existing functional relationships and interdependencies. Of course, these are not really very simple, and executives often do not know some of the switches they flip. Also, much that they do that is of the utmost importance bears little resemblance to flipping switches. Creating brand images, developing customer loyalties, cultivating harmonious relations with resellers, and creating favorable price impressions are not simple matters and cannot be likened to manipulating switches.

Strategy formulation consists in selecting attractive and feasible goals and then developing effective means to attain them. In marketing and pricing, both of these include a major qualitative element. They succeed or fail according to the content of the communication made, rather than the amount of effort made.

Regrettably, no known body of doctrine or proven procedures would lead an executive to the best price for his offering. Nevertheless, this book develops a general approach—a near-method—by which an executive should set prices in most cases by drawing maximum direction and guidance from what he knows about his market. There remains, however, the chance of error due to limited understanding or unexpected environmental changes.

The viewpoint adopted here is that of an executive in a private, profit-oriented firm—rather than that of a manager of a government-owned, philanthropic, nonprofit, or cooperative enterprise. It emphatically does not adopt the viewpoint of an economic theorist who seeks to explain basic economic forces.

Some general observations will be made to differentiate the focus of this book from others on the same subject.

1. Pricing is not mystical. A price is not set by impersonal market factors that combine to produce a result that reflects inexorable market forces. The setting and changing of price represent a species of human behavior that reflects perceptions, cogitations, aspirations, and preconceptions. It also reflects methods of making business decisions, the quality and availability of information, and also motivations, environment, and prior experience.

2. The subject of price has become closely associated in many writers' minds with competition, free enterprise, and business ethics. It therefore has acquired an emotional aspect that often obstructs understanding. We shall be careful to avoid that trap.

3. The level on which pricing should be discussed is a central one for both author and reader. Most readers of this book seek help for quite specific problems. I do not know what specific problems are facing all of my readers, and detailed help for any one reader would almost certainly bore most others.

I expect the reader to add to what I say and to select from what I say those things that apply. The reader knows vastly more about the detailed facts, behavior patterns, perception biases, and so forth, in his industry situation than any author could know.

4. The subject of pricing is treated here from the same viewpoint—and applies many of the concepts, research techniques, and management procedures—discussed in writings about advertising and personal selling. Thus the subject is treated as one of many interrelated marketing instruments that pose most of the usual problems of management—rather than as a basic economic factor that determines the general level of business activity or the manner in which resources are allocated.

5. Most of what is said here is too general to resolve a specific issue or dictate a specific pricing decision. On the other hand, most of the things said here are sufficiently general to apply to a large majority of business pricing problems. Readers must select the concepts and discussion that do apply most to their problems.

6. Despite point 5, the treatment of pricing here is far more detailed, specific, and concrete than is now found in the business literature. That is the chief difference between this book and others on the subject. It is by trying to push the discussion of pricing to the point of actual decision in a concrete context that I have selected the aspects of the subject to treat in depth. The result has been a very different mix of subjects than is found in existing treatments.

7. This book may be viewed as an almost equal blend of pricing and decision making. Underlying the discussion of price-setting presented here is a decision methodology that is central to the price-setter's task. Recognition that markets are dynamic, data are faulty and costly, and business goals are multiple and conflicting makes pricing a very different kind of activity from what it would be if the price-setter knew his costs and demand and sought to maximize short-run profits. Decision making in the face of ignorance, uncertainty, organizational constraints, time pressures, and so on, is what price-setting means in practice, and the subject is discussed in that context here.

8. This book often touches on nonpricing matters, inasmuch as price is at least a partial substitute for and a constant complement to advertising, product quality, personal selling, customer service, and marketing channel decisions. To treat price in isolation is to pass over perhaps the most central concern of a price-setter, namely, the interdependence of price and other elements in the marketing mix and the problem of choosing among them when a choice is possible.

Readers who are impatient to learn the author's views on how to set price are encouraged to skip Chapters 1 and 2.

This book was written largely because of the invitation and encouragement of Ernest Miller of the American Management Associations.

Beyond this, Mr. Miller commented on the outline of the book and read large sections in early draft. His suggestions were most helpful and his reassurance was most welcome.

L. Scott Miller (no relation to the first) of Exxon Corporation researched the recent literature on pricing for me and almost derailed the project by asserting that "Nothing I've read about pricing will really tell an executive how to set price; all [those] writings . . . only give broad general guidance on how to do part of the job but not nearly as much help as a price-setter needs and should be given." The validity of this statement led me to discard my outline for the book and reconceptualize the project altogether, a task which delayed its completion for a year. Scott Miller has read the final version of the manuscript and says that his earlier assertion no longer holds.

Dr. Arthur R. Burns, my teacher 35 years ago, gave the manuscript and proofs a very searching reading and made many suggestions and criticisms, large and small. The book probably would have been better if I had accepted all of his suggestions; it has been greatly improved because I carried out most of them. Anthony O. Kelly and Stanley Kostman read parts of the manuscript in an early version and indicated opportunities for improvement.

I am most grateful for all of the help these people have given me. Inasmuch as none of them has volunteered to accept responsibility for the shortcomings of the book, I do so reluctantly, for I fear they are many.

Alfred R. Oxenfeldt

CONTENTS

The Price-Setter's Responsibilities

THE PEOPLE WHO ARE RESPONSIBLE for setting price on behalf of private businesses, public utilities, and government enterprises perform very different functions, engage in highly dissimilar activities, and occupy diverse positions within their organizations. Given its importance, the pricing function is performed in a surprisingly haphazard way, and the people who are actually responsible for price decisions often have titles that make no reference to pricing. Regardless of title, however, we will refer to such executives as price-setters.

Under the circumstances, it would not be particularly helpful to describe what a cross section of price-setters do. Far more helpful would be a description of what a price-setter should do and the qualities he should have if he is to do those things well. Accordingly, we shall discuss the skills, abilities, knowledge, and personal qualities of a top-notch price-setter, the responsibilities he should bear, the kind of organization he should manage, to whom he should report, the kinds of difficulties he usually faces, and the kinds of opportunities he should seek.

WHERE THE PRICE-SETTER FITS IN A BUSINESS ORGANIZATION

The price-setter becomes deeply involved in at least three usually quite separate areas of business: costing, finance, and marketing. In most cases

2

his functions are primarily concerned with marketing, and so they require the application of marketing principles and a close association with marketing executives. Ordinarily his involvement with costs is as a user of data assembled by the accounting/control department; not infrequently he is an important critic of cost data. He is also involved in matters of active concern to the finance department, because his decisions commonly affect both the firm's cash flow and its estimated future rates of return. Again, however, his concern with financial matters is not as a decision maker. Here he serves mainly as a provider of data; in particular he estimates what the rates of return would be if different price schedules were adopted. Thus the price-setter would seem to belong in the marketing department, rather than in accounting or finance. But where does he belong in the marketing department?

In general, the price-setter appears to perform functions very different from but closely related to those of the director of advertising, the sales manager, the manager of customer service, and the product planner. If we had to place him in an organization chart, he would report to the vice president of marketing who, in turn, would report to the executive vice president or a group vice president (see Figure 1-1). Other firms are organized quite differently; they have what is called a product manager organization. The responsibility for pricing—as well as for marketing planning, advertising, personal sales, packaging, special promotions, customer service, and product design—is vested in a brand manager. The brand manager reports to a product manager who supervises several

Figure 1-1. Price-setting responsibility in the usual business hierarchy.

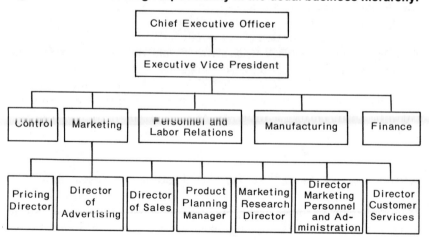

Figure 1-2. Price-setting responsibility in a product manager setup.

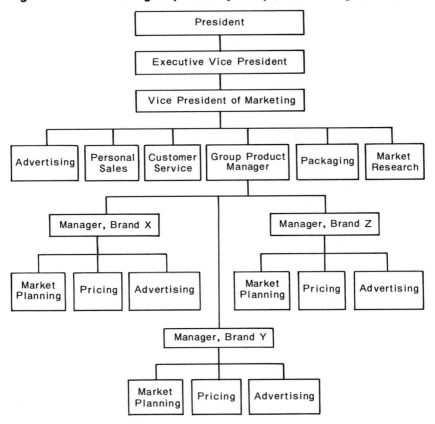

brand managers and, in turn, reports to the marketing VP. The arrangement is charted in Figure 1-2.

The pricing function is often combined to advantage with other duties. It can be the responsibility of the product planner or the brand manager, or it can be discharged by the vice president of marketing or the advertising manager. In a large firm, however, carrying out all the responsibilities for pricing one product line or a few related product lines is nearly a full-time job. For our purposes we will assume a price-setter reports to the vice president of marketing. He has no staff other than a secretary and possibly a clerk, but he is assured of easy access to information gathered by other divisions of the business. That arrangement seems to be suited to most large firms.

WHAT A PRICE-SETTER DOES

A price-setter does much more than simply recommend the dollar-and-cents amounts that a firm should charge for its products; he generally manages a fairly broad pricing program. In this chapter, the elements of such a program will be sketched. Few firms would be wise to employ all of the elements, although the executive responsible for pricing should know their potential benefits as well as their costs. The pricing program suitable for a particular firm depends mainly on the firm's market context and its internal resources and skills. The functions of an executive responsible for pricing are mainly the making of price-related decisions and the administering of the pricing function. Those functions will be discussed in turn.

Price-related decisions

Price-related decisions range from broad company philosophy and credo to special charges for product changes made at a customer's request. The broadest decisions are usually made exclusively by top management; the intermediate ones are made by top management with the help of marketing executives and the price-setter; the routine ones are made by the price-setter alone.

The decisions related to basic business philosophy and values typically concern such questions as these: Should we drive rivals from business if we can? Should we inflict serious injury on rivals who have been struck by such misfortunes as strikes, natural disasters, or production failures? Should we violate the spirit of the law to make a large profit? At a somewhat lower level are these questions: Should we seek price leadership for ourselves or foster a leadership pattern with some other firm as leader? Should we try to shake out the weak firms in the industry to achieve price stability and higher profitability? Should we foster a spirit of cooperation among rivals and an avoidance of most kinds of competition? Should we take the lead in forming a trade association and try to have that association gather sales information and cost data that would contribute to increased uniformity of cost estimates and demand forecasts? When decisions on such questions are not made explicitly by top management, the price-setter may be forced to make them. Presumably he will try to judge what decisions top management would have reached, although he often will have little basis for his judgment.

Probably the most important decisions about price relate to substrategies, the broad determinations that inform, direct, constrain, and guide specific price decisions and provide the basis for price policies. The potential contribution of substrategies is so great that we will examine:

1. The benefits that a firm might reap from developing effective substrategies.
2. What firms do in the absence of explicit substrategies.
3. What is involved in the development of substrategies.

Several terms similar to "price strategy" are used almost synonymously but always with considerable ambiguity: "approaches to pricing," "price policy," and "pricing methods." Let us therefore be quite specific about how we use the term "price strategy."

Price strategy: What? For our purposes, "strategy" is an "explicit line of thinking and accompanying actions designed to achieve a stated objective by effective means." Its key elements are (1) a specific objective, (2) a nonobvious logic or line of thinking that would achieve that objective with particular effectiveness, and (3) a program of action that implements that line of thinking. This definition will become clearer as we discuss what is gained by developing a strategy.

In defining price strategy we can take two quite divergent views. Price strategy can be considered to include any line of thinking in which price plays an important part. That view would make much of marketing strategy price strategy also; for price plays a significant role in most marketing strategies. Or it can be considered to include only lines of thinking that lead to a desired price result; that is, a result related to price is the goal of the strategy. For example, a scheme for giving a firm either a low-price image or an image as a producer of only high-price and high-quality brands would qualify as a price strategy.

The term "price strategy" as used here denotes both views, because a price-setter must be concerned with both. He must employ price in active support of the firm's marketing and even financial strategies, and he should propose strategies whereby product design, advertising, personal selling, customer service, and other measures beyond price are employed to attain price goals.

Price Strategy: Why? It is almost self-evident that actions in business in general and in marketing and pricing in particular should be goal-oriented and that an executive should always take action for a purpose. An executive should not only know clearly what he is trying to achieve but also be able to identify the most effective means available to him. Usually any objective can be pursued by different means; novel and imaginative ones can sometimes be devised. The applicability of any means should be examined critically. Finally, when a decision maker has found effective means of attaining desired ends, it is clear that those means should be used. Thus it is obvious that a price-setter, or any decision maker, should try to develop strategies. And it is equally obvious that his personal success will depend heavily upon his skills in strategy development.

Another way to answer the question, Why have a strategy? is to ask what an executive might do if he had none. The following are the most common alternatives:

- ☐ Make decisions on an ad hoc basis. That means deciding each issue on its individual merits and taking account primarily of immediate benefits and costs.
- ☐ Continue to do what you are doing at present if that seems to be working satisfactorily. When it ceases to work, find some other basis for making decisions.
- ☐ Imitate what successful firms in the industry are doing, even though you may not understand why they are successful or whether their actions are suitable for your firm.
- ☐ Transplant actions taken by successful firms in another industry.
- ☐ Just do everything more effectively than other firms do—succeed by "brute force of superior performance."

None of these alternatives inspires much confidence. Decisions made on an ad hoc basis are often inconsistent with one another. Also, an ad hoc approach to decisions commits a firm to a very short-run perspective. Often it requires a firm to forgo a large future gain for a far smaller current advantage.

Some firms have performed relatively well by employing the second, third, and fourth strategy alternatives. But because he fails to isolate and understand the forces that are operating, the decision maker runs considerable risk that he has misread the relationships or that the conditions that created them no longer prevail. Reliance on sheer superiority of performance is not risky, but only the rare firm can rely on that approach.

It is difficult to understand why an executive would not make strenuous efforts to develop a pricing strategy. His efforts might not cause him to change his actions, but in that event they would be reassuring. Moreover, his very efforts are likely to produce considerable new understanding. If he is open to new ideas and learns quickly from experience, he will continually devise new and better ways of pursuing his goals.

Price strategy: How? The process of strategy development can almost be inferred from the definition of strategy. A strategy is developed by identifying attractive and feasible subgoals and then seeking ways to achieve them. Ordinarily that calls for capitalizing on a firm's special advantages and strengths and exploiting the weaknesses of its rivals. Also, it provides opportunities to gain from original ideas on how to do things. At the base of strategy development is a hierarchy of carefully planned objectives each of which is established for a specific reason. The development of such a hierarchy and its use in obtaining benefits from ultimate customers, resellers, and rivals will be discussed in later chapters.

Lower-level decisions related to price

Beyond matters of basic philosophy and strategy, management must answer a series of important questions about price before it can set individual prices. For example, it must decide how much to emphasize low price in its appeal to the ultimate customer. The decision is sometimes described as assigning a role to price in the firm's marketing mix. It reflects a conclusion about the relative importance of price in securing the patronage of the ultimate customer. If, for example, price is believed to have only a trivial effect on a woman's choice of lipstick, a manufacturer would presumably stress quality-image advertising and make strong efforts to gain the support of high prestige retailers. Conversely, if management is convinced that customers regard all brands of a product as equal in quality, it would presumably avoid costly promotional efforts and concentrate on low production costs, low margins for distributors and retailers, and a low-price appeal. Usually the price-setter is involved in such a marketing mix decision, although primary responsibility for it lodges with the top marketing executive, who presumably can evaluate the alternative appeals.

   With the guidance and within the constraint of all the preceding decisions, the price-setter would be responsible for a large number of specific determinations: the list price for the firm's individual offerings; the differentials in price for individual items in the company's line; the number, timing, and nature of price promotions; the number of items that should be included in the company's line; the company's discount structure, including both functional and quantity discounts; whether or not to publicize prices in the firm's advertising; under what circumstances to initiate price changes; whether the firm should fair-trade when possible; and whether to include loss-leaders in its offerings. Associated with such decisions are problems like the following: Should we maintain price and alter the quantity or quality of what we sell, or should we maintain the quality and quantity and alter the price? Should we sell at a price that includes transportation costs, or should we make transportation a separate charge? Should we sell to captive jobbers (agents who buy for large retail concerns) at the same price as to regular jobbers? How much extra should we charge a customer who asks for specific features or changes in our regular output? To what kinds of outlet should we not sell in order to protect our regular resellers from strong price competition?

The preceding long list does not include all the decisions about price in which price-setters can become involved. It does suggest the broad range of issues with which they should be able to deal competently and the kind of understanding of marketing problems they must have if they are to meet their responsibility efficiently. In connection with those decisions, the price-setter badly needs current and accurate information. His requirements cannot usually be met from the data accumulated in the mere course of doing business. Accordingly, he must make decisions about the kinds and quality of market information that would be worth collecting and determine the best way to collect it. He must also decide how that information is to be processed and interpreted.

Periodically, most price-setters are required to submit an annual plan or program. That plan ordinarily calls for a list of the different items that the price-setter believes should be included in the company's offerings and the price at which each should be sold. He is also expected to set down an annual promotional program, and he will usually be asked to submit an estimate of the markdowns that must be expected during the period covered by the promotional plan. Beyond the kinds of decisions outlined here, the price-setter usually participates in the formulation of general marketing strategy. Few major promotions or changes in product features should be undertaken without his consultation.

ADMINISTERING THE PRICING FUNCTION

The pricing function is administered with less uniformity from company to company than virtually any other business activity. Very great differences exist in the background, training, and position of persons responsible for pricing. Sales managers seem to exert greatest influence on pricing, but production planners, finance specialists, production managers, and even accountants sometimes dominate the price-setting process. In some companies the administration of the price function is virtually nonexistent; that is, no one is formally responsible for the tasks we will discuss, but individuals are asked to do something from time to time. In other companies, price-setting represents a substantial and carefully administered activity. What is described here is a maximum program rather than the usual or the minimum one. Large differences in the way firms organize their pricing function might be expected, but the extreme variation that is found seems far greater than necessary.

Administration of the pricing function primarily involves an efficient assignment of responsibilities, the selection of personnel with the necessary skills, the monitoring of events relevant to pricing (particularly the activities of rivals), and the creation and testing of new approaches to price. Perhaps less important but certainly more time-consuming are the preparation of price lists and catalogs, the checking of price discounts given, the marking and re-marking of merchandise, and the arranging for the announcement of price changes. In some kinds of business—supermarkets and department stores particularly—the mere marking of prices on merchandise is a very costly activity in which errors can be quite wasteful. Often the costs are increased by alienating customers who find the price marked substantially higher than the price advertised or by failure to restore the usual price when the promotional period has ended.

This brief sketch of the responsibilities of a price-setter for a firm with a large-scale pricing program has indicated the kinds of issues that will be discussed here. Clearly, we will not be able to deal directly with all of the decisions and administration issues mentioned. Hopefully, the matters that are discussed will provide the concepts and principles that should be applied to those that are not.

WHAT PRICE-SETTERS NEED TO KNOW

Much of the great variation in the responsibilities and activities of price-setters results from differences in market situations. Some firms sell many products and introduce new ones frequently, utilize a variety of marketing channels, face competition from overseas and domestic producers, deal with a volatile technology, and sell mainly to customers who are spread across the nation and are highly sensitive to price appeals. Other firms are small factors in their industry, have rivals who are highly disciplined and not predatory, offer products that are few in number and almost unchanged from year to year, and sell to uninformed customers who are not deeply concerned with price. Executives responsible for pricing on behalf of the first type of firm have very weighty and time-consuming duties; those who price for the second type have duties that are relatively simple and unchallenging. Accordingly, it is not possible to specify what a price-setter needs to know without knowing in detail the situation he faces.

We will discuss the skills required by price-setters who face difficult problems rather than those required by price-setters whose responsibilities are simpler. Every reader can then determine what he might find of value. Also he may take pleasure from the fact that he need not know all of the things discussed here.

Pricing is a specialty. Although, in some businesses, pricing is perhaps the most complicated function that must be performed and managed, it still is not regarded as a specialty in the way that advertising, product planning, or sales force management is. Whatever the reasons for that may be, the individuals who are responsible for pricing often lack the special training and experience that would equip them properly. The executive responsible for a firm's pricing function, when it is complex, could benefit from mastery of certain cost and demand concepts and would find particular models and theories illuminating. He should be informed about alternative pricing policies and strategies and be familiar with alternative methods of measuring cost and estimating demand. He should study the experience of firms with unusual pricing approaches and problems.

Without that training and experience, he will surely perform far below his potential. He can no more administer the pricing function without special training than he could direct product planning without special training. If anything, the contrary is true. Pricing is more complex than product planning, and an executive will benefit more from a study of abstract concepts and models if he is responsible for price-setting than he would if he were responsible for almost any other business function. After all, pricing has been written about in great depth by economists for centuries.

It could be argued that even though a price-setter faces very complicated problems and badly needs help, it is unlikely that he will be able to get it. Many price-setters who have looked for help in a study of price theory and the literature on pricing have not found the effort too rewarding. What kinds of things, specifically, should a price-setter know and from what sources might he learn them? In very general terms, he should have a fairly deep understanding of the following:

☐ The many effects of a change in price on the various parties to the business process. Those parties include his colleagues, ultimate customers, rivals, resellers, suppliers, and the government.

- ☐ The manner in which price differs from the other available ways to influence sales.
- ☐ The manner in which price changes interact with other marketing actions.
- ☐ The circumstances in which customers and resellers are most responsive to changes in price.
- ☐ The difference between the initial impact of price changes and the longer-run effects.

It is not suggested that we know the answers to these questions or even that we know a great deal about how to look for the answers. Still, there are many concepts and models that a price-setter could apply with profit. They are drawn mainly from an ill-defined field called business economics or managerial economics. Marketing management is another field that offers help. For the most part, however, the concepts and models that apply to pricing are general, and it is not always clear when they apply and how best to apply them. More than that, the models frequently are very complicated; they deal with the interaction of price, sales volume, production output, sales costs, and profit. Like all other models, they represent simplifications of reality but are difficult to master and apply.

The general and conceptual nature of what a pricing specialist could learn to assist him in his duties has been stressed. Is it not possible, then, for a price-setter to learn a few procedures that he can apply in most, if not all, situations? Very flatly, no body of techniques, no formulas, no routine procedures will lead to a best price in *any* situation except by sheer accident. Almost by necessity a routine system will produce a less-than-best solution. Let us see why that is so. In the process we will acquire a better understanding of the complexities of pricing.

Why pricing decisions cannot be made by formula

Many different parties are involved in and affected by almost every price decision; we refer to them as parties to the business process. They usually include colleagues, resellers, ultimate customers, rivals and potential rivals, and government agencies. Colleagues sometimes resemble rivals because they give the pricer so much trouble; they include people in advertising, sales, accounting, finance, manufacturing, and even top management. At least in large firms, they play particular roles and are almost predictable as to behavior and viewpoint. The pricer must gain their acceptance for his decision or be forced to compromise—even if he is right. The ultimate customer represents many quite different types of individual usually called market segments. Rival firms are far from homogeneous in managerial skills, resources, customer favor, and financial power; and resellers, including distributors and retailers, are perhaps even more different from one another than ultimate customers and rivals.

To arrive at a "best price under the circumstances," * a price-setter must track down the specific consequences of any action he might recommend to determine how each of the affected parties will react. To do so, of course, he must have a thorough understanding of the motives, needs, capabilities, bargaining power, situation, attitudes, and fears of the affected parties. He is really in the position of trying to find a single acceptable solution to six separate pricing problems.

To forecast the reactions of the six separate parties who represent those problems, he faces these difficulties, among others:

1. Appraising the reactions of the various parties involves enormous forecasting difficulties. After all, can anyone forecast accurately how customers or rivals will respond to a price change?
2. That the effects of any particular action will conflict is nearly inevitable. What will help with, say, ultimate customers is likely to be injurious to reseller relations.
3. There is a likelihood of a major difference in the short- and long-term effects of any price action.
4. Price may be used to reach a variety of goals that often conflict.

Beyond the difficulties that result from the conflicting interests of the many parties involved in the pricing process, the price-setter manages only one of a group of marketing tools. The tools include all of the factors under the control of the firm that might be used to influence sales; among them are advertising, point-of-sale materials, personal selling, customer services, credit, product quality, product design, and distribution arrangements. These many tools, often called elements in the marketing mix, must be used together. That means two things: A price-setter must not employ price to attain ends that could be attained more efficiently by the use of some other marketing device. Second, he should consider what might be done in conjunction with a change in price. Frequently, price changes become far more effective when they are combined with a change in advertising, personal selling, or product design. The price-setter must recognize and be able to capitalize on those possibilities.

* This notation means what it appears to mean but is more complicated and important than it appears to be. It is discussed in some detail in Chapter 2.

Other difficulties that make pricing too complex for a formula arise from the differences in the market structures within which firms try to sell. The wide variations in the products sold, the types of customers cultivated, the power and managerial skills of rivals, the degree of foreign competition, and the nature and form of government regulations affecting the industry all exert influence on the decisions and actions of price-setters.

Clearly, no formula or procedure could take all those variables into account. Unless an executive is prepared to delegate his pricing responsibilities to another firm—by simply adopting its prices—he must be prepared to make an extremely complex and multidimensional decision.

In the course of explaining why no formal routine would produce a good price decision, we met some issues that deserve elaboration because they suggest the kinds of things that price-setters need to understand if they are to perform effectively. First we saw that the price-setter must understand the response patterns of the parties to the business process. Without question, that is the most difficult aspect of pricing. We will develop some concepts that help to deal with it; but helpful though they may be, they leave many problems unresolved. Second we saw that the price-setter must understand wherein price differs from other elements in the marketing mix so that he can determine whether price is the most suitable tool in any situation. The next chapter is devoted to this issue. Third we saw that he must understand the interaction among the various elements in the marketing mix, and particularly those involving price. Here again, he can learn something of value, but we mainly raise questions and offer no answers. Clearly it is not easy to know all that a price-setter would like to know.

Not all successful price-setters are in command of all the issues involved. Many, on the other hand, have learned a great deal that has not yet gotten into the literature of business. They are able to reach intuitive conclusions that are superior to the best conclusions reached by persons who are highly informed about the literature on pricing. However, it is not possible to teach intuition; until something is made explicit and communicable, it remains an individual's personal property and is inaccessible to others. Accordingly, a price-setter would want to learn what he can about pricing, even while he enriches his intuitions through experience. As implied, even if he learns all there is to learn about pricing, he will find a gap between what he has learned and what is required of him. Training can carry a price-setter only part of the way toward what he needs to know. He must adapt what he has learned to the very specific and unusual situations he faces.

Learning how to be a price-setter

Some individuals learn most by drawing conclusions from a detailed examination of individual situations; such people are clinicians of a sort and
would benefit most from use of the case method of study. Others learn
best from a combination of approaches. Clearly, a highly abstract discussion and a preoccupation with special circumstances are equally to be
avoided. Still, individuals learn in different ways and no single method is
best for all. How, then, might an experienced and successful pricer help
someone who wants to learn how to set price? Clearly, it would not help
much if he were to tell the novice about every pricing situation in which
he had played a part. Such an autobiography would be a hodgepodge of
undistilled fact that the novice would find difficult to assimilate and
apply. He could, however, give several valuable types of assistance.

First, he could present the fundamental concepts and ideas involved
in pricing as he views the process; the ideas would necessarily be general
and therefore presumably applicable to many pricing decisions. The
simplest of such concepts would include the notions that unit sales ordinarily go up as price goes down and that sunk costs should be ignored in
computing costs for a pricing decision. Those concepts would indicate
what things a price-setter should consider, how they are interrelated, the
types of error they should help him avoid, and the chief elements that
should govern his price decisions.

He could also present the most typical situations in his experience
and explain the essential elements of each. He would not dwell on special circumstances but instead would concentrate on their usual features.
Each of these typical situations would presumably represent a simplifica-
tion of reality even while it duplicated reality to a considerable extent.
These typical situations would be considered models. By mastering the
models, the inexperienced person would gain intellectual tools that
would equip him to handle more complicated cases.

It must be emphasized that both the concepts and models that might
be acquired from a highly experienced and analytical pricing specialist
are only intellectual tools that can be used in arriving at answers. They
are emphatically not answers in themselves, and their application requires considerable skill. Once mastered, however, they can be put to
use in making diverse price decisions.

Price-setters need more than a mastery of the concepts and models
that apply to pricing. As an important part of their training they should
learn what information they require, how to obtain and analyze it, and
how to interpret it. Concepts and models must be given empirical content if they are to be useful in reaching concrete decisions. As will

emerge from later discussion, the price-setter need not be sophisticated in high-powered statistical techniques so much as he needs to know how to extract qualitative information from the most informed persons to whom he has access. Although he seeks a highly quantitative solution—a specific number—he will usually be forced to rely heavily on rough data, broad impressions, and logic rather than on numerical computations.

Thus the reader should be prepared to meet a strange combination of materials in this book. Much of what follows is highly conceptual and theoretical; almost as much deals with specific information gathering and interpretation. It is in the combination of the two that a solution to pricing problems is to be found. If a price-setter is going to become equipped to solve highly complicated pricing problems, he must become quite expert on both levels.

When the pricing function is most vital to business

The importance of a business function to top management is determined by two factors: complexity and contribution to the firm's success. It is very difficult to make valid price decisions; that is, the probability of being able to find someone who can make such decisions is low. The contribution to the firm's success arises from the fact that large sums of money are involved, errors are very costly, and small differences in decisions have large repercussions. Clearly, some decisions, such as what tie to wear with a particular suit and shirt, can be absurdly complicated, whereas others, like the wisdom of avoiding an on-rushing car, are self-made. It is when complexity is combined with inherent importance that management must devote greatest attention and resources to the pricing function. When either complexity or intrinsic importance is alone present, the function is far less deserving of executive attention and support.

Now let us take a closer look at the notions of complexity and intrinsic importance as they apply to the pricing function. The examination is intended to illuminate an important management decision with respect to price: how carefully must we train and supervise the executive responsible for pricing? How much support—personnel, information, and funds—should we devote to the activity?

The complexity of the pricing decision

Earlier we discussed the impossibility of arriving at a valid price decision by using a formula. The market situation implied was one in which a firm enjoyed many price options. Beyond a bare mention, we ignored one option, namely, to imitate the prices charged by another firm. Any executive who elected that course would make his price decisions so simple that they would require almost no effort or expenditure of time or money.

Apart from imitation, price decisions are most simple when the firm has no control over prices because they are either fixed for it by some administrative authority or are determined by market forces over which the firm has no influence whatever. In such situations the price decision function virtually does not exist; the option is to sell or not sell at the prevailing price. Similarly, if prices are established by a price leader under circumstances such that conformity is clearly in the firm's long-run interest, any clerk could arrive at the correct price decision. If in any of these situations a mistaken price is set, the signals that an error had been made would arise promptly and clearly and the error could easily be corrected.

Pricing decisions are less simple, but still not very complicated, when a viable price—one that a satisfactory number of customers will pay—falls in a very narrow band. Especially in some industrial markets, customers are highly informed and extremely sensitive to slight differences in the prices they must pay. Moreover, they regard the offerings of different suppliers as virtually identical in value to them even when they take account of the differences in services offered by and the convenience and pleasure of doing business with the several suppliers. In such circumstances the range of prices at which a seller might get some business is extremely narrow; at one extreme, it could be limited to a small number of dollars or even cents. Here again the price decision approaches a clerical task. An important exception occurs when a firm can get a slight price advantage for superior service, better reputation, likable salesmen, cordial management, and so on, although many executives would not recognize that possibility. It is usually difficult to know when a firm could obtain a premium price, because many customers surely would complain and the firm might lose a few. On the other hand, the firm might be better off with the premium price and the loss of some customers. Only a skillful price-setter can recognize and exploit such opportunities.

It is only when a price-setter has numerous options—that is, when he could select among many different prices and, even more, when he might devise an ingenious approach to price—that the pricing function is highly complex. Paradoxically, the more alike the options are in their total effects, the more difficult the task of selecting among them—no great skill is required to choose among alternatives that are manifestly unequal in their effects. Ordinarily, price-setters face some vexing strategic decisions: They can advocate a strategy of low profit margin with high sales volume; they might push for a strategy of high profit margin with small sales volume; or they might recommend a strategy of medium margin with moderate sales. Those approaches might be almost equally promising in some situations, and then the choice would be difficult. One could, however, argue that the choice is not important because it does not affect profits much.

The intrinsic importance of the pricing decision

It is difficult to imagine a firm whose profitability is unaffected by the prices it charges. When there are rivals, small changes in price could often result in major changes in profitability. It is only when customers are almost indifferent to price that the risks of loss from poor pricing are small. But then price decisions have a different importance because the firm could charge higher prices without fear that its sales and possibly its profits would be depressed by the price increases.

The importance of price comes from the influence on behavior of important participants in the marketing process, who could be ultimate customers, resellers, competitors, suppliers, or government. When the price appeal moves resellers or ultimate customers in large numbers, it is important. If a shift in price could provoke rivals to take strong and painful measures, price decisions must be considered vital. As suggested earlier, it is difficult to imagine situations in which at least one of the three major parties to the pricing process would not react strongly to a change in price. And if all parties are insensitive to price, then skillful sellers can substantially increase their profits by charging their customers relatively high prices.

Thus the pricing function is almost always important to a firm; that is, it involves large potential gains and risks of damage whether parties to the process are sensitive or insensitive to price changes. Accordingly, a management in deciding how much of its resources to allocate to the pricing function would be well-advised to base that decision mainly on the complexity of the task. Only if a firm is compelled to adhere to some price by either market forces, government power, or the decision to conform to some industrywide pattern of behavior can it consider the function simple. If it has a variety of options and enjoys opportunity for innovative approaches—for example, if it sells many different items in diverse markets—it must be prepared to devote very large resources to the pricing function to achieve the potential benefits of skillful pricing.

2

How Price Differs from Other Marketing Mix Elements

ECONOMISTS STRESS THE DISTINCTION between price and nonprice competition. They maintain that sellers prefer to avoid the first and rely more on the second. They see price as a very special competitive instrument—one that can be applied quickly and by everyone, unlike most other forms of competition. In the economists' view, the businessmen's preference for nonprice rather than price competition has injurious effects, mainly in the form of wasted resources.*

Our interest differs from that of the economist. We want to know when and whether a firm should employ price or some other marketing instrument to attain *its* objectives in any given situation. We view price as one of many devices that a firm might employ to further its economic interests. It *could* be effective or it *might* work poorly; it *might* work well at certain times but not at others. It *might* be more effective than, say, advertising or personal selling in some cases but not in others.

---

* This distinction and its implications were first discussed and developed at length by Arthur R. Burns in *Decline of Competition* (New York: McGraw-Hill, 1936). The more traditional position taken on this subject is derived from Edward Chamberlain, *The Theory of Monopolistic Competition* (Cambridge, Mass.: Harvard University Press, 1962, 8th edition).

The purpose of this chapter is to determine when price is the most suitable tool for a seller to use and when he should use an alternative one. Any marketing executive who recommends the use of price presumably has already decided that the firm's interests would be better served by a change in price than by some alternative action.

The thesis advanced in this chapter is that price and the other elements in the marketing mix have many consequences beyond an effect on short-term sales. To manage the pricing function, an executive must understand the full effects of each element in the marketing mix and select the one whose total consequences are most advantageous for the firm when its costs are taken into account.

An analogy to an executive's selecting among price, advertising, customer service, personal selling, product design, credit accommodation, and broader assortment to increase his firm's sales may be instructive. Imagine a physician who finds that his patient is suffering from a severe viral infection. He knows five different drugs that have been marketed for that disorder, and all have proved to be efficacious although they differ considerably in their side effects. They vary in the speed with which they give relief from pain, in the speed with which they eliminate the basic infection, the extent to which they remove the danger of reinfection, the severity of side effects, the number and kinds of people who are allergic to the drug, and the cost of the medication itself. If all of the patients suffering from the disease were identical, presumably one of the five drugs could be considered best for all. However, patients differ widely in their tolerance of pain, their susceptibility to reinfection, the kinds of chemicals to which they are allergic, and their ability to bear financial cost. Consequently, the best drug for one patient might be the worst one for another. The doctor must prescribe for individual patients on the basis of their particular characteristics.

The same kind of complexity is found in marketing activities. Before a marketing executive prescribes a change in price, he will compare that action with other marketing actions in suitability for the prevailing situation. He presumably will recommend a price change only when he is convinced that it would achieve the company's goals better than any substitute. Marketing mix elements should be evaluated in specific contexts on the basis of (1) their cost characteristics, (2) their administrative characteristics, and (3) their effects on the behavior of customers, rivals, resellers, and possibly others. We will discuss these three attributes of marketing mix elements and compare price with advertising and customer services in terms of them.

COST CHARACTERISTICS OF MARKETING MIX ELEMENTS

A marketing executive wants to know the cost of any benefit he might obtain. Apart from the amount of the cost, he is also concerned with its timing and its form and his opportunity to get others to share the cost with him. The amount of cost is a clear enough concept; it need only be specified that an executive should be concerned with incremental cost rather than fully allocated or standard costs. The costs appropriate to price decisions are discussed in Chapter 7.

The timing of cost is often important to sellers, especially when their liquid resources are limited. When the seller employs certain marketing mix elements, he must make sizable outlays long in advance of any possible benefit, as in training salesmen, preparing and testing advertising copy, and acquiring and cultivating strong distributors and retailers. Expenditures for other marketing mix elements are made at about the same time that benefits are obtained. For some elements the seller usually pays after the marketing effort has been undertaken; suppliers commonly extend credit for some marketing outlays.

A cost represents the sacrifice of something that a firm prizes. Usually that is cash, although it could be leisure, peace of mind, or reseller goodwill. One question about the cost of carrying out a marketing change is whether the firm could make the effort simply by using its own resources more intensively, as by making greater demands on its employees and executives, or must go outside for the resources.

Sharing the cost of marketing effort involves such possibilities as (1) reducing the price to ultimate customers by reducing the firm's own margin of profit and asking its distributors and retailers to reduce their margins also, and (2) using co-op advertising programs in which the manufacturer shares advertising costs with the reseller. In some respects, co-op advertising allowances resemble price reductions.

ADMINISTRATIVE CHARACTERISTICS OF
MARKETING MIX ELEMENTS

To undertake almost any marketing effort, a seller ordinarily must perform some tasks. The activities required to carry out different marketing mix elements differ in important respects including (1) the speed with which they can be enacted, (2) the risk that the effort will be conducted poorly, and (3) the extent to which the effort can be directed to selected customers or resellers.

Some marketing decisions can be put into action almost immediately; for most sellers that is true of price changes. On the other hand, the adoption of a new advertising approach may take months to work out and implement, whereas the continuation or extension of a given promotion might take very little time. The decision to add salesmen or offer better customer service could involve many months of preparation.

The risk of getting a poor quality of effort may be considerable when an advertising promotion is undertaken. The execution could be poor or the underlying idea could be misguided or not implemented. In contrast, a price change of 10 percent either way can be achieved without risk of poor quality of effort.

Conditions that permit a seller to direct his efforts to relatively few selected customers offer important advantages: lower cost, greater speed of implementation, and the possibility of designing the effort for individual customers rather than for some hypothetical average. Secret price cuts can be selective, but they are generally illegal. The seller can, however, usually give certain customers more service than he gives others without creating legal difficulties or incurring the animosity of those less favored; for such special benefits are not likely to be visible.

THE CONSEQUENCE NET: A MODEL OF
MARKETING MIX ELEMENTS

The following discussion can be clarified by keeping in mind a simple structure that is used to tie the key ideas together; it is the consequence net (see Figure 2-1). Each element in the marketing mix generates a whole set of consequences that can be grouped by the parties to the business process who are affected. A price reduction, as already described, would sometimes affect ultimate customers, distributors, retailers, rivals, suppliers, colleagues, and government regulatory agencies. Although most marketing mix elements affect the same parties, the amount and form of the effects usually differ markedly from party to party. Advertising, for example, affects ultimate customers very differently than price, product quality, or customer service. Of course, the differences represent the chief basis on which a marketing executive decides which marketing activity to conduct in a given situation.

The consequences of each element in the marketing mix can be shown diagrammatically and elaborated to include subgroups of major parties to the business process and different kinds of effect. The major customer segments cultivated by the firm are likely to respond differently to

Figure 2-1. The consequence net.

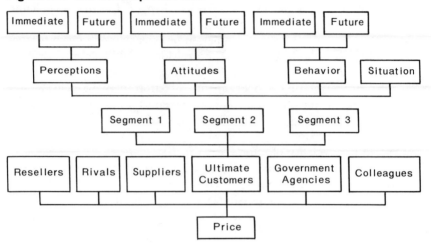

price changes and should be considered separately. As to different kinds of effect, does the marketing action lead directly to changes in behavior or to shifts in attitudes, perceptions, and information, or does it change the situation in which the parties find themselves? In addition, it is advisable to take account of the timing of the responses to different marketing actions. Do customers ordinarily respond more promptly to changes in price or to offers of customer service, to advertising, or added salesmen? Figure 2-1 is concerned with only one party to the business process, and it suggests the kinds of effects that a marketing specialist must consider. In particular it suggests the myriad questions related to the effects of a change in price on ultimate customers that a price-setter should take into account when he is evaluating a price change.

The model of Figure 2-1 is essentially empty of content; it offers only a series of boxes that require filling. But a skillful, experienced marketing executive can give it content for his firm and meaning for particular situations and specific contemplated actions. He can, for example, forecast the consequences of price changes—whether increases or reductions, large or small, or for a limited or extended period—on each party to the business process and on subgroupings of those parties. He can do the same thing for different kinds of advertising programs and personal selling efforts. The ability to conjure up effective marketing actions and to forecast their consequences represents the chief skill of the marketing executive. It follows that the main function of a marketing executive is to discover the relations between the individual elements in the marketing mix and their various consequences. Better than anyone else in his organization, a marketing executive should be able to forecast what consequences will follow a particular price, advertising, product quality, or customer service action.

It is, therefore, mainly in its consequences that price differs from other elements in the marketing mix. Since an understanding of the consequences of marketing actions represents the essence of marketing skill and the practice of marketing requires an ability to forecast the consequences of different marketing actions in specific contexts, an experienced price-setter should be skilled in forecasting and managing the consequences of his firm's price actions. That is far from easy. Each element in the marketing mix has many effects, not simply one. To use any element in the marketing mix effectively, and especially to select among the elements wisely, it is necessary to understand the following: How does the action exert its effect? Which parties to the marketing process does it affect? To which parties can it be directed? Might it have a pronounced effect on the party affected? What is the timing of the effect; how soon after it is carried out is it likely to produce its chief intended benefits? What is the form of its impact; in particular, what kinds of behavioral change might it produce? What are its main attitudinal effects? The next section is concerned particularly with the last two questions, which are both important and complex.

HOW MARKETING MIX ELEMENTS EXERT THEIR EFFECT

We want to understand the means by which the chief marketing mix elements lead people to act and think differently. In particular, we want to know the process by which a price change would alter the behavior of ultimate customers, resellers, and rivals. As already indicated, sellers' marketing actions usually affect the individual parties to the business process in dissimilar ways. That means several things. In the first place, certain marketing actions can be directed selectively at particular targets and have almost no effect on other parties. In the second place, when certain other elements in the marketing mix are directed at a particular party, they inevitably affect other parties. In the third place, some marketing actions are easily perceived by their targets and are likely to be interpreted and evaluated in the manner desired by the seller, whereas others are easily misinterpreted and often not perceived. (The significance of "perception," "interpretation," and "evaluation" will be explained presently.) Accordingly, to manage marketing mix elements effectively, an executive must understand the factors that determine how many and what kinds of persons will perceive the elements, how quickly they will be perceived, by how many they will be interpreted favorably and by how many unfavorably, and among those who perceive and interpret them favorably, how many will evaluate them in a manner that will achieve the result sought by the seller.

These issues are too complicated to consider here in depth; the best we can do is explore the chief differences in the way marketing mix elements operate. Sellers recognize that the prices they charge influence the behavior of their customers. Typically, they believe that customers will increase their purchases if prices are low and will decrease their purchases if prices are high, though they may not know why or how a price change has its effect. (At times, surprisingly, the effect is the reverse of the expected one.) Something happens between a change in price and the purchase or nonpurchase by a customer that a price-setter should understand so he can predict the effect of price changes and devise effective price strategies.

First let us acknowledge that price affects individual customers in dissimilar ways, and that a given price change might have a decidedly different effect on distributors and retailers than on ultimate customers. A full account of the way in which price influences behavior would, therefore, take account of the separate effects on individual customer segments and on all parties to the business process. Later chapters analyze those effects, so here our discussion will be quite general. Its main purpose is to contrast price, as an influence on behavior, with such marketing activities as advertising, personal selling, customer service, and product changes.

In the layman's view, price reductions influence customer behavior by "bringing the product within the reach of more customers" because more people can "afford the product" when the price is lowered. No doubt that is actually true for some customers, but for a great majority the problem of being "able to afford" any single product simply does not arise. If the product sells for a few dollars or less, most potential customers could really afford it. When the price is reduced, some people find the product worth purchasing at the lower price. Apparently they had put a value on the product such that only after the price reduction was it worth buying, given their set of values. Others may never have even considered a purchase of the product but were moved to action when they saw it on special sale. They may have been attracted by the possibility of "getting a bargain" and would not have bought the product at a higher price even if that higher price had itself been a bargain.

Here we see the customer as a more or less rational calculating individual who is comparing the value—to him—of money with that of products that are for sale. He is also comparing the value of different products that he might buy. Depending upon the prices charged, he will prefer owning certain products to holding his money, whereas in many cases he will prefer holding his money to purchasing. Even after he has decided to purchase, he must decide how much of the product to buy. Price changes, then, alter the penalty of holding money and so influence behavior. They also affect not only what is purchased but how much.

We can imagine other ways in which price might affect customer behavior, as by changing attitudes, impressions, and desires. A price change may attract the customer's attention to a product that he had not actively considered buying. Having given the product attention that he would not have given it otherwise, he might purchase it as an indirect result of the price change. Similarly, an increase in the price of a product he had considered purchasing for some time might cause him to fear the price would rise still further and so prod him into an immediate purchase.

Much has been written about the effect of price on the quality that most customers will attribute to a product. It seems that most customers reason as follows: "If that brand costs more than the others, it must be better; otherwise, no one would pay more for it. And no retailer will sell something at a high price when he could sell something equally good for less. After all, he doesn't want his customers to be angry with him." With many customers, no reasoning is involved; they simply associate high-priced brands with high quality, though some logic on a subconscious level may associate those two ideas in their minds. On the other hand, some customers—perhaps a majority for certain products—do not assume a high correlation between price and quality. It has been suggested that many housewives retain very extensive information about the prices of products they buy frequently, especially food. When they see a lower price marked for an article of food, they feel a strong impulse to purchase it, perhaps to gain pleasure from the fact that they are paying less than they would have paid previously.

Proving that one is "smart," and especially that one is "smarter than other people," seems to be one of the operative factors when a price reduction influences purchases. The knowledge that, only a few days before, many people were paying, say, 15 percent more than they will pay may induce some customers to make a purchase. It is widely be-

lieved—and many customers readily acknowledge its validity for them—
that purchasers fear being bested by the seller. Also, they do not want to
pay more for something than others in their acquaintance have paid.
They look on purchases as a test of their intelligence, and they don't
want to flunk the test.

We have suggested some ways in which price changes might influence purchases. Our terminology would offend behavioral psychologists,
who object to discussions about psychic states. The effect of price
changes on customers could be expressed in terms of positive and negative reinforcement schedules, but that would require exceedingly awk-
ward expression. Furthermore, such statements would not help to differentiate cases in which a price reduction would spur sales from those in
which it would depress sales. Price clearly affects the dispositions of
many customers—their attitudes, fears, expectations, and judgments—in
ways that alter purchase behavior.

We should ask whether price changes have the same effects on distributors and retailers as on ultimate customers. Are the effects mainly
related to valuation or are they more subjective, representing a disposi-
tional change? Ordinarily, sales by manufacturers to their distributors
are conducted on a highly businesslike basis by parties who are mainly
concerned with profitability. Price changes have quite realistic and readily recognized effects on distributors. Possibly some distributors would
interpret them in ways unjustified by the facts, and it is almost certain
that individual distributors would interpret the same price changes in
different ways. Nevertheless, the processes involved would ordinarily be
conscious and logical.

A distributor will usually forecast the effect of a manufacturer's
price change on the sales he will make. He will do so first by estimating
the effect on his retailers' sales to ultimate customers. Next he will calculate the effect of the price change on the value of his inventory. A price
reduction will reduce its value, and that will often have emotional consequences wholly out of line with the change in value. Not infrequently,
resellers are totally outraged by price reductions on items of their inventory even though their added profit may in a relatively short time offset
the price reduction. Thus the chief effects of a price change on ultimate
customers and on resellers apparently differ only in degree. The value
that both place on the product relative to their valuation of money will
dictate their rational response. Beyond that valuation some attitudinal effects often occur and have consequences that run counter to rational considerations.

The following chapter will elaborate on the preceding discussion of

how price affects the behavior of ultimate customers and re:
however, the diverse effects of price changes will be cleare1
ine two hypothetical marketing programs that revolve ar(
reduction in one case and a price increase in the other. T₁ι￼ pιυgrams
also indicate the value of combining other marketing actions with price
changes to realize the opportunities they offer for increased sales or
higher net revenues.

MARKETING PROGRAM BASED ON A PRICE REDUCTION

1. Circumstances leading to the price reduction.
   a. Sales have been disappointing.
   b. Inventories are building at several levels in our hands and in the hands of
      distributors and retailers.
   c. We need cash.
   d. Top management and the board of directors want action.
2. Rationale behind a reduction in price.
   a. A reduction in price will spur sales mainly to ultimate customers and only in-
      directly affect sales to resellers.
      (1) The lower price might be used to attract the attention of ultimate cus-
          tomers through dramatic price offers that would be advertised.
      (2) The lower price would make it possible for more people to buy inasmuch
          as price is an obstacle to purchase.
      (3) The lower price would induce customers to purchase who otherwise
          would wait until some retail store ran a sale.
      (4) The lower price would increase traffic in appliance stores; it would in-
          crease the number of shoppers or lookers.
      (5) At the lower price a larger proportion of shoppers would purchase our
          brand.
      (6) The price reduction should increase the sales of some of our models
          that we would continue to offer at regular prices.
3. Actions required to implement the price reduction.*
   a. Negotiate with distributors and retailers to go along with the program, that
      is, persuade resellers to accept shorter margins on selected sets to permit a
      more dramatic price reduction than would be possible otherwise.
      (1) To do so, we might hold meetings with panels of distributors and re-
          tailers and with the most influential resellers who are not represented on
          those panels.
      (2) In support of the effort to secure reseller cooperation, we might under-
          take a strong advertising campaign that would both communicate the
          price change and reassure the resellers that they could expect larger
          sales volume to compensate for the shorter margins.
   b. Communications activities to inform the relevant persons of the change in
      price.

---

* All of these actions, taken together, would be termed a price-oriented marketing program, or POMP.

      (1) Broadcast advertising (possibly on a co-op basis) to ultimate customers.

      (2) Indoctrination of distributor salesmen and their indoctrination of retailers and retail salesmen to announce the price changes.

4. Expected effects of the price reduction on different parties to the pricing process.

    a. Ultimate customers: effects are expected to vary by individual market segments.

      (1) Price-sensitive customers would be tempted to buy the models whose prices were reduced most.

      (2) Quality-sensitive customers might tend toward greater doubt of the quality claims of the sellers because of the price reduction.

    b. Resellers.

      (1) Distributors would resent the price reduction in rough proportion to the amount of inventory they were holding. They would also welcome the opportunity to offer a stronger price appeal and thus stimulate unit sales.

      (2) Retailers would not welcome the need to re-mark their merchandise. They too would resent the reduction in price if they were holding sizable inventories, even though they appreciated that sales would be stimulated by the price reduction.

    c. Rivals.

      (1) They presumably would regret the price reduction and would view it as an attempt to transfer the impact of poor sales onto them. They would carefully weigh the wisdom of retaliating.

MARKETING PROGRAM BASED ON A PRICE INCREASE

1. Circumstances leading to the price increase.
   a. Sales at or above expectations.
   b. Costs higher than expected; company is suffering a profit squeeze.
   c. The factory is having some trouble in keeping deliveries abreast of orders.
2. Rationale underlying price increase.
   a. Seek higher profit contribution through a price increase.
   b. Get greater sales support from the retailer by sweetening his margin a little and thus offset the sales-dampening affect of the price increase.
   c. Take the higher profit on the best-selling models, and not simply on those whose cost has increased.
   d. Under the circumstances of tight supplies most rivals will go along with the price increase.
3. Actions required to implement the change.
   a. Revision of price lists, catalogs, price tags, and so on.
   b. Consultation and negotiation with representatives of resellers.
   c. Selection and implementation of the change in cosmetic product features.
   d. Development of an advertising program for ultimate customers and perhaps retailers also to persuade them that product quality has been improved.
   e. Add a trivial product feature change—perhaps some cosmetic change—to provide a justification for the price rise.
   f. Give added sales support to resellers via broadcast advertising.

4. Expected effects of the price increase on the different parties to the pricing process.
   a. Ultimate customers: different effects on individual market segments.
      (1) Price-sensitive customers would be discouraged from buying the models whose prices were raised, but they might believe they were getting a better buy if they purchased a model whose price was not increased.
      (2) Quality-sensitive customers and those interested in getting the very latest model might be attracted by new cosmetic features and believe product quality had been improved.
   b. Resellers.
      (1) Distributors would gain and would like the program because their dollar and cents margins would be increased, the value of their inventory would be raised, and they would welcome the greater sales support from the manufacturer via advertising.
      (2) Retailers would welcome the sweetened margins on some models and the advertising support. They should not find the re-marking of merchandise much trouble.
      (3) Their sales might decline at the higher price.
   c. Rivals.
      (1) Presumably rivals would welcome the price rise and might raise their prices also.
      (2) Differences in the reactions of individual rivals are to be expected.

PARTIES AFFECTED BY MARKETING MIX ELEMENTS

As already suggested, certain marketing activities affect more than one party to the business process, even though they may be directed at only one party. A marketing executive should ask how each marketing mix element affects each of the six key parties involved. The question to be discussed can be stated this way: When a seller directs a marketing effort to a particular party in the business process, which other parties are usually affected and in what way? To be more specific, what effects might a price reduction addressed primarily to ultimate customers have on the other five parties?

We can approach the problem in several ways; its importance suggests that we should employ all of them. First we might ask about all forms of influence that marketing actions *might possibly* exert to insure that we would not overlook anything important. Then we could ask the following questions about each element in the marketing mix separately:

1. If we direct a marketing effort at, say, ultimate customers, in what ways would it influence their behavior directly and indirectly? What circumstances determine the degree of its influence on behavior? Typically, these questions lead to considerations of perception, interpre-

tation, and evaluation and the factors that create favorable as opposed to adverse effects.

2. When we direct our marketing effort to one party to the marketing process, in what way are the other parties affected? What, that is, are the byproduct effects? Are the byproduct effects strong or weak? Are they likely to be favorable or unfavorable?

3. How do the different marketing efforts compare in the nature and magnitude of their byproduct effects? In their exposure to adverse effects?

We will adopt a mixed strategy in approaching this problem. First we will itemize the most powerful claims made for each marketing mix element. For example, the chief claim for personal selling is that the salesman can force the potential customer to make a choice by asking for the order; a dramatic price offer can attract attention; the offer of something for nothing both attracts attention and unleashes the feelings of near-avarice that are latent in many people; advertising creates images and associations and can strongly stimulate desire—one wants to drink beer and eat peanuts after seeing someone else doing it. Marketing channel actions often influence behavior by confronting potential customers with products in a way that stimulates their impulses to buy and makes the indulging of those impulses effortless.

Now we will examine the many different influences that marketing mix elements might exert on parties to the business process. In general terms, marketing mix elements can affect dispositions and circumstances as well as behavior. Under the head of dispositions is a very long list of establishments of mind or psychic states that might be created or altered by marketing actions; they include attitudes, values, desires, associations, fears, motives, expectations, and impulses. The circumstances that might be altered by elements in the marketing mix include convenience, accessibility, the ability to finance a purchase, and the cost of the purchase. Mainly these effects are brought about by the use of price, the provision of credit, and the management of marketing channels.

Verbal modes of communication are potentially powerful creators and changers of dispositions; that is particularly true of TV advertising and direct personal selling. Price, packaging, marketing channels, customer service, and most other marketing actions also communicate, although more indirectly. Indirection of influence does not necessarily mean a weakness of effect, but it does usually suggest an ambiguity that causes different reactions from the various parties engaged in the business process.

PRICE VERSUS ADVERTISING AND CUSTOMER SERVICE CHANGES

When a manufacturer alters his prices in order to influence ultimate customers, he almost always influences other parties as well. In an effort to reduce the cost of its products to the ultimate customer, the manufacturer may, for example, lower his price to his own distributors. He will then expect the distributors to lower their prices to retailers who, in turn, will reduce the price to the ultimate customer. Indeed, the manufacturer will sometimes reduce the list price—which might be advertised—on the product in conjunction with a reduction in price to his distributors. In that case the manufacturer will have compelled the distributor and retailer to change their prices. Thus a price change by a manufacturer will ordinarily affect other parties than the one to which it is mainly directed. The indirect effect may be favorable, but at other times it may be a cause of resentment by the parties who are indirectly affected. Beyond effects on distributors and retailers, a manufacturer's price change will usually affect competitors and even government regulatory agencies. Again the effect might be favorable or unfavorable, speedy or delayed, certain or problematic. What has been said about price changes by manufacturers applies to price changes by distributors. Changes in price by retailers, on the other hand, rarely affect other members of the vertical chain very directly.

Can price be used selectively to affect certain ultimate customers and not others? More specifically, can a price change by a retailer be limited to certain ultimate customers while others continue to pay the same price? Secret price concessions to favored customers do occur, but they are rare in retailing. When manufacturers offer them, secret price cuts rarely remain secret for long. Can a manufacturer raise his prices to distributors without the distributors changing their prices to retailers and so to ultimate customers? With rare exceptions, a price change to distributors affects either the prices the distributors charge or the amount of sales effort they give to the product. Some effect of importance to the manufacturer is almost inevitable after a significant price change. On the other hand, certain forms of open price discrimination are possible. An example is the quantity price discount that limits the availability of certain special models to particular distributors and retailers.

Does advertising directed at the ultimate customer affect other parties to the marketing process also? Will an advertising program that is intended to increase ultimate customer awareness or desire for a particular product also affect distributors and retailers of the product? Will it affect competitors? Might it influence regulatory bodies? The answers will vary with the specific advertising program, but ordinarily they will be affirmative. Distributors of a brand are even more likely than the ultimate customer to perceive advertising of that brand, and the knowledge that a manufacturer is supporting sales through advertising will usually win a favorable response from distributor and retailer. Occasionally, however, distributors and retailers resent a manufacturer's heavy expenditures for advertising. They may claim that the mass advertising produces no benefit and that, instead of it, they should be given larger profit margins so they can put greater effort into selling the product. That reaction to a manufacturer's advertising is far less common than the favorable response, but it does illustrate the possible diversity of marketing action effects. Advertising by a manufacturer differs from a manufacturer's price change in its effect on resellers; it requires no change on their part. They need not re-mark their merchandise, change their price list, or make any change in their method of operation.

Would the effects of increased customer service be more like those of price changes or of advertising changes? Would a manufacturer's offer of increased service to the ultimate customer be regarded as a burden on retailers and manufacturers, or would it mainly create an expectation of greater sales on their part? Can customer service be directed to a few specific ultimate customers more easily than advertising or price changes can be? Is the risk of prosecution for the discriminatory use of customer service less than for the discriminatory use of either price or advertising? General answers to those questions are dangerous because customer service offerings are so diverse; they range from guarantees of repair parts and labor to gift-wrapping. What is true for one form of customer service is false for others. In the main, manufacturers can offer special service to preferred customers far more safely than they can make either price or advertising changes. In such cases the special services are not announced publicly; they are offered and carried out in private. They might be known to very few people in the firm that receives them, and they would certainly not be matters of company record. In that respect, they differ substantially from secret price differences.

PERCEPTION OF MARKETING MIX ELEMENTS

The marketing executive wants to know about the perception of every marketing mix element both before customers undertake to make a purchase and when they are on the purchase site. How many customers will perceive a price change for TV sets, canned peas, or tennis balls before they enter a store where they might make a purchase? Usually very few unless the price change is accompanied by some effort to make it widely known. On the other hand, advertising is likely to have its primary effect before the potential customers reach the purchase site. If a seller decides to offer better customer service, more sales help, or better credit terms, he must communicate those changes to the potential customer before the customer reaches the purchase site if he is to achieve their main benefit. In other words, if only those who go shopping for a product will learn of a marketing effort, then relatively few will perceive the effort and even fewer will be influenced by it. On the other hand, if the changes are communicated to people who have not looked for the product, they are likely to affect more persons—those who have not as well as those who have decided to look for the product.

The difference between being exposed to something and perceiving it can be enormous. It is possible for a person to be in the presence of advertising, actually pass his eyes over it, and still not perceive it or, having actually read it, to miss its essential message. Similarly, he might see a price marked on an item and not realize that it represents a sizable change from a short time before. A customer, say a distributor or retailer, might be sent literature that describes added services available from the manufacturer without cost and not even see it because his secretary had discarded it as junk mail. All these risks of nonperception and misperception must be considered in assessing alternative marketing efforts. The size of the risks varies from one element in the marketing mix to another and also from situation to situation. Generalizations about those differences are dangerous, because little supporting evidence is available. Also, it appears that many special circumstances would exert a major influence on the visibility of a marketing action—the probability that it would be perceived.

SUMMARY AND CONCLUSIONS

So far, price has been compared with other marketing instruments, and particularly with advertising and customer service, in three respects: (1) cost, (2) administrative characteristics, and (3) effects. Differences exist among marketing instruments in all three respects but most particularly in their effects. Unfortunately, although we know that the marketing mix elements differ considerably, we are not aware of all of the differences among them, nor can we forecast them in individual cases.

Most marketing instruments have varied consequences and affect several parties to the business process. The timing, qualitative nature, and magnitude of their impact also vary considerably. Moreover, the different marketing instruments vary greatly in their amenability to control by the firm intent on applying them to certain customers and not others. As suggested, our understanding of the full consequences of the individual marketing instruments is extremely limited in general and even in concrete marketing situations. The consequence net is a very simple but flexible and useful notational device for setting down the important known effects of any marketing action.

Perhaps the traditional approach to any subject, which is to place it in its proper setting before attacking it straightaway, is dysfunctional. And often a reader cannot see a subject's true setting until he fully understands that subject. Very possibly the reader should review Chapters 1 and 2 after completing the rest of the book.

The chapters that follow discuss in considerable detail and depth the concrete specific decisions about price that confront most price-setters. They were intended to bring the discussion very close to the desk of the price-setter so that the reader would find most of the discussion relevant to the issues he confronts when he is sitting at that desk. Accordingly, the reader will find a considerable change in the level and focus of the subjects treated in the following chapters.

3

Pricing Products
in Their Prime

AN OVERVIEW

THIS CHAPTER RAISES KEY QUESTIONS that price-setters confront in setting prices for products in their prime and shows why the questions must be answered if a "correct price" is to be found. The nature, role, and design of a pricing and marketing strategy are discussed in general terms. Also discussed are the data relevant to pricing decisions—their availability and reliability and the problems of their interpretation. It turns out that the central issues in arriving at price are these:

1. What objectives and subobjectives might be achieved by price action?
2. What are the consequences of price changes other than those sought?

The chapter begins with a definition of correct price and then explains the many interrelated parts of a price decision, including the fact that the decision must be acceptable to other members of the firm, ultimate customers, resellers, and rivals. In that sense, a correct price has some of the characteristics of a piece in a jigsaw puzzle. Later sections discuss what is involved in identifying the correct price for each key party to the pricing process, and the final section in this chapter discusses the problems involved in reconciling the potentially conflicting best prices.

CORRECT PRICE

We will refer again and again to the correct, right, valid, or best price and, at some points, to a mistaken, poor, or wrong price. The two sets of words represent opposites of the same complex notion, namely, that competent, informed, reasonable, and highly motivated people would select one price to be most suitable under the circumstances. Our goal is to identify that price, for it represents the best decision that an executive might make if he were in the situation. Expressed in operational terms, the right, valid, best, or correct price is the one that a panel of jurors drawn from a group of highly informed, objective, intelligent, reasonable, and motivated persons would select under the prevailing circumstances.

It is, of course, not feasible to determine a best price by appealing to such a jury. Apart from the mechanics of selecting and assembling the jury, the outcome of a price decision is an unreliable test of validity. The separate effects of a given element in a marketing program are impossible to assess, and, under the circumstances, the price-setter's decision may have been the most reasonable one. Also, the right thing is often done for the wrong reasons and the best decisions often turn out badly because of unpredictable developments. Other difficulties would bedevil an effort to evaluate a particular price decision. Serious errors in product design, packaging, and distribution channels—and mistakes in the *execution* of price decisions—may produce unfortunate results that could mistakenly be blamed on defective price decisions.

The right price depends upon circumstances beyond the control of anyone in the firm and also on the activities of the price-setter's colleagues. The price-setter is expected to forecast changes in the market environment and base his price decisions on those forecasts. He must adjust prices when the entirely unforeseen occurs, and he is expected to coordinate his pricing decisions with the actions and decisions of his colleagues in product design, customer service, advertising, and credit. His colleagues' errors require compensating errors on his part if he is to be right. Thus the notion of the right price is subtle and elusive and difficult to apply in concrete situations.

This notion can be expressed in another way: Unless someone can show that something is wrong with a particular price decision or can show that another decision would have been better, that particular decision will be considered right, valid, correct, and the best no matter how it turns out in practice. If an informed, objective, and motivated jury could be convinced that other decisions would be equally effective under these circumstances, then those decisions too are right, valid, correct, and the best.

Assembling the pieces of the pricing puzzle

Many writers have prescribed general methods for setting price. Among those methods are markup or cost-plus pricing, pricing to attain a target rate of return, pricing by marginal analysis, psychological pricing, the selection of strategic pricing points, and demand pricing. The methods generally affect the price to be charged to the ultimate customer. Most firms, however, do not sell directly to the ultimate customer; instead they sell to firms that purchase for resale sometimes after, but more often without, a modification of the product. Even they, however, are deeply concerned with the price that the ultimate customer is charged; for unless the ultimate customer purchases the product, the manufacturer and his middlemen cannot endure. Accordingly, manufacturers and distributors often try to influence the prices that retailers charge. Sometimes they actually dictate retail prices by marking the price on the merchandise, advertising the price, or using the legal right to establish resale prices that is enjoyed by producers of branded products in certain jurisdictions. As a general rule, manufacturers' price decisions strongly influence the prices charged by distributors and retailers.

An excellent price for the ultimate customer would actually be a poor price if it left paltry margins for distributors and retailers and thus elicited little sales support from them. Moreover, that excellent price for ultimate customers might lead to damaging actions by rivals, especially if it drew away many of the firm's customers. It could even adversely affect the amount of funds available to the firm for such things as advertising and personal selling. Thus a price-setter must develop a price that is acceptable to several different parties that are affected by his price decisions. Chief among those parties are colleagues, rivals, resellers, government, and ultimate customers, all of whom have conflicting goals. What helps one might injure another.

The chief reason why price-setting is so terribly difficult is that the price-setter must somehow balance the interests of all the parties involved while he pursues his firm's goals. Anyone who concentrates on one part of the problem—generally the price to the ultimate customer—oversimplifies the problem grotesquely. Again, pricing is like a jigsaw puzzle: the price-setter seeks one piece of the puzzle—a price—that can fit well with all of the other pieces, some of which may be in place.

In one way, however, the jigsaw puzzle analogy is misleading. A puzzle is a highly static device: the parts are fixed. The person working the puzzle may shift them around, but he cannot change their shape. Some price-setters act as if all the various parts of their problem were fixed. They are not. In most cases the price-setter can alter the attitudes, motives, and behavior of at least some of the parties involved in the pricing process. He can set price and employ other tools to gain support from distributors and retailers; he can change customers' valuations; and he can create loyalty. Especially if he adopts a long-run viewpoint, he can make major changes in the various pieces of the puzzle confronting him.

PRODUCTS IN THEIR PRIME

Products pass through a fairly predictable life cycle. We are interested in three phases of that cycle, for each poses some special price problems. First we will analyze the pricing of products that are well established and have not yet been superseded by other products. The reason for that departure from life cycle order is that the essential price-setting principles and procedures can be understood best when they are applied to a product with a fairly long history, a product in its prime.

By the prime of a product's life we do not mean that the product is particularly profitable. Instead, it is a product that has been offered for sale during a sizable period of time even though its physical form may be changing with some frequency. Accordingly, most people who might benefit from its purchase know about it, know where it might be purchased, and have a general idea of the terms on which it is available. Another way to define the prime of a product's life is to say that the product is no longer new. As we shall see subsequently, the essence of newness is great uncertainty about the extent of the total market for the product—how many units will be sold each month and in roughly what price range.

Now let us consider what is involved in arriving at the right price for a product in its prime. We will be particularly alert to the presence of many parties involved in the pricing process and their frequently conflicting interests. As our hypothetical situation, we will imagine that our hero has just been made executive in charge of pricing for a large electronics manufacturer. His firm has operated in the radio, Hi-Fi, and TV industry since the middle 1930s and has enjoyed considerable success measured both by growth and profitability—with some ups and downs

of course. It markets a fairly long line of TV sets, including small porta-
bles at one end and large consoles at the other. All together, the firm's
line includes 40 different models, each of which comes in cabinets of different color and material. In the preceding year the firm enjoyed relatively good business and met both its sales and profit goals. In other
words, when our price-setter assumes his responsibilities, his company
appears to be facing no special pricing difficulties. At least, no one in the
firm is pressing for a revision of prices.

Before we follow through our hypothetical example, let us note that
no one pricing problem is representative of all such problems any more
than one building, painting, or person is like all others. In fact, no three
or thirty products could embody all significant types of pricing problems. A sizable gap is likely to exist between the examples discussed
here and the product of chief concern to each reader. No matter how
many examples are discussed, none will perfectly match the particular
situation with which the reader is concerned. Moreover, the larger the
number of products used as illustrations, the more brief and superficial
the treatment each can receive. For that reason, only one product will be
used consistently throughout the book as an illustration—the TV set.

TV sets admittedly pose somewhat different pricing problems than
do razor blades, eggs, autos, neckties, meals in restaurants, garbage
pails, electric clocks, typewriters, frozen orange juice, residential apart-
ments, real estate commissions, wristwatches, and lipsticks. Still, they
are about as representative of all goods and services as any one product
could be, at least from the standpoint of their pricing problems and opportunities. The TV set happens to be one of a relatively small number
of products about which the author knows considerably more than the
average layman, and it also offers advantages for our purposes, particularly in highlighting pricing problems involving resellers.

What are the most important differences among products that
should influence decisions about price? How important are they, individually and collectively? The author contends that the basic notions—the
concepts, models, theories, and so on—that a price-setter would find
helpful are the same, regardless of the product characteristics. That position may appear to be inconsistent. On one hand, it is contended that the
price-setter must know in great depth and detail the circumstances surrounding a product—its customers, history, competitors, and technology—if he is to arrive at the correct price. General concepts and models
obviously cannot substitute for that type of detailed information. On the
other hand, it is argued that the price-setter cannot be effective if all he

possesses is detailed information. To apply detailed information to the setting of price, he requires mastery of a body of concepts and models that are usable with anything offered for sale.

The resolution of the apparent inconsistency is that most price-setters are in greatest need of concepts and models; they already are well informed about the markets in which their firms operate. Accordingly, the product characteristics listed below pose no special problems and call for no deviation from the concepts discussed. A thorough analysis of one illustration should therefore be more illuminating than a cursory discussion of many. The product characteristics that most price-setters should take into account include:

1. Size of the ticket—does it represent a small purchase or a large one?
2. Volatility of technology embodied in the product.
3. Cost of servicing the product relative to the purchase price.
4. Cost of operation of the product.
5. Inconvenience, pain, or damage caused if the product is not in service.
6. Durability.
7. Nature of customers—are they industrial or household?

From the standpoint of price-setting, what products differ in significant respects from TV sets? Industrial products, packaged goods, and personal services come to mind at once. Nonetheless, the apparent price-setting differences between such products and TV sets turn out to be largely illusory. As an illustration of one important similarity in the face of apparent differences, take pricing as it applies to such products as machine tools and basic raw materials on the one hand and imported perfume, cigarettes, deodorants, and toothpaste on the other.

The prices of both industrial and consumer products depend heavily on customer valuations, whatever the basis or validity of those valuations. Some ultimate consumers are better informed about the advantages of particular products than are purchasing agents who buy hundreds of items for large corporations. Customers for all products can be expected to include some who are highly informed and discriminating, some who are exactly the opposite, and some who fall in between. The fact is that the proportion of customers in those categories varies with the product. What matters is that the extent to which customers are well informed is certainly germane to the price that should be set. That applies to both consumer and industrial goods.

Now we can return to our newly promoted price-setter for a TV set manufacturer. Presumably, an executive who assumes new duties would start by assessing the state of his responsibilities. He would want to know whether he had inherited a healthy situation, and he would search out needs for change and opportunities for improvement. To assess his firm's pricing arrangements, our new price-setter would need to recognize when his firm's prices are correct and when they are wrong—that is, when they are too high or too low. He would need to know when the firm should change price and when it should stand pat. How is he to know? What are the indicators of a wrong price? How might our price-setter determine whether his firm has a price problem? What are the usual symptoms of price difficulties?

To know when something is wrong, it is necessary to know when things are right. To know that requires a comparison of the existing conditions with the established goals. If the goals are being achieved as nearly as possible under the circumstances, even though they are not being attained, we would say there is no problem. If a firm could achieve its goals more easily, we might say that the goals were set too low.

We concluded then, that a price-setter can assess prevailing prices only by determining whether they are contributing as much as possible to the attainment of his firm's objectives. To do that, he must understand how price can contribute to the attainment of business objectives in general and be able to recognize when it is not doing so. Now he faces the following questions: What is the firm trying to accomplish by its pricing actions? How does it seek to employ price to attain its goals? What are its ultimate goals and what contribution is price expected to make toward their attainment? What effects might price, or price changes, have that can contribute to or impair the attainment of a firm's goal?

BUSINESS OBJECTIVES AND THE ROLE OF PRICE

Few business subjects are more complex and subtle than that of objectives; it involves problems of level, conflicting goals, trade-offs, and the balancing of short- and long-term considerations. At the risk of getting stuck in the quagmire surrounding this broad subject, we must investigate how price can help to attain a firm's goals.

In simplest terms, the higher a firm's price, for any given sales volume, the greater its revenues and the larger its profits or the lower its losses. That simple view is behind the frequent businessman's wishful thought: "If we could only get a little more for our products, we might double our net profit." We might indeed, provided our sales volume held up. But price-setting is fairly complex for the good reason that changes in price usually *do* affect sales volume, and sometimes very strongly. So price can be seen to affect a firm's profitability at least in the following ways: It affects sales volume, which in turn affects sales revenue and possibly unit costs of production and marketing as well. (Sometimes the effects of a price change on volume just offset the change in price and leave total revenue unaffected. That is called a condition of unit price elasticity of demand.) All of these effects of price would ordinarily influence a firm's short-term profitability. Accordingly, price is quite directly related to a firm's short-term profit goals.

The connection between a firm's prices and its medium- and long-term profitability is often quite indirect. Let us look at some of the more important connections by considering some hypothetical situations.

☐ A firm holds large inventories and is so short of cash that it cannot take advantage of its opportunities to obtain discounts for prompt payment of bills. To do so, it would have to borrow at unattractive rates and might suffer some damage to its credit rating. A promotional price reduction for a short period might represent an inexpensive method of borrowing, and it might provide interesting demand information and yield other benefits.

☐ A firm sells in a market that has been beset by price-cutting by a few firms. Some other firms have responded by lowering price, with the result that all firms have either been operating with minimal profit or suffering losses. This firm wishes to reverse the price trend. It announces a general price increase in the hope of persuading all rivals other than the price-cutters to accept some loss of business to the price-cutters while earning an attractive margin on the sales that are made. It even hopes that the price-cutters will welcome the opportunity to raise prices once they have gained some sales by their price cuts.

☐ A firm has been selling mainly to price-sensitive customers and finds that it is in a segment of the business that is eroding rapidly. Its management determines to cultivate other kinds of customers and resolves to upgrade its brand image. As part of that program, it raises its prices.

☐ A firm introduces a major new feature in its line of products and thereby has an opportunity to gain a reputation for offering products of high quality. Even though the new feature actually results in a reduction in production cost, management elects to raise prices so that it is associated in customers' minds with an improvement in quality.

Accordingly, we see that price affects far more than per unit profit and sales volume; it affects cash flows, a firm's inventories, its customers' inventories, its brand image, its quality image, the competitiveness of its markets, the likelihood of government regulation, and customer awareness of and concern with price. Thus price has many implications for a firm's goal achievement.

Figures 3-1 to 3-5 present some hierarchies that should help most executives construct a list of the goals that their firms can pursue through the intelligent use of price. The first hierarchy, Figure 3-1, indicates the ultimate objectives of most firms; the hierarchies presented in Figures 3-2 to 3-5 indicate how the ultimate objectives relate to price. Ultimate objectives represent value judgments on the part of a firm's top management and large owners. They are the outcomes that those persons want "simply because they want them." That is, they are not desired because they lead to some other result. They are ends in themselves.

As Figure 3-1 shows, business success is composed, for many top managements and boards of directors, of an amalgam of long-run profits, growth, survival, and social responsibility. The relative importance of each would vary from time to time even for the same firm; surely it varies widely from firm to firm. Let us explore the lower reaches of this hierarchy to see whether and how price might be used to attain the four top-level objectives.

Price has been shown to be very closely connected with profits, but the different paths that connect price and long-run profits have not been identified. Figure 3-2 shows that price affects total revenue by affecting unit sales volume, profit margins, and product mix. By affecting sales volume, price usually also affects unit costs. Beyond those effects, price affects marketing costs, since most sellers must make a greater marketing effort to sell items at a high rather than at a low price.

We have asserted that a connection exists between price and unit sales volume. In that we are simply accepting the general proposition that price is usually negatively correlated with unit sales. Even in the odd cases when more is sold at high than at low prices, price does have a

Figure 3-1. Ultimate business objectives.

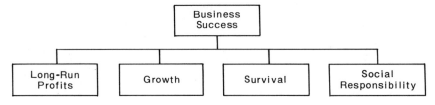

direct effect on sales; rarely does a change in price have no influence at all on sales. However, price also has an indirect connection with sales, and that connection runs along the following path: The price at which a product is offered for sale—especially its relationship to the price charged by rivals—affects the value that customers place on the product; one might say it affects the image that customers form of the brand. Some manufacturers of luxury products consider it an advantage to have the most expensive of all brands. Price affects the images that customers develop of individual brands, and their images affect their purchases.

Product mix—the proportions in which the firm sells different items in its line of offerings—affects profits and is also affected by price. In particular, the price differentials among individual offerings in a product line often strongly influence what is sold. A price-setter can easily adjust price differentials to make particular offerings especially attractive or very unattractive. Also, the product features incorporated in the different offerings usually reflect the prices charged for them; the higher the price the more features incorporated.

Figure 3-3 explores growth, another ultimate goal of many firms. This hierarchy also accords a place to price. A firm's size is often mea-

Figure 3-2. Relation of price to long-run profits.

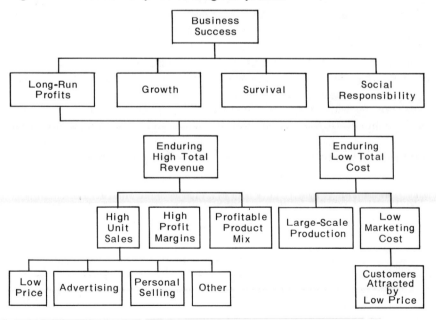

Figure 3-3. Relation of price to growth.

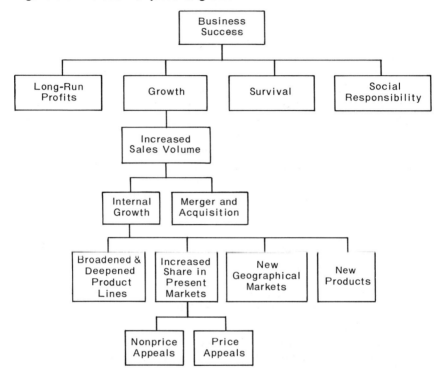

sured by its sales volume, which we have already seen is affected by price. In addition, by contributing to long-run profits and cash flow in the way already sketched, price might help to finance growth. Finally, a firm could employ price to deter other firms from entering the market or check their progress in the market and thereby contribute to its own growth.

Figures 3-4 and 3-5 sketch how price might figure in the attainment of the goals of survival and social responsibility, respectively. Nothing that these hierarchies indicate is surprising, but they do demonstrate that price can have objectives beyond the maximization of long-run profits, a fact that is not usually recognized. In the balance of our discussion we will assume that price is set with only one objective in view: the maximization of profits over a long period. Certainly that appears to be true of the overwhelming majority of concerns. If a firm has other goals, the price-setter should find the principles discussed in the following pages applicable to his problem.

In pursuing the goal of long-run profits, a firm will sometimes forgo short-run profits. In other words, a firm can often increase its long-run profits by actions that lower profits in the short run. That kind of trade-off frequently occurs when price is concerned and also when many other marketing expenditures are involved. Put simply, many firms increase their long-run profits by investing in the creation of market demand for their output. They may do so by building brand image, by strengthening their ties with distributors and retailers, by winning the support of people who are engaged in servicing the product, or even by arrangement with government regulatory agencies. Once this kind of long-run objective is recognized, the appraisal of prices becomes extremely complex and in fact is almost impossible if account of multiple objectives is taken.

If our executive newly appointed to responsibility for TV set prices inquires about the firm's short-run objectives, he might receive the following statement from the marketing VP for the firm, together with an indication that it was taken directly from the company's annual marketing plan.

The firm is planning to increase its dollar sales by 7.5 percent this year and increase its return on investment (ROI) from 8 percent after taxes to 8.5 percent.

During this year it plans to open at least 30 new major retail accounts by cooperating with distributors. It will lend strong support to distribu-

Figure 3-4. Relation of price to survival.

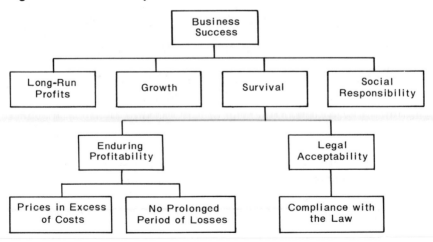

Figure 3-5. Relation of price to social responsibility.

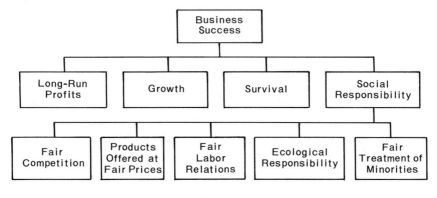

tors who request it and will also search out opportunities to obtain stronger sales support from old retail accounts.

In addition, the company will develop at least five new regional salesmen so that it can reduce the size of the territory entrusted to each of its salesmen.

During the year, the firm should increase brand awareness of its TV line among families of middle income and above from the present level of 82 percent to 93 percent and brand preference from 14.0 percent to 16.5 percent.

Observe that, although nothing in this excerpt from the marketing plan speaks of them, several specific pricing objectives may be implicit. For example, the commitment to aid distributors to develop new retail accounts could imply some price concessions, or the equivalent, to induce new retailers to take or to push the brand. Also, brand awareness and brand preference among consumers might be directly affected by a firm's prices.

How might our newly appointed price-setter move from such a statement of objectives to an assessment of his firm's prices? He has no indication whether the increase in brand awareness and brand preference has primary importance or is secondary to the projected increase in unit sales and the return on investment. He is not likely to have available to him current and reliable information about customer brand awareness and brand preference, and the company's total growth and profitability would reflect conditions in its radio and Hi-Fi divisions almost as much as in its television division. Clearly, he needs more guidance and some specific information if he is to assess the firm's TV prices against its stated objectives. Actually, he would appear to face multiple objectives: management has decided to accept temporarily lower profits in order to increase customer awareness and preference and obtain new major retail accounts.

It would be unusual if a firm were to achieve all of its goals or to underachieve or overachieve all of them by the same proportion. It might attain its sales target but not know how well it was performing with respect to some of its other goals. For example, it might have information from its district sales representatives that active and promising efforts were under way to get some major new retail accounts but have only a few new accounts already in hand. Will it obtain the 30 it seeks? Maybe it could if it were to offer more price concessions or other inducements, but that would compromise its profits goal. Also, if brand awareness and brand preference are to be increased then it might do well to rely on increased promotional expenditures rather than price changes.

Our executive now faces some fundamental and frustrating facts of life. First, the goals of organizations usually conflict. Getting more of one thing usually means giving up something else. Second, it is often difficult to determine how well objectives are being achieved until long after the fact. Third, objectives are frequently hopes rather than attainable goals. Fourth, unless objectives are given relative weight, they give the decision maker very little guidance. Finally, the appraisal of a pricing situation requires comparison of the present with realistic alternatives. Situations are not good or bad in themselves, they are better or worse than the available alternatives.

OBJECTIVES AND PRICING STRATEGIES

We have just discussed the objectives that an executive may try to achieve for his firm by the use of price and related marketing instruments; in Chapter 2 we explored the many possible consequences of price-related actions. We should expect a close connection between consequences and goals, but our discussion did not seem to reflect one. The reason is that the consequences we discussed were on a lower level than the objectives. For the most part, the objectives considered were very general and on a high level, whereas the consequences of price changes were quite specific and detailed.

The result was a gap that is of great significance for the development of marketing/pricing strategy. (We are concerned with marketing/pricing strategy rather than pricing strategy alone, because it is almost unthinkable that the second could be formulated in absence of the first.) In our terminology, the gap represents the subobjectives, the objectives that are desirable because they contribute to the attainment of higher-level objectives. In other words, the actions of a decision maker can be usefully conceived as a means-end chain. Actions are taken to achieve results that, in turn, produce other results, and so on until, at some point, the consequences are those that are desired for their own sake, the ultimate objectives.

For example, a retail price-setter lowers the price on one of his promotional items with the immediate goal of increasing the traffic in his store. His higher-level goal is to increase sales of the promotional item and, more particularly, of other items that customers may buy on impulse while they are there. He will also usually seek to create, perpetuate, and reinforce the impression among potential customers that his store offers many excellent values. Perhaps he will emphasize good values of a particular type, such as well-known brands at reduced prices. In that way he will try to establish an image of his store as a place to obtain high-quality merchandise at relatively low cost. His hope will be to attract a clientele that will almost routinely patronize his store. All of his subobjectives contribute to the ultimate goals of higher long-run profits, security, survival, and growth.

Because subobjectives represent routes that management might follow to attain the firm's ultimate objectives, they represent highly strategic choices. If a firm seeks long-run profits, it must decide what to do in order to attain them, and it has many choices. It could offer wall-to-wall low prices, carry an extraordinarily broad assortment of merchandise, employ highly skilled and persuasive salesmen, feature the latest styles, or offer unusual repair and alteration services, easy credit, rapid delivery, or pleasant surroundings. Which choices were made would have a strong effect on the firm's success.

Here we have started with a price action—the reduction of price for a promotional item—and examined its potential consequences by relating them to the firm's ultimate objectives of long-run profit, survival, and growth. It is possible, and desirable, to approach the matter from the other end. Specifically, a useful starting point for the development of a marketing and pricing strategy is the selection of high-level subobjectives. To approach strategy development in that way, a decision maker must construct a means-ends hierarchy of objectives.* If he does so, he

* For a discussion of the procedure followed in constructing a hierarchy of objectives and its rationale, see Charles Granger, "The Hierarchy of Objectives," *Harvard Business Review,*

will face a series of related means-ends questions that will force him to
set down the most feasible means of achieving his goals. Furthermore, he
will be forced to choose what he considers to be the best means. That
process is at the heart of marketing strategy formulation, and it is neither
mechanical nor simple. It provides an orderly and structured process by
which a careful, informed, imaginative, and experienced executive can
squeeze out of himself (1) many alternative means of pursuing any objective that he sets for himself, (2) an accurate assessment of relative effectiveness, and (3) effective ways of carrying out the course of action he
selects. The process sketched so far calls for the following steps:

1. Set down the firm's ultimate objectives—long-run profits, security, growth, social contribution.
2. Set down all feasible and attractive means of attaining each of the
   ultimate objectives. The marketing strategy will revolve around
   increasing revenues and sales, as well as lowering marketing
   costs.
3. Select the most effective of the feasible means or the best combination of means.
4. Set down the best alternative ways to put into operation the
   means selected in step 3.

We can now address ourselves more specifically to the development
of a pricing strategy and the marketing strategy of which it would be a
part. We must recognize that a firm will and should have many pricing
strategies rather than one and that they should be consistent with one
another; that is, they should be part of a more general marketing and
business strategy. More specifically, a marketing VP would benefit from
developing separate strategies toward these ends:

1. To cope with special circumstances in which he finds himself.
Examples are a general inflation, price control, unavailability of credit,
increased foreign imports, the advent of a strong new competitor, the introduction of a new product that is very well received or the opposite,
increased taxes, a scarcity of raw materials.

2. To permit the firm to market its wares effectively with regard to
the main parties with which it must be concerned. In most cases those
parties include ultimate customers, resellers, rivals, and the firm's own

May–June 1964, pp. 63–74, and A. R. Oxenfeldt, "Business Objectives: Why a Hierarchy?" and "Financial Objectives: Differences in Level and How They Conflict," in Oxenfeldt, *Decision-Making Concepts*, Columbia University, Graduate School of Business, 1973,
4th edition, pp. 39–49 and 57–70.

salesmen. Those main parties represent separate as well as interconnected problems that the firm must surmount, so a strategy is needed.

3. To indicate the relative emphasis—resources, personnel, and time—that will be devoted to each of the individual parties.

4. To determine what particular subobjectives will be sought with respect to each party to the business process. The subobjectives might consist of market segments, particular types of reseller, or particular prizes sought from each segment or type.

5. To provide the basis for selecting the means to be employed to pursue each subobjective.

The fourth step, the identification and selection of subobjectives, is often omitted or overlooked. For that reason, marketing/pricing strategies often lack sharp focus and direction, and so particular emphasis will be devoted in the following chapters to the identification and selection of subobjectives for pricing. The reader will be reminded to relate those discussions to the preceding discussions of objectives and consequence nets. In summary of those discussions a few facts should be stressed. Above all else, the price setter must understand the consequences of price actions or of price decisions in general. Second, he should be fully aware of the benefits that a firm might achieve by price actions. He should, therefore, have a profound understanding of the role of price; he should possess good models of business processes in which price is an element. Such models gain maximum power when they are incorporated into a means-ends hierarchy. In constructing such a hierarchy, the price-setter will identify many subobjectives each of which represents a useful potential starting point for the development of a marketing/pricing strategy.

THE APPRAISAL OF PREVAILING PRICES

Now that the newly appointed price-setter has clarified his firm's objectives and decided how price might contribute to their attainment, he will presumably analyze the prices for which he is responsible. He will appraise the current prices for the TV line as a whole as well as the price of each individual model. But what questions will he try to answer as the basis for his appraisal?

He might appraise a price by asking whether it is too high or too low. If the answer is no, the price will not require change. But certainty in a concrete situation is rare. Usually the answer to the question would be, "Yes, it might be a little too high [or low], but it isn't clearly so." The price is not clearly wrong, but neither is it clearly right. Yet most price-setters would settle for that answer.

On what basis, then, can anyone say that a price is not too high or not too low? That question implies the following subsidiary questions: What would happen if the firm were to change its prices upward? What would happen if it were to reduce prices by varying amounts? Even those questions imply subsidiary questions. What would happen to short-run sales? What would happen to sales in the longer run? What would happen to brand awareness? What would happen to brand prefer- ence? What would happen to the firm's cash flow? Even more questions than those must be answered to determine whether prices are too high or too low. All are implied by the fundamental question: What would be the consequences of the many feasible price changes we might make?

Accordingly, the price-setter should determine what alternative price changes might warrant consideration. (He would not be of much use if he felt that all potential changes were equally promising; hope- fully, he could isolate a small, manageable number.) And he would also identify the particular consequences that he would try to forecast. Hav- ing done that, he could then decide whether the prevailing prices met the firm's objectives as well as any of his reasonable alternatives would meet them.

To make more precise what is involved in assessing prevailing prices, we will start with a relatively simple example. We will assume that the firm seeks only maximum current profit. Since no other goals figure in the decision, the price-setter need only consider the profit im- plications of other prices that he might reasonably charge. Let us assume that, given what is known about the competitive situation, production costs, and customers' valuations of rival brands, the price-setter con- siders price changes of more than 15 percent in either direction wholly out of the question. Also, he believes that changes of less than 5 percent at retail are pointless; for they are either not perceived or considered triv- ial by customers. Accordingly, he decides to explore the profit effects of changes in prices, both upward and downward, of 5, 10, and 15 per- cent—six changes in all. For each price, he will want to forecast the total sales in units, the total revenue (sales times unit price), and the total costs of production and marketing costs. In other words, he will fill out a schedule like the one shown in Figure 3-6.

The items listed in Figure 3-6 are only the top of an iceberg. Be- neath the estimate of the change in unit sales as a result of, say, a 15 per- cent increase in price are the following elements.

Figure 3-6. Layout of a forecast of price change effects.

Price Change, %	Unit Sales	Total Revenue	Total Mfg. Cost	Total Mktg. Cost	Total Mfg. and Mktg. Cost	Net Profit
+15						
+10						
+ 5						
− 5						
−10						
−15						

The initial impact on purchases by distributors and retailers for inventory.

The initial response of ultimate customers to the price change.

The longer-run response by distributors and retailers. That includes the extent to which they pass along the price increase.

The responses of rivals to the price changes by distributors and retailers.

These elements are difficult to forecast, but only if all are forecast can the effect of the price change on unit sales be forecast with reasonable accuracy. But here we need not dwell on the difficulties of forecasting the effect of a price change on unit sales; we will discuss them subsequently. Suffice it to say that a price-setter can assess a price only when he assesses other feasible prices and the extent to which they attain a firm's objectives. The task is highly complex even when only short-run profits are considered; it is vastly more complicated if multiple goals are considered.

We have thus reached the fairly obvious conclusion that the price-setter's main task is to forecast the consequences of charging different prices and picking the particular price that best meets the firm's goals. We have also seen that the forecast involves a series of interrelated sub-forecasts. The price-setter's task is not easy; he is required not only to forecast the consequences of different prices but also to come forward with price-oriented marketing programs that hold special promise of achieving the firm's goals. The first is essentially routine; the second is potentially innovative.

The full effects of a price change occur at different places and times. Some of them were presented in connection with the consequence net in the preceding chapter. First, when management decides to alter price, it generally adopts special measures to support or accompany that price change. Salesmen are instructed on how and when to announce the change; price lists are revised; advertising is employed to reinforce the effects of the price change. Thus the first effects of a price change are usually changes in the firm's other marketing activities. We will call the totality of these changes a price-oriented marketing program (POMP).

Second, a forecast of the response of distributors to the price change is wanted. The short-run distributor response will take two main forms: (1) a change in purchases due to a change in inventory policy or in ability to hold inventories and (2) a change in price to customers. Distributors are legally free to charge what they will for their merchandise, and they may pass on the price change to their customers or respond in some other way.

Third, it is necessary to forecast the reaction of retailers to the change in price charged them by the distributor. They too might vary their inventories as well as the price they charge their customers.

Fourth, the ultimate effect of the price change depends heavily upon the manner in which ultimate customers respond to the change in retail price. Presumably it is this particular effect that was sought originally by the price-setter.

Fifth, it is necessary to forecast how rival sellers will respond to the changes in retail price. They might match the price change or ignore it or make some intermediate price move; or they might respond with some nonprice action.

Sixth, if rival retailers were to match the price change, the ultimate-customer response might be changed. The customers might, for example, have been strongly attracted by the initial retail price change. Once the change had been matched, they might no longer be induced to purchase the product because it no longer appealed to them as a bargain.

Seventh, as a result of the responses of ultimate customers and rivals, distributors and retailers might reinterpret the effect of the price change on their business and revise their prices. If such a revision takes place, further responses from rivals and ultimate customers must be anticipated.

Ultimately, the full effects of the price increase would presumably have been absorbed and become stabilized. It would be those full effects that the price-setter would try to forecast simply to estimate the short- and medium-run effects of each reasonable price change on profits. If the firm pursues nonfinancial goals as well, the problem of assessing prevailing prices—that is, forecasting the full effects of price changes—is far more complex. Can we offer the price-setter some escape from such an onerous task? Is there an easy way out? If not, how might he get a reasonably reliable answer at a reasonable cost? Those questions lead directly to the matter of availability and use of pertinent price-related information.

PERTINENT DATA

We have listed the chief questions that price-setters try to answer; they relate to the responses of various parties to a change in price. No firm or price-setter has enough data to forecast those responses with high accuracy. Anyone who is responsible for pricing should know that is so and not berate his data collectors or feel inadequate himself. When we have examined the matter, we will sketch alternative sources of help for price-setters who face difficult data problems.

In making most pricing decisions an executive can benefit from inputs to the decision beyond his memory of facts, his own understanding of the situation or models of it, and his logical processes. Outside sources of assistance range from the views of persons near at hand to the fruits of lengthy conferences, the findings of national surveys, and the net result of elaborate statistical procedures. As a rough rule, an executive confronted with a significant decision should always obtain some outside help, especially when the facts of the situation are not clear or when he feels great uncertainty.

That rough rule does little good unless it is combined with an indication of how much help and of what kind and from what sources it should be sought. Obviously, the answer depends upon the particular circumstances in which the decision maker finds himself. In particular, it depends upon (1) the degree of uncertainty he feels about the validity of his own views, (2) the relevance of available information to the decision at hand, (3) his view of the validity of the available information, (4) the effect of the particular decision on the goal attainment of the company, (5) the amount of time available to make the decision, and (6) the accessibility of sources of information to the decision maker. In other words, many factors should dictate when, whether, in what way, and from whom a decision maker should seek assistance. He may seek factual information from one set of sources, insights from others, and a review of his logical processes from still others. It is emphatically an error to believe that executives should obtain factual information only from formal research surveys; ordinarily such surveys are among the most expen-

sive and time-consuming forms of assistance available. For every market
research study or market test he authorizes, the decision maker should
place at least a hundred telephone calls to colleagues and acquaintances
who might have something of value to contribute to his fund of information.

Most important of the nonfactual types of information that the
price-setter should gather are forecasts, views about the factors operating
in the market and their prevailing relationships, and reviews of his reasoning. Of the many ingredients that go into a decision, factual information is perhaps least important. Almost any business organization includes individuals who can help others with difficult decisions, even
though that is not their specialty. A good decision maker learns who
they are and how to obtain their help.

To make good use of the information sources available to him, an
executive must first identify the assistance he requires. The starting
point is a very clear and rigorous formulation of the specific questions
he seeks to answer. He must take particular pains to insure that the answers to his questions would actually influence his behavior, and not
simply satisfy his curiosity. Once he has made clear what he wants to
know, he will usually find that other questions, subsidiary to those he
seeks to answer, must be faced. As we have said, the question "Are our
prevailing prices correct?" raises the double question "Are our prices too
high or too low?" There are other subsidiary questions: How would our
distributors and retailers react to, say, a 5 percent reduction in our price?
How would our competitors respond? How would ultimate customers
respond if our retailers and rivals were to react as expected? All these
questions help to develop a forecast of the financial effects of changes in
price. The action implications of the forecast are clear; they suggest
whether price should be changed or held constant.

Having identified the questions he wishes answered, the decision
maker must decide what sources of answers he has. If the question is distributor and retailer response to lower price by 5 percent on all TV sets,
he might talk to a panel of distributors that his company had established,
he might speak to the vice president in charge of distribution for the
company, he might call the company's distributors whom he knew best,
or he might speak to the executive secretary of the industry's trade association. He might also consider the possibility of having the market
research department interview a cross section of the company's distributors. In selecting from those alternatives he must estimate the value as
well as the cost and timing of the help he can expect. More specifically,

he might evaluate each of the alternative sources of information on these points:

Timing of the help received—when would he get the results?
The form of the help. Would he get data, ideas, suggested methods of collecting data, or forecasts?
The amount of help—how many data, what kinds of ideas?
The reliability of the information.
The likelihood of receiving new information or ideas.
The cost of the information, including nonfinancial debts that would have to be repaid.

At least in theory, the decision maker could rate each alternative source of information for its suitability under the particular circumstances he faces. If speed is most urgent, he would put high value on the sources from which he could get an immediate response. If he had a large budget available, he would put a relatively low value on economy. Many of his judgments would be highly subjective. Persons who were ordinarily reliable might not be reliable in that specific instance; individuals who usually were most anxious to help might be unwilling or unable to do so because of the circumstances. Accordingly, the assessment of alternative sources of information is difficult and subject to considerable error. However, it might be a far greater error to treat all potential sources as if they were equally valuable or to conduct elaborate studies to assess the timeliness, reliability, and cost of each alternative.

Having decided where to solicit information, the decision maker will usually obtain conflicting answers. Indeed, if he finds a consensus about something that is manifestly unknowable, he must suspect a common source. All the people he consults may have read the same forceful article in a trade journal, so all he gets is a replay of that article. But given the conflicting views he should expect from several equally reliable sources, what must he do? Should he strike an average? Should he toss a coin? Should he change his job?

Suppose that our newly appointed TV price-setter wanted to estimate the effects of reducing each model in the line by roughly 5 percent. How might he best proceed? Typically, a large TV manufacturer would not have much applicable experience. Its past price moves would ordinarily have been associated with some marked change in demand or a shift in the prices of a major rival. In neither case would the effects of a price change be very much like those of a marketing program built around a 5 or 10 percent price reduction. Even if the manufacturer had ever made such a general price reduction, it may have been so long before that the same reactions from rivals, resellers, and ultimate customers could not be expected.

Among the changes in a market that could alter ultimate customers' responses to price and price changes are: the entry or departure of firms, increased emphasis by sellers on price appeals, the appearance of substantial items, the number of persons who already own the product (if it is a durable), shifts in value systems, and a change in anticipated future price and quality of the product.

Other factors would make a reliable estimate of the effects of a 5 percent price change from a study of the historical record almost impossible. In the first place, markets for many products change substantially over fairly short periods of time, so that the effect of price on sales to ultimate customers would differ between the beginning and end of, say, a ten-year period. Statistical generalizations about the relationship between price and sales would be based on the presumption of an unchanged relation. Second, firms sometimes change the emphasis that they themselves place on price appeals. In that case, the relation between price and sales would usually change over time. Also, such market developments as the entry and departure of rivals would ordinarily affect the responsiveness of customers to changes in price. Few if any manufacturers, then, could accurately estimate the effects of a general price reduction of 5 percent on the basis of a statistical analysis of the firm's market history. What alternatives are available?

In recent years, specialists in decision making have come to rely on the intuitive judgments of informed individuals, and they prescribe how those judgments are to be obtained and processed. This reliance developed because the record of historical events is quite inconclusive, often irrelevant, and usually full of statistical pitfalls. Moreover, market experiments can be conducted with only a few alternatives in any reasonable period of time. In the absence of reliable historical data and market experiments, many management scientists are prepared to accept a consensus of informed individuals.

The line of reasoning suggested here may not be employed by any major corporation, nor would all specialists in management science agree with it. Nevertheless, it represents the author's recommended solution for the problems faced by executives—price-setters no more or less than others—who lack the information they require. The decision maker should systematically use the judgments of the best-informed individuals within and outside the firm to whom he has access. That means he must (1) determine whose judgments would be of value, (2) develop a method for obtaining those judgments in a form that permits them to be used, (3) refine and strengthen the original judgments received, and (4) develop a composite judgment in the likely event that the individual judgments vary significantly. These steps will be discussed briefly in turn.

Whose judgment to seek

Ordinarily only a limited number of individuals within any firm are either concerned with or have direct experience with issues similar to those facing the price-setter. Who within a large manufacturing concern might be able to make a useful judgment about the response of ultimate customer, reseller, and rivals to a marketing program revolving around price reductions across the board? Perhaps the marketing VP, the general sales manager, the director of advertising, the manager of customer services, and some of the firm's district and regional sales managers could qualify. Typically, a price-setter might identify ten such persons, although he might have to ask for the views of others in the interests of good personal relations.

Some individuals outside the firm might also be of help in forecasting the effects of price changes. The firm's largest distributors and retailers might be more valuable than the firm's own marketing executives, and they would typically be willing to cooperate. Beyond them, a price-setter might get valuable judgments from persons not directly connected with his firm, including members of trade associations, the trade press, and possibly regulatory agencies also.

How to obtain judgments

Once the price-setter has decided whose judgments he wishes to use, he must develop a method for gathering the judgments in usable form. Obviously, he must solicit the judgments, which means either a spoken or written inquiry. He will have to motivate the selected individuals to respond, and he must explain his purpose and pose his questions clearly enough to elicit valid responses. We need not discuss the difficulties of questionnaire construction and the reluctance of some people to express their views frankly. Fortunately, some relatively good procedures have been developed to deal with those problems. The recommended procedures and line of reasoning are associated with the Delphi technique developed by Helmer and Bilkey. The effect of the technique is to distill the intuitive judgments of highly expert persons in a way that will yield a best forecast. A composite forecast is developed by securing an independent set of answers from each expert, summarizing all the responses, and distributing the summary to the individual experts who are asked to comment favorably or unfavorably on the answers of the others and, if they wish, revise their own initial forecasts. Those responses are then summarized and distributed for further comment, reflection, and revision.

Helmer and Bilkey were anxious to secure and process the intuitive judgments of experts without permitting undue influence by contributors who might hold high positions or be particularly aggressive or persuasive. They were also anxious to get the benefits of interaction among the experts. The method they devised avoids the danger and assures the interaction. They believe—and some research bears them out—that their procedure will produce a consensus. And they further believe that the consensus reached will be far more accurate than, say, an average of the initial responses. In the intercommunication process, the participants learn from one another and sharpen their thoughts.

How might our TV price-setter apply the Delphi technique? What questions might he ask of his experts? The answer depends on the particular issue and the strengths of the price-setter, for he will want to limit the burden he places on his experts. As we shall see, the questions that he might raise relate mainly to three chief sets of parties to the pricing process: ultimate customers, resellers, and rivals. In the following chapters, which deal with each party separately, we will consider the specific questions that he might raise and the sources from which he might get the best answers.

OCCASIONS FOR PRICE DECISIONS

Up to this point, we have explored the evaluation of an existing price; for such an evaluation raises all the issues involved in establishing price to begin with. We adopted the viewpoint of a newly appointed executive who is appraising the price arrangements that he had inherited, a highly unusual situation. Price decisions are usually made when the responsible executive believes that the prevailing price is in error. Accordingly, we will want to identify the occasions that call for a change in price and determine whether a price-setter would uncover such situations quickly.

When to change price

A price cannot be allowed to remain unchanged for long periods in a volatile economy. Accordingly, a price is set, knowingly or unknowingly, for an indefinite but limited period—that is, until there is good reason to believe it should be changed. Under what circumstances should it be changed? How can anyone know when a price no longer achieves the firm's objectives as well as some other price would? Although this last question sounds very much like the one discussed at length earlier in this chapter, it focuses on *timing*—that is, *when* the prevailing price no longer is acceptable rather than the amount, the proper level of the price. We approach this question first by asking when most price changes actually take place and then asking when it is appropriate to change prices.

When most price changes take place

Some price changes are made openly and others secretly; the latter are sometimes, but not always, illegal. Most open price changes occur when (1) the firm introduces a new set of models, (2) substantial changes in the environment have taken place, or (3) the firm has undergone major internal changes in management, strategy, or conditions of cost. Secret price changes are less easy to categorize; they typically arise out of negotiations between a seller and individual customers. Most of them occur in response to shifts in the bargaining power and skills of the buyer and seller.

Note that both open and secret price changes occur primarily when circumstances of buyer, seller, or both have changed in some important respect, and so the situations that frequently give rise to a price change can be identified:

☐ Substantial changes in costs. Not all changes in costs would occasion a revision of price. Those that are likely to be short-lived or that occur shortly before a new line of product is to be introduced might not call for a price change.

☐ Artificial shortages of output. These might be due to a reduction in supply of some vital raw material, a calamity, or a strike or shipping tie-up.

☐ Sharp jumps in demand, possibly resulting from buyers building inventory in anticipation of a strike.

☐ A change in behavior by one or more rival firms such as a change in prices charged, expansion or announced expansion of capacity, worsened financial condition, or a new firm entering the industry and seeking a sizable market share.

Even when none of these changes has occurred, price changes may nevertheless be made as part of the periodic marketing plan. Responsible executives reappraise the firm's market position and financial needs, and as a result, decisions are often made to alter the offerings of the firm. Accordingly, the reexamination of market circumstances in conjunction with the annual marketing plan gives rise to many changes in product and marketing effort. Many open price changes take place at that time. However, a common price decision made in connection with a marketing plan is to leave prices and product as they were. Secret price changes are made when market circumstances alter substantially; the timing of such changes can be very flexible—far more so than that of open price changes can be.

When market circumstances change, generally the first effect on price is a change in discounts. A strengthening of demand is reflected in a reduction or elimination of discounts; a weakening of demand shows up first in the granting of secret discounts to customers who never received them before and also in an increase in discount size.

When price changes should take place

A broad general answer to the question of timing is that prices should be changed when market circumstances have shifted substantially. However, price changes involve costs that may offset the benefits obtained by changing price. Also, if a firm does produce annual marketing plans, management will often be wise to delay a modest price change until the planning period to avoid the frequent price changes that are disturbing to customers. Shifts in discounts are indeed the best way to alter price, because the seller can be highly flexible with respect to timing. A price-setter is wise to view price discounts, or increases in their size, as the first step in the process of changing list price lest list prices become excessively flexible.

Certain conditions are particularly favorable for price increases; when they occur, a price-setter would be wise to explore the effects of raising price. Particularly favorable conditions are created by substantial increases in major cost elements to all producers—as by wage settlements, increases in prices of important raw material components, and obvious shortages of materials.

As a seller obtains further information about customer reaction to his product, he may learn things that call for price change. For example, he may learn that his product changes have been received very favorably—or very unfavorably—by ultimate customers, and he may develop ideas for exploiting his market opportunities that he had not recognized before. Some of those factors may call for a change in price.

Summary and conclusions

We have examined what is involved in appraising the prices of a firm, in particular the prices charged by a hypothetical TV manufacturer. We found ourselves asking a long series of questions—starting with "Are the prices too high or too low?"—about the average price of the entire line as well as the price of each model. The answers to almost all questions about price turned out to revolve around two general issues: the objectives sought by the firm via price and the responses of the various parties to the pricing process.

We also found that the responses of the parties to the pricing process are interrelated and that those responses are not uncontrollable—a firm can indeed influence the response patterns of ultimate customers, resellers, and rivals. Accordingly, we might say that a seller must know how the chief parties to the pricing process will respond and also know how and at what cost he might alter that response. Both involve a forecast of human behavior, something that is perilous in any connection. Most sellers, however, need only forecast the behavior of ultimate customers en masse and not the behavior of individuals. If possible, however, they should forecast the behavior of groups of similar customers rather than the average behavior of all customers. The individual customer or distributor usually bears little resemblance to the so-called average. Accordingly, price-setters are wise to analyze the response patterns of subgroups of ultimate customers, rivals, and resellers separately.

We saw further that data about past market behavior often are difficult to obtain, are of poor quality, and are extremely difficult to interpret for purposes of forecasting the near future. A price-setter cannot base his decision solely upon analyses of past sales data; beyond data, he requires an ability to conceive innovative actions. A wealth of understanding and logical reasoning can help to support a price decision. But a price-setter would do well to draw upon resources beyond his own knowledge and understanding. He must learn to solicit help from other individuals inside and outside his firm who might have something to contribute to his decisions. He generally needs their intuitive judgments more than their factual knowledge.

Price-setting clearly involves multifaceted decisions that cannot be made by routine procedures. The interests and responses of many parties must be balanced, and a price-setter would do well to develop a marketing/pricing strategy and substrategies to guide and inform his decisions. Beyond that, many price-oriented marketing programs that combine price with other marketing actions in a way that achieves synergy might be adopted by the seller. The ingenuity with which the price-setter conceives of such programs is perhaps the most vital determinant of his success.

We can define price-setter success to be the setting of the right price, a highly elusive concept. For working purposes we can consider the right price to be that which achieves the firm's goals better than any other possible prices in the prevailing environment and in the context of the other marketing actions of the firm. In practice this usually means that the price must be paid by a substantial number of customers; it must yield a profit to the firm—that is, it must exceed the firm's relevant costs; it must gain strong sales support from resellers; and it must elicit behavior from rivals that is not seriously damaging to the firm. No price will meet all those requirements fully or equally. If one requirement is to be met, another must be sacrificed at least partially.

Consequently, the right price may be considered a compromise. The right price for ultimate customers is related to costs, which may vary with output. The right price for resellers is related to the margins that resellers add to the prices they pay, the amount of sales support and exposure that they are willing to give to an item, and the kinds of reseller that are willing to sell the item. The right price to charge in respect to competition takes account of rivals' responses to any action the firm might take, including the possibility that at least one rival will take counteraction.

The following chapters will extend the TV set example developed in this chapter and discuss the three main elements involved in price decisions: ultimate customers, resellers, and rivals. The way in which these separate sets of considerations fit together will then be discussed. Specific hypothetical data will be developed, and an effort will be made to face some of the problems that plague most price-setters in dealing with detailed information and also its absence.

Pricing Products in Their Prime

ULTIMATE CUSTOMERS

THIS CHAPTER ANALYZES the ultimate-customer considerations that a price-setter should take into account in arriving at a price. One focus will be on the objectives and subobjectives that might be achieved through the use of price. Another focus will be on the possibility of using price in order to obtain greater benefits from ultimate customers—purchases, loyalty, and word-of-mouth advertising—without winning customers from its rivals. The use of price to expand market share will be discussed in the next chapter.

This chapter is *not* addressed to the determination of retail price by a firm that has no rivals or possesses a very strong distribution system. Such a firm could charge prices far higher than are otherwise feasible. To make the analysis of price-setting for the ultimate customer quite realistic, we will assume that the firm (1) retains its present distribution system and existing margins and (2) will obtain essentially its current market share. Later we will explore what the firm might do to alter those circumstances in its favor by means of price.

The fundamental approach is the one developed in the preceding chapter: to match the firm's pricing and marketing objectives with the consequences of price changes. Given the firm's objectives, a series of questions is raised; the answers will indicate whether the prevailing price is proper or right. Once the questions are formulated, the price-setter must find sources of information that will help him answer them. The quality of evidence available for that purpose is assessed. Emphasis is placed upon problems of data interpretation with an eye to avoiding the pitfalls into which the unwary often fall.

HOW ULTIMATE CUSTOMERS RESPOND TO PRICE

The ultimate customer is the final determinant of a product's success. No matter how the other parties to the business process react, if the ultimate customer is not induced to make the purchase, the product cannot survive. The test that every price must meet is whether ultimate customers will buy enough units at that price to support the enterprise.

Marketing executives must, therefore, understand fully that a price must be acceptable to large numbers of customers. What makes that very difficult is that prices that would be acceptable to ultimate customers very frequently alienate distributors and retailers, are unprofitable for the manufacturer, or are out of line with competitors' prices. Nevertheless, the logical starting point for an appraisal of a price is at the ultimate-customer level.

When a customer purchases a product, he generally obtains a variety of benefits and makes some sacrifices. He usually obtains a physical product and also some services during the act of purchase, typically from the retailer's salesmen. He obtains the right to return his purchase if it is unsatisfactory, with varying degrees of inconvenience. He ordinarily purchases service from the manufacturer or the distributor in the event the product fails to function properly. He may obtain credit accommodations. All that he gets at some price. The price itself can be viewed as a potential benefit inasmuch as a low price can be a benefit that is lacking when the customer pays a high price. Of the many benefits that a customer seeks from a purchase, low price is only one, and not necessarily the most important one. We will call these benefits the customer benefits mix.

The importance of price cannot be generalized either for all individuals or for all products. Certain customers are far more sensitive to price appeals than others. Paradoxically, better educated and more affluent customers typically exhibit greater price sensitivity than do persons of low income and education. Similarly, most buyers of products purchased frequently are far more sensitive to price changes than are buyers of products purchased less frequently. For example, modest changes in the price of milk, butter, coffee, bread, soap, men's shirts, and sheets seem to be widely noticed and give rise to strong responses. Proportionate changes in the price of pimentoes, shoe laces, scarves, coffee percolators, and window shades lead to relatively little response.

Just as price is only one element in the customer benefits mix, so it is only one element in the seller's marketing mix. Of course, most of the benefits in the customer benefits mix are put there by the seller, and to that extent, the customer benefits mix and the marketing mix are similar. They differ mainly in that some of the seller's expenditures, constituting part of his marketing mix, are intended to persuade the customer to buy rather than to provide benefits. Examples are advertising, personal selling, and costs associated with developing channels of distribution.

The importance that the seller attaches to the price component of his marketing mix is roughly equivalent to the importance that he believes the ultimate customer attaches to it. Unfortunately, that generalization, even if valid, is exceedingly difficult to apply. In the first place, persons who buy the same product do not place equal emphasis on price appeals. Second, sellers attempt to change customers' values. Indeed, one important use of advertising is to divert customers' attention from price to product features, quality, or service.

DETERMINING CUSTOMER RESPONSES TO PRICE CHANGES

A black-box approach to customer responses to price changes is possible. It consists in observing the responses of customers to changes in price and formulating generalizations about them, but it is also necessary to understand those responses. For some purposes it is enough for a seller to know, for example, that if he lowers price by 5 percent, his unit sales will increase between 6 and 7 percent. But if he is trying to formulate a pricing strategy or is trying to employ price in a novel and cunning manner in conjunction with other promotional devices, he must understand the process by which customers are affected by price changes. In other words, he must know what goes on inside the customer, the black box, when the price changes so that he can feed in the right prices. In Chapter 2 the way in which different elements in the marketing mix work was sketched in general terms. We will now examine that important issue in some detail as it applies to ultimate customers

Model of price effects

A price-setter who wishes to forecast and perhaps alter consumer response to change in price and to price-oriented marketing programs (POMPS) must understand how price changes affect potential customers. More specifically, he should be able to explain the process by which a change in price induces certain customers to alter their purchase and use of a product and how it affects their view of the product's quality, their opinion of the manufacturing company, and so on. In modern parlance, he should have a model to explain how the behavior and attitudes of customers are affected by price.

Some price-setting executives seem to perform quite well without such a model. They do so on the strength of strong intuitive abilities, which presumably means that they possess an excellent model on an unconscious level, or on the strength of long experience that provides them with a black-box understanding of how price and POMPS operate. That usually means they operate in a field in which the responses of ultimate customers to changes in price are reasonably consistent over time; they are intelligent and careful about drawing conclusions from past experience and can forecast successfully even though they do not understand how price affects sales, usage, perception of quality, and opinion of producers. Even if the price-setter does not understand what happens inside the black box, he can perform relatively well if he knows what will come out of it. However, a knowledge of what happens when price changes can help a decision maker to know what kinds of customers will be influenced by a price change, the circumstances under which they will be influenced most, the actions they will take when they learn of the price change, their subsequent behavior, and so on. Such understanding is very helpful in deciding what kinds of price actions to initiate and when and to whom they should be directed.

Human behavior is extraordinarily complex and intractable to efforts to understand it. If an executive's success depended upon his accurately predicting the behavior of specific individuals, all executives would be failures. On the other hand, some things have been learned about customers' behavior in general that are helpful for most businessmen and, in specific contexts, industries and markets. We have observed some moderately consistent behavior that permits us to understand at least partly how price affects customers. Accordingly, we will sketch the models that some price-setters may find helpful.

Models of response to price

The simplest model of the operation of price on behavior depicts price as a barrier or hurdle that customers must overcome if they are to purchase something they want. It is assumed that almost everybody wants almost every product and is kept from buying it only by the penalty he must incur—its price. Accordingly, price holds buyers back from purchase and only those who value the product most are likely to incur the penalty of purchase.

Another model in wide use is based on the assumption that price can affect behavior only if it is perceived, interpreted, and evaluated in particular ways. Many products are unknown to some potential customers; also, many price changes are not *perceived* by other potential customers. In addition, customers ordinarily attach a meaning to each price change; they try to explain why it took place—they *interpret* it. Beyond that, each customer tries to determine what meaning the price change has for him; that is, he decides what he should do about it. His *evaluation* might lead him to conclude that he should take no action, or he might conclude that he should make a purchase quickly lest he miss the opportunity to do so on favorable terms.

This behavioral model does not explain why certain customers perceive price changes while others do not. It does not explain the process by which individuals make particular interpretations, nor does it indicate how they decide what the price changes mean to them. And that lack is not altogether surprising; for the process by which people perceive, interpret, and evaluate any event surely varies greatly from one context to another. One cannot expect generalizations that would be applicable to all cases. The behavioral model simply directs a price-setter's attention to three essential behavioral processes—perception, interpretation, and evaluation—as they operate in his particular industry.

A third model may be called a decision-making model; it explains the effect of price on customers in terms of a rational calculation by customers of the costs and benefits of alternatives open to them. The assumption is that customers are familiar with all alternatives and can make accurate appraisals of them; that is, they are getting something they require to accomplish a clear goal as efficiently as possible. A customer can therefore appraise any purchase reliably as to its merits. We know, of course, that many people might be better off without things they desire. We know too that many place an unreasonable value on the items they wish and recognize that fact only after they have made a purchase. The valuations of products by some customers fluctuate substantially over small periods of time. Many customers value money not for what it is or does but for its symbolic value. All those factors explain why most customers exhibit strange buying behavior from time to time.

Many individuals who behave in a manner that seems irrational to others are simply reflecting their unusual personal values and tastes. The values of specialists in purchasing behavior are almost at the opposite pole from those of young, optimistic, impulsive, fun-loving adolescents. Any adolescent who behaved like an elderly, theoretical economist and shared the latter's values would be considered strange if not clearly irrational. Accordingly, rationality has meaning only in the context of some individual's values, and those values vary widely. Given the great ambiguity in the term as applied to particular purchase situations, the decision-making model does not help greatly to explain the behavior of most customers.

The decision-making model therefore suggests that the price-setter familiarize himself with the factors that most consumers will consider to be the costs and benefits associated with his product and how they value those things. Again, this model mainly raises interesting questions, but at least it leaves the price-setter free to search for elusive answers that may apply in his particular situation.

To use all of these models in combination, it is necessary to forecast the responses of ultimate customers to a particular price change. But do these models isolate the key questions that a price-setter should raise and help him make reasonable guesses at the right answers? Let us try to answer that question.

From the first model the price-setter would conclude that any price increase would discourage purchases whereas a price reduction would increase them. (Subsequently we will note exceptions to that generalization.) The first model would also suggest that the larger the change in price the greater its effect on sales.

The second model would direct the price-setter to estimate the percent of potential customers who would perceive his price change; further, it would suggest that he try to determine how people learn of changes in price and how quickly they do so. Given that understanding, he could draw inferences about how he should announce his price changes, as to both the media and the terminology to employ. Presumably, he would also try to determine what kinds of customers are the quickest to learn of price changes and what kinds are the least likely and the last to do so. He might then have clues to how he might quickly reach those who ordinarily are slow to learn of price changes. Simply with respect to the problem of perception, then, the behavioral model suggests specific questions and possible research that could help a price-setter who is trying to forecast the results of a specific price decision. However, the answers to those questions and the suggested research rarely would provide the basis for very accurate forecasts of customers' responses.

The behavioral model is most suggestive with respect to the interpretation of price changes. It suggests that different potential customers will not attach the same meaning to a price change. Indeed, certain kinds of people are more or less routinely unfavorable to or suspicious of a price change, whereas others tend to view a price change favorably. Subsequently, we will indicate the conflicting interpretations that customers can and do place on the same price event.

What was previously applied to perception and interpretation applies to the evaluation of price changes as well. An executive errs badly if he believes that almost all his potential customers have similar situations. Two customers who perceive a price change and interpret it in the same way might behave very differently because one is heavily in debt and the other is not.

The third model, which accounts for customer responses by assuming that they are rational, could help a marketing executive explain the evaluation process. However, he must avoid the trap of considering as rational only the things that he does himself and recognize the many powerful and legitimate influences on behavior beyond those of finance and economics. Many people cherish their illusions, want desperately to believe in minor miracles, and place enormous value on what others would consider trifling benefits. Nevertheless, a price-setter should look for uniformities in the way particular types of customers approach purchase decisions. If the main types of customers were studied in depth as they made particular purchases, some generalizations of great value to price-setters might emerge. Through such studies an executive might learn how different types of customers value the benefits and sacrifices associated with a given product, and especially the importance they attach to price.

Thus the three models reviewed do illuminate the effect of price on customer behavior, even though they mainly raise questions rather than provide answers. Careful application of the models to individual situations should help a price-setter understand the many and complex factors that influence the behavior of his potential customers and their response to price. However, beyond such understanding, a price-setter must take account of the special circumstances that prevail when prices are changed, the special position occupied by each firm, and the special reactions of each type of customer to any price stimulus. General models, however illuminating, require considerable elaboration if applied to specific tasks.

Price-setters who wish to determine whether prevailing prices are correct as far as they affect and are affected by ultimate customers will largely retrace the path taken in the preceding chapter. That is, they will ask whether prices are either too high or too low with respect to ultimate customers. Their next questions will be what goals the firm could achieve by means of price and what symptoms would reveal whether price was too high or too low.

ATTAINABLE ULTIMATE-CUSTOMER GOALS

The varied consequences of price changes can be depicted by a consequence net, Figure 4-1, that shows that price has several distinct areas of influence when only its effect on ultimate customers is considered. (Price also affects the firm internally—its production costs, marketing costs, cash flow, inventories, and salesmen's morale—and its competitive relations and resellers as well.) Customer behavior, for example, might include one or more of the following: amount of product purchased, use of

Figure 4-1. A price change consequence net.

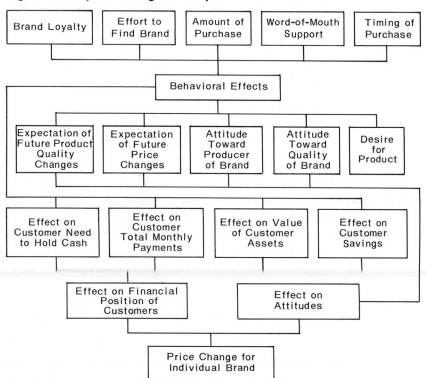

the product, timing of the purchase, inventories of the product held, and word-of-mouth advertising of the product.

Another area of price influence is customer attitude. A change in price often communicates ambiguous messages to which the customer attaches meanings of his own that change his attitudes and possibly his subsequent behavior. Among those possible meanings are these:

The quality of the product has been changed.

The product is about to be superseded by another.

This price change is a precursor to another change in the same direction.

The price change indicates a change in customer responses to the product.

The manufacturer of the product is in financial difficulty.

A change in price, especially for a product that represents a major element in most consumer budgets, also alters the financial position of customers by reducing the funds available for other products. Accordingly, a price change might have these effects on ultimate customers:

It alters their financial resources and affects their other outlays.

It requires them to borrow.

It increases the monthly payments for which they are liable.

A price-setter should be alert to the intended consequences of his price changes, but he should also recognize that changes in price often have unintended effects that are no less significant because they are unintended. To return to whether a particular price is right vis-à-vis ultimate customers, the price-setter must ask such questions as these: Is the prevailing price inducing customers to buy *when* I would like them to buy? Could a change in price significantly alter the use of the product? Could a modest price change substantially increase the inventories held by ultimate customers? Would a slight decline in price make the monthly payments for our product appear significantly smaller?

The rightness of any price for ultimate customers can be determined only by measuring the price against the seller's objectives. More specifically, a price is right if it results in the desired timing of purchase, use, inventory holding, attitude toward product quality, view of manufacturer reliability, word-of-mouth advertising, perceived size of installment charges, and availability of funds for other purchases. The price-setter must not only consider all those goals but also assign them weights that reflect their importance to him.

As has been stressed repeatedly, an executive rarely knows the full effects of a price change in any given situation. However, a valid appraisal of any price requires that the price-setter estimate the effects of his firm's prices. Since such estimates are difficult in the extreme, most price-setters limit their concern and forecasts to the areas of influence that are crucial and ignore those that are minor. The difficulty is that a minor area may become a major one. For example, the timing of purchase becomes very important to a company that needs to raise funds from customers when financial institutions are curtailing credit.

Again the correctness of a price for ultimate customers is shown to depend on a clear identification of price objectives. Because price exerts a variety of effects on ultimate customers, a variety of subgoals are possible. To appraise any particular price, as was seen earlier, the price-setter requires a forecast of the full potential consequences of a change in price and a comparison of those effects with the probable effects of the most attractive alternatives. Only in that way can he determine whether matters would be improved or worsened by any price change, and there is no shortcut through the labyrinth.

Symptoms of a wrong price—for the ultimate customer

The clearest symptoms of a price that is wrong from the standpoint of ultimate customers are great disparities between output and sales. An inability of the manufacturer to produce as much of the brand as is being sold over a period of time is almost conclusive evidence that the brand is underpriced. On the other hand, the manufacturer's inability to sell a sizable proportion of what he can produce is not proof that the brand is overpriced unless the price is far above relevant costs and a reduction in it would not result in many rival firms also lowering price. In other words, the relation between sales and productive capacity can indicate that prices are too low but not that they are too high.

A price-setter must usually look for symptoms of wrong price in the views that ultimate customers express about price and also in the views of retailers and retail salesmen. Both ultimate customers and retailers might be expected to behave in particular ways when they regard a brand price as too high or too low. First, then, what symptoms would be observable among ultimate customers and retailers if a brand were selling at too high a price?

Rarely is a product priced so high that virtually not one customer will buy it or so low that almost everyone would prefer it to any competing brand. Accordingly, some customers who do not consider a brand too high in price will always be found, even though they are a minority.

When a brand is overpriced, many of its potential customers will be saying things like the following:

> That brand isn't worth as much as other brands that sell for less.
> Other brands offer better quality at the same price.
> The product just isn't worth what it costs.

Such statements indicate that the customer believes rival brands offer him better value. Since quite conflicting brand preferences are numerous, there must be many such statements. How can the instances in which a brand is overpriced be separated from simple customer preference for one brand over another?

When the quality of the product offered for sale is virtually identical with that of competing products and that uniformity of quality is widely known, almost any price differential is suspect. On the other hand, many customers have the impression that quality is different even when it is not. Accordingly, if price differences are to be matched against quality differences, the price-setter must deal with *perceived* quality rather than actual quality.

Thus the fact that many customers believe that certain brands offer better values than others is not proof that any of the brands are overpriced. On the other hand if many customers, each of whom favors different brands, agreed that one particular brand was overpriced, that brand would appear to have a pricing problem vis-à-vis ultimate customers. The expectation would be that only small amounts of that brand would be sold, but even then exceptions would be found. Many an overpriced restaurant or resort hotel, piece of jewelry, or article of clothing becomes desired and admired simply because it *is* overpriced.

Retailers and retail salesmen can be valuable sources of information about the correctness of price, especially retailers who carry several brands. They can indicate which brand in their opinion offers customers the best value—a feeling they are likely to transmit to customers. They can also describe customer reactions. Ordinarily they sell only a few rather than all brands, and so their views have limited scope. Nevertheless, if most retail salesmen say, "I think your brand offers good value compared with other brands we carry," that brand's prices probably are not too high.

What are the indications that the price of a particular brand is too low? One would accept as evidence the fact that one brand was named far more often than any other as representing the best value. A censensus to that effect among retail salesmen would usually carry more weight than similar statements by ultimate customers. Actual sales figures that showed a rapid rise in market share would greatly reinforce verbal statements.

The foregoing questions and answers buttress a conclusion stated several times already: A firm rarely has clearly identifiable price problems; its marketing problems may derive from many sources other than price. Price is special in that a price adjustment frequently would overcome many difficulties that really do not stem from wrong prices. For example, poor product features, mediocre design, and ineffective advertising would ordinarily create serious marketing problems. They might, however, pass unnoticed if price were set sufficiently low to offset them; then the low price would conceal but not solve the firm's true problems. The following examples indicate the great difficulty in detecting pure price problems.

1. A firm is earning profits well below average in the industry and is losing market share to two other firms that are much more profitable. When asked, most customers say that the firm's product is too expensive, although it is equal in quality to the products offered by the other two firms.

This firm appears to be a relatively inefficient producer, so that its management is forced to charge prices that seem to be out of line with competitors' prices. The real trouble apparently is not too high a price but excessive costs; other firms have demonstrated that lower costs are feasible.

2. This firm is losing market position even though it offers a good-quality product at prices that are as attractive as those of competing brands. Its advertising, however, has been ineffective, and its brand has suffered some loss of prestige and drawing power.

Although the situation described might be improved for a time by a price reduction, an enduring solution to this firm's problem is better advertising. Put differently, the brand's price is too low from the long-run standpoint, and its advertising is too ineffective.

3. This firm offers first-rate product quality, durability, and ease of service at a price somewhat below the average charged by other firms in the industry. However, the design of the product is considered unattractive by many customers who purchase other brands in preference to it. If the brand's prices were reduced moderately, however, sales would expand and possibly profits as well.

This situation could represent both a design and a pricing problem. Clearly, poor product design is hurting the company's sales badly. But if a lower price would increase the firm's profitability, despite the poor product design, the product also suffers from a pricing problem.

4. This firm finds its sales declining steadily even though it offers product quality equal to that available from rivals and charges no more than rivals. Its product happens to be sold through distributors who are not able to sell the brand to first-rate retailers. The firm is suffering from a weak distribution organization rather than a price problem.

5. Like the firm in (4), this firm is losing ground despite correct price and quality. Other firms in the market are also losing ground to newcomers that have entered the industry. In this case we may have an inevitable loss of sales due to an influx of competitors that the firm could not have prevented. We would say that no price problem exists and that the problem is simply one of increased competition or increased production capacity.

These five examples illustrate that it is rarely obvious whether a firm's sales problems are due to faulty price or some other reason. Certainly a correct diagnosis cannot be made from a study of sales data alone. Only if considerable information were collected especially for the purpose—usually by interviewing both consumers and retailers—could the problems resulting from defective price be uncovered. And in most cases, even after such interview studies, an executive would not know whether a sales problem was truly the result of defective price.

Market-by-market evaluation. The correctness of prevailing price vis-à-vis the ultimate customer is likely to vary from market to market. The national market is composed of many decidedly different regional markets; almost every seller fares much better in certain regions than in others. Accordingly, the price-setter must distinguish between two sets of decisions and actions. One set concerns the national moves that he might make and the other the regional moves.

Although the power of sellers to behave differently in individual markets is limited somewhat by law, sellers need not and actually do not sell on the same terms in all markets. A seller is not required to make the same number of sales calls in separate markets; nor must local advertising efforts be the same in all markets; nor must sellers offer identical service to buyers in widely separated areas. It is not even clear that the Robinson-Patman Act requires sellers to change price in the same way in all regions, in view of the wide differences in the competitiveness of individual regions. As already implied, a national brand of TV sets will meet far stronger competition from its rivals in some markets than in others and will be forced to behave differently with respect to price and other factors in different markets.

Accordingly, when our hypothetical price-setter attempts to evaluate the price he inherited from his predecessor, he must treat each region separately. As a consequence, he will become highly dependent upon data that are available for individual markets. And inasmuch as certain models are usually more successful in certain markets than others as well as more successful nationwide, he will be forced to evaluate his prices model by model and market by market.

Our price-setter might well be impatient to get his hands on solid data so that he can make factual judgments about whether he has a price problem with any of his models in any regional markets. If he has had experience in marketing, he will know the kinds of data—qualitative and quantitative—that would ordinarily be available to him and that might permit an appraisal of prevailing prices. The most commonly available data that might be relevant to an apprasial of prices from the standpoint of their appropriateness for ultimate customers include:

- ☐ Sales by the firm to its individual distributors by individual model.
- ☐ Sales by distributors to their retail customers. (These data are obtained from distributors who handle one manufacturer's line exclusively.)
- ☐ Costs of production by individual model, which usually take the form of standard cost computations. Also available are the records of the actual costs of individual runs of specific models in the recent past.
- ☐ Field reports about customer reactions from regional salesmen and regional sales managers.
- ☐ Reports of special market research studies.
- ☐ Reports from a trade association on total sales of the association's membership, which permit computations of market shares.

From the data sources listed a price-setter could draw an avalanche of factual information that possesses at least an apparent relevance to price but which will not help much in an appraisal of price other than possibly to identify gross errors. Let us see why that is so and identify some of the pitfalls in using data, especially sales data, to determine whether a firm has a pricing problem,

Sales data

A major appliance manufacturer provides its executives with a computer printout of its sales of all models of TV sets in all its markets. Usually the models that are sources of trouble in one market are doing well in others. An hour spent studying these data typically would leave anyone deeply confused; for individual markets show very little order. The price-setter must wonder whether the chaos reflected in the sales data could be reduced by anything he might do about price. Should he lower the price of model X32C in Atlanta, where sales are down, and possibly raise it in St. Louis, where sales of that model are far ahead of expectations? Is the situation he now faces very different from that which existed in the markets served by his company during, say, the past month? During the past year? If he instructed the computer to give him similar sales information for a date three, six, and nine months before, he would find the reports very similar in describing what appears to be near-chaos. In some markets sales would be very strong whereas others would seem to present serious problems, and almost every market would have a model that sold well below expectations and another well above.

The price-setter would wonder what his colleagues were thinking and doing with the same computer printouts. He would know that the sales manager, the advertising director, the market research director, and the VP's of distribution and of product planning received the same data. Were they expecting him to clean up the problems in the various markets by suitable price adjustments? Had he been elevated to his responsibilities for pricing to rectify a serious situation that had gone uncorrected for at least nine months? If he had been and if he asked for a computer printout for two, four, and eight years earlier, they too would reflect no less chaos in the marketplace than the most recent reports.

How could his colleagues be resigned to such chaos? Could it be that they had just stopped caring and now accepted serious imbalance in the market? Or were these really his problems primarily? Would his colleagues expect him to take action, if not leadership? If he were to meet the sales manager and director of advertising in the executive dining room and mention that he had been reviewing the sales data for the last few quarters, he might be told that they wished that business would always be as good as it had been for the last twelve months.

A price-setter in this hypothetical inherited situation who reflected deeply might reach the following tentative conclusions:

☐ No one can tell what is going on in a market from a description of sales during a fairly brief period. Even a month is too brief. Accidents with respect to order dates, especially at the beginning and end of the period, produce deceptive results.

☐ When a firm sells many models of its product in a large number of markets, it is exposed to a very large number of potential problems—instances in which a model seems to be selling very poorly. If there are over 200 markets and 20 models, there are 4,000 possible problem spots each week. It would be remarkable if, during a short period, dozens, if not hundreds of models, did not seem to be selling far below expectations.

☐ When long periods and groups of models are considered, the number of sales problems shrinks sharply. Similarly, apparent sources of strength prove to be flashes in the pan.

☐ Although an executive cannot get reliable clues to real trouble from such sales data as he had been studying, it would be unthinkable that he would not scan them.

☐ When a persistent sales problem shows up in a quick analysis of sales data, its source cannot be identified; it could be a pricing, sales, service, product quality, advertising, or retail efficiency problem. All anyone could say with confidence is that a problem apparently exists. It might be called a marketing problem, although possibly the company was not able to ship merchandise into that area because of a local trucking strike.

☐ Any sales/marketing problem is as likely to stem from other sources as from mistaken pricing.

Given the last two conclusions, how would a price-setter be able to know whether the prices his firm was charging were wrong from the standpoint of ultimate customers? Was he looking at the wrong information in the first place? Maybe he shouldn't be looking at his firm's sales to distributors at all. Those sales need not run parallel to sales by retailers to ultimate customers.

From a discussion with the firm's sales analyst a price-setter would learn quickly that sales to distributors do not vary directly with retail sales. He would also learn that if his company conducted a sample study of sales by retailers, it could not provide reliable information for any single market area with the possible exception of metropolitan New York. That is, the number of retailers surveyed in any market would be too small to describe that market reliably. By that kind of study—which the firm might conduct monthly—the company's sales would be shown to be holding up quite well both in total and as a share of the total, as we have assumed.

The price-setter might learn that his company depended mainly on its field salesmen to discover quickly if sales at retail were in trouble. The salesmen would get their information by checking distributor sales to retailers, by talking to distributor salesmen, and even by calling directly on retailers. A price-setter would be wise to spend a few days out in the field with one of the company's best regional sales managers to discover what information could be obtained from field reports—if the salesmen were asked to provide it—and to understand what is and is not included in the firm's periodic sales reports. The price-setter might make several resolutions after his study of available sales data and discussions with his colleagues. First, he might decide not to worry much over the monthly sales reports; second, he might pay very close attention to the reports of the regional sales managers; and, third, he might try to insure that regional sales managers would pick up symptoms of a pricing problem in their markets in their earliest incipiency. It is this last resolution that requires development.

We are again asking how an executive in the home office might identify a pricing problem; now we assume that he has access to persons highly informed about the industry and the product who could easily speak to retailers, retail salesmen, distributors, and even persons in retail shops who are looking at TV sets. As stressed earlier, the suitability of price must be judged by more than its effect on current sales; for top management might be pursuing other goals.

The starting point in developing regional sales managers as an early warning system for price difficulties must therefore be an identification of the firm's pricing goals with respect to ultimate customers. Almost always, current sales are a primary objective and are often stated in clear, quantitative terms, even for individual retailers. Sometimes the firm even specifies the competing brands that it seeks to displace, so that the sales of particular rival brands represent another indicator of whether the firm is achieving its goals. Retail salesmen's evaluation of rival brands, as indicated, is another clue to the correctness of price, but often the salesmen cannot divorce their evaluations from the size of the rewards they obtain for selling different brands. Of course, the remarks by potential customers when different brands are mentioned is one of the best sources of brand image information obtainable from the field. However, very little such information is obtained, and only extreme instances are likely to be remembered and reported. The foregoing line of reasoning might induce a price-setter to develop something like the following list of questions to be kept in mind by regional salesmen:

Do the retailers who carry our brand regard it as offering good value for most customers?

Are retailers who carry our brand assigning it enough space and is the space fairly choice?

Do retail salesmen know the strong features of our brand and state them effectively to prospective customers?

What impression do most customers seem to have of our brand? What features seem to trouble them most? What features seem to attract them most?

Which of our models do retail salesmen like most to sell?

For which rival models do retail salesmen have strong preference?

Are rival manufacturers or distributors doing anything unusual? If so, what is it?

If a firm's regional salesmen asked many retailers and retail salesmen such questions and reported the replies accurately, their firm would obtain a valuable body of marketing information and would possess an excellent basis for deciding whether and where it faced a pricing problem and opportunity.

CLASSIFICATION OF ULTIMATE CUSTOMERS

As has been stressed repeatedly, potential customers for virtually everything differ significantly in respects that have some bearing on price. Some customers place heavy emphasis on price appeals, whereas others give them little weight; some are highly informed about the prices, quality, service, and availability of rival brands, whereas others know very little; and some are very responsive to price changes, whereas others are not. Individual customers vary greatly in the brand they favor and the degree of their preference for it—that is, how much more they would be willing to pay for it than for their next most-favored brand—and the degree of their trust in and loyalty to retailers. These large differences among customers suggest that a price-setter would be wise to classify potential customers according to the characteristics most germane to the setting of price. When he has done that, he can decide which of the classes he has identified he should try to cultivate and whose business he should not expect to get, and then make his price decisions with a specific group of customers clearly in mind. It is very difficult to set prices without knowing for whom they are being set. How then might our hypothetical price-setter for a TV set manufacturer classify ultimate customers for the purpose of making valid price decisions? What would be the result of setting price for the average customer?

Diversity of ultimate-customer response to price

To begin with, the price-setter would classify potential customers *for pricing purposes only;* that is, he would identify groups of potential customers *within the firm's customer segments* who differ in ways that are related to price. An awareness of differences among subgroups of customers whose patronage his firm is seeking would help him select among alternative price decisions. For example, he would know that certain options available to him would please a particular group of specific estimated size while it displeased another; the same option would lead one group to defer purchase and another to hasten purchase. Certainly any marketing executive must recognize the diversity of his prospective customers and must not expect his pricing actions to affect all of them in the same way.

The price-setter's classification of customers for pricing purposes would usually represent a further subdivision of an already select group of customers. Presumably the firm's top management would have decided to cultivate a particular customer segment that represents a subgroup of all potential customers for TV sets. In selecting a particular group of customers for cultivation, top management usually employs a price criterion. For example, it might define its target customers as families that will pay the average price for TV sets or a little above. In addition, it might define its target customers as households with one or more children under school age, a head who is either a professional or an executive with a promising future, and a home that is in a suburb and that stretches the family's resources.

Is further classification of target customers possible or desirable *for pricing purposes?* Certainly if all customers within the target group were homogeneous with respect to price-related characteristics, further classification would be pointless. But if the segment included potential customers who differed in respects that would affect the firm's decisions about price—that is, if individual customers would be affected differently by price decisions—the price-setter could not evaluate alternatives unless he took account of those differences.

Important distinctions can be made among customers for pricing purposes, even within a group whose members would be willing to pay about the same price for the item. The distinctions can be made by answering these questions about customers:

Are they sensitive to price; do they respond to bargain offers?

Have they information about the prices of different brands?

Do they depend on credit; do they usually translate price into monthly payments?

In what kinds of store do they buy? Do they patronize stores that have a price identity, such as discount houses and warehouse stores?

Do they take pride in buying at low prices and fear being over-
charged?

Do they believe that competitive forces cause all sellers to charge essentially the same price?

Do they like to shop around or do they feel pressure to buy at the
first store?

Are they susceptible to sales talks that might persuade them to
purchase a step-up model?

Do they judge the quality of a product mainly by its price?

Are they trusting of sales people?

Are they very loyal to a particular retailer? Do they defer to his advice?

Not all these distinctions are pertinent to all price decisions, but
many of them would be relevant at least to some. Important differences
among potential customers homogeneous from many other standpoints
would be expected. For example, not all people who ordinarily pay the
average or slightly above average price for major appliances are equally
attracted by bargain advertising. Not all trust salespeople and so might
get some reassurance from a list price on the item itself. The price-setters' purpose in classifying target customers is *both* to describe how different types are responding to the firm's current offer and to suggest actions that might attract certain subgroups.

Although our price-setter has made some progress, he is still a long
way from knowing whether the firm's present TV prices are right. The
data he has examined prove to be only partially relevant to his needs and
very difficult to interpret. At most, they show what happened and what
seemed to cause it to happen. Reports of regional salesmen prove to be
his most fruitful source of information. He cannot find data that indicate
what would happen if he did certain things in the future; the company's
sales, cost records, and reports of its field sales force apply to the past.
But he mainly requires forecasts, especially of the effects of the changes
in price that he might recommend. Such forecasts cannot be based on
the firm's recent history alone, though that history provides the best
basis for making them.

As was discussed in the preceding chapter, our price-setter could
take refuge in the wisdom, largely intuitive, of the most informed and
experienced members of the firm. On occasion he could obtain similar
help from individuals outside the firm. Accordingly, let us assume that
he decides to employ the intellectual machinery outlined in the preced-

ing chapter. Our purpose is to indicate in some detail what is involved in employing that procedure and to suggest the kinds of results it might produce. He recognizes that he lacks the information needed to appraise prevailing prices. He has decided what he needs to know and from whom he must get it in order to make a valid appraisal. For example, he knows that he must forecast the reactions of ultimate customers, resellers, and rivals to any change in price by his firm.

At this point our price-setter would be wise to solicit the views of the most qualified members of the organization on two scores. First, he must learn what goals the firm should pursue by means of price action. Specifically, he must determine how much importance he should attach to such goals as increased current sales, the development of longer-run sales, improved brand image, and more favorable impressions about product quality. He must also know the relative importance of each of those goals. Those matters should be decided by top management and the board of directors, for it is their right—and within their power—to set objectives and determine their relative importance.

Second, he should solicit intuitive estimates of the likely effects of selected price changes from the members of the firm who are most directly involved and best informed. In addition, he should develop a procedure for obtaining the most considered opinion of his best-qualified colleagues as to what would happen if he were to adopt each of several price decisions. What questions should he raise? What methods should he employ to obtain answers?

A promising approach is the following one. The price-setter should assemble a list of price-related objectives accompanied by measures of their relative value, that is, the trade-offs among them. They would provide the basis for a numerical measure of the effectiveness of each pricing strategy. Second, he should collect the best estimates of the effects of the pricing actions under consideration. With those two components he can compute a score for each strategy. He then adopts the strategy with the highest score.

PRICE STRATEGIES TO OBTAIN BENEFITS
FROM ULTIMATE CUSTOMERS

As indicated in the preceding chapter, a firm will usually price its products more effectively if it develops a series of marketing and pricing substrategies. Also, it was suggested that an executive would be wise to develop such substrategies by examining his subobjectives. They would represent the goals of the substrategies, and the executive would select those that were most valuable to the firm and for which he could devise some potentially effective line of thinking and associated program of action.

Accordingly, Figure 4-2 presents in diagram form some subobjectives related to ultimate customers that a price-setter might elect to emphasize. The somewhat more complete Selected Subobjectives Related to Ultimate Customers might serve as starting points for the development of substrategies. Presumably a price-setter would examine such a

Figure 4-2. Subobjectives related to ultimate customers.

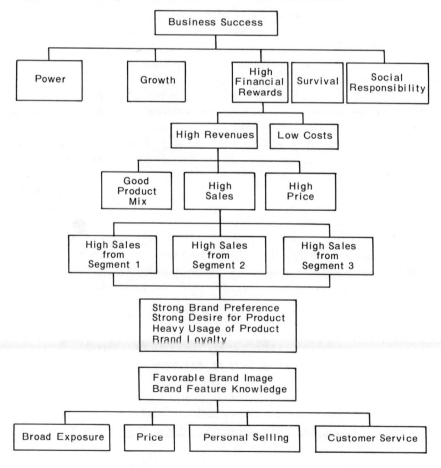

list and select the substrategies that seemed to be most promising. He would then develop a logic and a program of action that would attain them. He would choose for action those that promised to yield the greatest benefits in relation to costs.

SELECTED SUBOBJECTIVES RELATED TO
ULTIMATE CUSTOMERS

Attitudinal Subobjectives
1. Attitude toward product that is wanted in ultimate customers.
    a. That product is essential.
    b. That the purchaser is expected to use it.
    c. That its use gives a person a desired social position.
    d. Favorable belief about the benefits to be derived from the product.
    e. Favorable belief about the kinds of people who use the product.
    f. Belief that the product is within the purchaser's means.
2. Attitudes toward the company that makes the product.
    a. Its preeminence in technology.
    b. Its concern for its customers.
    c. Its capacity to endure and its willingness to honor its guarantees.
3. Attitudes toward the brand.
    a. Belief in its high quality.
    b. Belief in its repair or replacement in the event of defect or failure.
    c. Belief in its social position—actually in the kinds of people who buy it.

Facilitating Purchase Subobjectives
1. The product is readily available.
2. Payment arrangements are convenient.
3. Packaging is convenient and delivery can be arranged.

Behavioral Subobjectives
1. High level of usage.
2. Large-quantity purchase at each transaction.
3. Purchase at time convenient for the seller.
4. Customer performance of service that reduces the seller's costs.
5. Favorable word-of-mouth support.
6. Large customer inventories of the product.
7. Customer purchase by cash or credit, whichever is advantageous for seller.
8. Quick customer response to special inducements.

Miscellaneous Subobjectives
1. Attract potential customer's attention to the product, the brand, special product features, or particular promotions.
2. Increase number of potential customers that consider patronizing you—win and keep a place on their list of acceptable suppliers.
3. Obtain valid market information about what customers want and how they would respond to different actions that the seller might take.

These subobjectives represent benefits that a firm might hope to achieve with respect to its ultimate customers. Some of them are essentially attitudinal, others are behavioral, and some would facilitate purchase by the ultimate customers. A firm could be expected to pursue attitudinal and facilitating objectives in order to induce the desired behavior in customers; accordingly, behavioral objectives are on a higher level than the other two categories (see Figure 4-1).

IDENTIFICATION OF ULTIMATE CONSUMER OBJECTIVES

Let us now specify the method by which a firm might compose a statement of its objectives. Selected members of top management and owners would be sent a Questionnaire on Company Objectives together with a letter to explain the purpose of the questionnaire, stress its importance,

---

SUBJECT: Questionnaire on Company Business Objectives

Dear Joe:

I've asked Bill Hart to take on the job of setting down the company's objectives—both short- and long-term—in a way that would help all of us devise and assess various alternative strategies. Bill has been told that he is not to settle for any vague, general, public-relations-type statements but to get down to specific goals that could be matched against actual achievement. He has also been instructed to flesh out our goals to identify means that will lead us to our ultimate objectives.

You are one of a few members of the firm who are being asked to help Bill put together this set of objectives. In replying, recognize that you are asked to represent the interests of the firm's stockholders and top management rather than your own goals or those of individuals who trade in our securities for a quick profit. And I should think you would want to consider such possible goals as service to the community, responsibilities to our employees and suppliers, and meeting the needs of our customers.

Please give this project your full support. It won't require much time, and it covers matters that you probably have given much thought to in the past. I urge only one constraint: Do not discuss your answers with anyone until Bill has completed his analysis.

The attached questionnaire is the first of several that you will be receiving. You will be given an opportunity to revise your responses after seeing the answers that Bill receives from others who are participating in the project.

Please get the completed questionnaire back to Bill by ———.

Cordially,

———

President

QUESTIONNAIRE ON COMPANY OBJECTIVES

Please answer the following questions to the best of your ability. In most cases, the question has no "right" answer and we only want your considered opinion. If you want to qualify or elaborate on your answer, please do so.

Broadly speaking, every corporation pursues business success. Ordinarily, success is defined to comprise some or all of the following objectives. Please add any objectives that you believe have been omitted. (See 10 to 12.)

1. Financial rewards for owners—dividends
2. Financial rewards for owners—capital appreciation
3. Growth
4. Security
5. Power
6. Service to the community
7. Good value to customers
8. Improved quality of products available to customers
9. Opportunities for employees to develop their capabilities
10. _____
11. _____
12. _____

Indicate any of the numbered objectives that you consider inappropriate or mistaken for this firm: _____

Now, in Table A, please identify the objectives that you would have the firm pursue. Please list them in order of importance.

Table A. Preferred objectives.

Objective	Points
1. _____	_____
2. _____	_____
3. _____	_____
4. _____	_____
5. _____	_____

In Table A please assign to each objective the number of points that measures its relative importance to you. Please distribute a total of 100 points among all of the objectives.

The objectives you have listed in Table A could be pursued in different ways. We seek the ones that capitalize on our particular strengths and minimize the effects of our weaknesses. In Table B please indicate the strategies that you believe would be best for us to pursue. Here's how to do it:

1. Add any strategy that you think has been omitted. See item 6.
2. Cross out any strategy that you consider inappropriate at this time.
3. To the remaining strategies that you believe our firm should pursue assign the number of points that measures their importance to you. Have the total of points you assign add to 100.

(Questionnaire continued on next page.)

Table B. Alternative marketing strategies.

                                                                          Points

1. Introduce new product features—rely on superior ability to in-
   novate.   _____

2. Offer products that best match consumer tastes—rely on superior understanding of their wants.   _____

3. Offer superior value—rely on superior manufacturing-engineer-
   ing capability.   _____

4. Achieve high sales volume—rely on superior marketing skills,
   especially advertising and strong distribution organization.   _____

5. Achieve high profit margin—rely on ability to create strong brand
   image and brand preference.   _____

6. Others (please specify):

   _____   _____

   _____   _____

   _____   _____

We also seek your views on the objectives that we should try to achieve by our pricing strategy. As we see it, we will use price to achieve our marketing objectives and our marketing objectives to achieve business success—our ultimate objectives. With that viewpoint in mind, would you please assess the potential objectives of Table C vis-à-vis ultimate customers as to their appropriateness for this firm at the present time. Do so by assigning a total of 100 points to the pricing objectives that you favor. Note item 4.

Table C. Potential pricing objectives.

                                                                          Points

1. Behavioral objectives:
   Increased short-run sales   _____
   Increased long-run sales   _____
   More favorable word-of-mouth support   _____
   Increased product usage.   _____
2. Attitudinal objectives:
   Higher perceived quality   _____
   Greater brand awareness   _____
   Greater trust of the company   _____
   Associations of brand with more prestigious users.   _____
3. Facilitating purchase objectives:
   Smaller monthly payments   _____
4. Others (please specify):

   _____   _____

   _____   _____

   _____   _____

(End of Questionnaire)

and emphasize the need for completely independent responses to it. The questionnaire would raise questions about potential objectives to be pursued in the sphere of price and matters related to price.

The persons participating in the exercise would be informed that they would have an opportunity to revise their responses after they saw the answers of others. Accordingly, responses to the questionnaire would be summarized and redistributed to them. This time, they would be asked to answer many of the same questions a second time and explain why they disagreed with some of the answers by others to the original questionnaire. Those responses would again be summarized and redistributed to the participants, who would be offered yet another opportunity to revise their answers and to comment on the responses of others. If no clear consensus emerged in this process, the participants would be brought together in the hope of achieving a consensus. In the absence of general agreement, the person responsible for the project would be forced to make his best guess, which would serve in its place. Presumably, his best guess would represent the most common response.

ASSESSING EFFECTS OF ALTERNATIVE PRICE PROGRAMS

The most competent persons available to the price-setter would be asked to estimate the effect of price changes under consideration on ultimate customer behavior, attitude, and situation. They would be sent the Questionnaire on Effects of Possible Price Changes together with an explanation of their involvement and the procedures they are to follow. The procedure employed to formulate price objectives, which is designed to secure interaction among the experts while avoiding undue influence by any one of them, would be used to forecast the effects of different pricing actions. If no consensus emerged, someone would set down a best answer that would be used to evaluate the strategies under consideration.

In Table 4-1 we have set down some assumed objectives with the values that might have been obtained from Table C of the initial questionnaire. We have also set down some hypothetical forecasts that might have been obtained with the second questionnaire. With those data as the basis, the price-setter would arrive at the results shown in Table 4-1 as weighted outcomes: the extent to which each of the four price strategies would meet the firm's objectives. Presumably, the highest weighted outcome indicates the best available solution to the pricing problem. We would therefore favor price strategy 2.

QUESTIONNAIRE ON EFFECTS OF POSSIBLE PRICE CHANGES

The marketing department is conducting a review of our current TV set prices—that is, our suggested retail prices—to see if they are on target for the retail customer. At this point, we are not concerned with the adequacy of margins for our distributors or retailers. Of course, in considering retail price, we must take account of the prices charged by our competitors, which means that we must take account of possible changes in their prices if we were to alter price.

We seek help in conducting this price review. In particular, we want your best estimates of the effects of four price changes that are under consideration. We recognize that such estimates are extremely difficult and only want to get your best thoughts on the subject. By the way, you will be given an opportunity to revise your first estimates after seeing the estimates of others who are participating in this price review.

Here are the changes in price—along with associated changes in advertising support, indoctrination of distributor and retail salesmen, and introductory promotions—that we are considering:

1. A 5 percent reduction in all TV set prices—with rounding of numbers. The reduction would be accompanied by an initial step-up in national advertising stressing best value. Funds available for local co-op advertising would be increased by 20 percent for three months. We would instruct our salesmen to put pressure on both distributor and retail salesmen to emphasize the price reduction and drive home our superior value. Point-of-sale displays would show our prices to be lower than those of other brands with comparable features.

2. A 10 percent reduction in all prices, again with appropriate rounding of numbers. The reduction would be accompanied by a larger increase in national advertising than in program 1, but national advertising would later be reduced to the same level. Co-op advertising would be increased more than in program 1 for three months—by 35 percent instead of 20. Indoctrination of salesmen and point-of-sale materials would be much the same as in program 1, except of course for differences in the sales story.

3. A 5 percent increase in all prices, with some rounding of numbers. The increase would be delayed until we add the new little circuit that will be called the eye-saver. We would increase national advertising by 25 percent—mainly on the eye-saver—for the balance of the year but would not do any more co-op advertising. Salesmen would be instructed to train retail salesmen—through indoctrination of the distributor salesmen on the eye-saver feature. Point-of-sales displays would be made available on the eye-saver feature, and special tags would identify sets as containing the feature.

4. A 10 percent increase in all prices, with some rounding of numbers. Otherwise, the same things would be done as in program 3 except that national advertising would be increased by 50 percent instead of 25 percent.

With respect to each of these four programs, please give your best estimates of the effects on the things itemized in Table A.

If you felt, for example, that our brand image would be improved by any or all of the programs, you might say "big improvement" or "moderate improvement" or "slight improvement." If you prefer, say that it would be improved by 25 percent or some other figure.

Table A. Estimates of effects.

Outcomes	Price Change			
	No. 1 (Down 5%)	No. 2 (Down 10%)	No. 3 (Up 5%)	No. 4 (Up 10%)
Sales within 3 months				
Sales 3 months to a year				
Brand Image				

In respect to each of the programs, which of our competitors do you think would change his prices? By how much and when? Please list your estimates in Table B.

Table B. Estimates of competitor reactions.

Competitor	No. 1		No. 2	No. 3		No. 4	
	Amount	Timing	Amt. Timing	Amt.	Timing	Amt.	Timing
Company A							
Company B							
Company C							
Company D							

Table 4-1. Potential pricing objectives.

Objectives	Weights	Strategy 1	Strategy 2	Strategy 3	Strategy 4
	Forecast Outcomes *				
Increased short-run sales	0.15	130	85	75	110
Increased long-run sales	0.35	90	120	120	70
Better word-of-mouth support	0.10	105	110	100	85
Higher perceived quality	0.15	105	90	110	95
Greater brand awareness	0.10	105	100	70	125
Smaller monthly payments	0.15	100	100	95	105
	Weighted Outcomes				
Increased short-run sales		0.195	0.128	0.113	0.165
Increased long-run sales		0.315	0.420	0.420	0.245
Better word-of-mouth support		0.105	0.110	0.100	0.085
Higher perceived quality		0.158	0.135	0.165	0.143
Greater brand awareness		0.105	0.100	0.070	0.125
Smaller monthly payments		0.150	0.150	0.143	0.158
Totals		1.028	1.043	1.011	0.921

* The average of the four strategies is taken to be 100.

SUMMARY AND CONCLUSIONS

At least in theory, a product has a right or best price if it is judged solely on the basis of its suitability for ultimate customers. To determine that price, a price-setter must estimate the full consequences of alternative prices. They include far more than short-term sales and profits. The price-setter must consider the effect of price on product use, timing of purchase, inventories held by ultimate customers, and word-of-mouth advertising. Price also affects the attitudes of ultimate customers toward the brand's quality, the producing company, and future changes in price and quality. Also, price affects the financial position of customers, mainly by changing their ability to buy other things. Presumably all these effects will have an influence on customer behavior. Accordingly, a price-setter will want to understand the functional relation between price changes and their possible consequences. Most price-setters rivet their attention on the connection between price and short-term sales, but that connection is poorly understood and is forecast with considerable error.

In an effort to determine whether prevailing prices are correct, a price-setter usually must make a market-by-market and model-by-model analysis. Although he will frequently have available a huge body of data, much of it will be only peripherally relevant to his needs. Ordinarily, he can at best isolate marketing problems—and that with considerable difficulty. The available sales and cost data will carry him only a short way toward uncovering price problems, and he must actually collect information especially for his purpose. One promising source is the reports of regional salesmen, but only if the salesmen have been carefully indoctrinated and are rewarded for their effort. In addition, a price-setter must consider the advisability of having market research information collected in a manner that relates customer behavior and attitudes to general psychological, socioeconomic, and demographic customer characteristics.

Whatever he may do, a price-setter will find a considerable gap between what he learns from the data available and what he needs to know to set price. One way to fill the gap is to squeeze out of the organization the valuable qualitative information that is contained in the intuitions of its most experienced and talented executives.

Considerable progress has been made in the use of qualitative (subjective, judgmental, intuitive) information in decision making in general and in price-setting in particular. On one hand, techniques have been developed that help executives extract relatively rich and reliable intuitive judgments from themselves; some specialists are highly skilled in tapping the intuitions of others to obtain valid and consistent judgments. On the other hand, such judgments can be processed routinely with the application of probability theory. In the use of intuitive material, a skilled decision-theorist can take full account of the information sources' varying degrees of confidence in their judgments.

It is not suggested that these techniques for generating and applying intuitive material in price-setting are highly reliable and that their use leads to uncontroversial results. On the contrary, highly divergent opinions often are uncovered in this process and much good ordinarily results from efforts to explain and reconcile such differences. These methods do, moreover, make the basis for decision highly explicit and specific and thus permit the injection of other individuals as sources of information and as critics of both logic and fact. They also make it possible to improve one's decision-making capability by reviewing past decisions to search out the sources of both success and error.

5

Pricing Products in Their Prime

RIVALS

BUSINESSMEN SHOW REMARKABLE SIMILARITY in answering the question "How do you arrive at price?" The most common answer is, "We compute our costs, and add a margin for profit. We then compare that price with what our competitors are charging and adjust it if it is out of line." Competitors' prices, then, are at least as important as costs in determining prices. Costs are a floor below which prices will not be set except in crisis situations. Competitors' prices are a ceiling above which most sellers hesitate to set price except in unusual circumstances.

Businessmen's descriptions of their price-setting methods are not very revealing. When an executive computes costs for pricing purposes, just what does he include? If he looks at competitors' prices, whom does he consider to be his competitors? If his cost-plus price is well below theirs, what price does he ask? If it is substantially above, what does he do? And with which items that his competitors sell does he compare his own? Does he charge exactly what they charge? Can he not charge more? Would he not be wise to charge less at certain times?

To understand how rivals should influence prices for products in their prime, we must find answers to such questions. For example, we must take account of the fact that most large firms sell in literally hundreds of separate markets in many of which they compete both with other national firms and with local firms that enjoy not only a loyal following but low transportation costs as well. We must also explore how sellers can determine which products of competitors are directly competitive with their own. That is not easy unless the products are highly standardized for technological reasons or are basic raw materials.

Of the utmost importance is the question that was raised earlier: How much more or less can one firm obtain from the particular kinds of customers it cultivates than its closest competitor is charging for its most comparable product? Substantial differences in price are often sustainable among offerings that seem essentially equal in value and even among products that are identical chemically or mechanically. Consumers buy more than physical products, and their evaluation of services and convenience vary substantially. Also, some consumers show remarkable inability to perceive that offerings are in fact identical.

A firm that sells products or services that are in their prime is usually constrained by other firms that seek the patronage of its customers. Accordingly, the effective use of price to avoid inroads into markets and to expand at the expense of rivals will be discussed in this chapter. In effect, we will address ourselves to all issues related to rivals that have a bearing on price. We will seek the price that would best meet the firm's objectives *if only the presence of rivals were taken into account.*

Our discussion can be realistic and have clear meaning only if we specify what we assume about the other main parties to the pricing process. With respect to ultimate customers, we assume that they will continue to evaluate rival sellers' offerings much as they do now and that they will shift their patronage only for good cause. As in the preceding chapter, we will assume the firm's continued use of the prevailing distribution system and the continuation of existing margins for all resellers. In the next chapter, however, the role of price in the design of a firm's distribution system will be examined.

We will now explore market competition as it should affect the person responsible for setting price. A big gap exists between the treatment of competition in theoretical writings about price and the competitive forces experienced by businessmen. It is therefore necessary to make clear what we mean by competition, and in particular to distinguish among the main types that pricing executives may face.

COMPETITION FROM A PRICE-SETTER'S STANDPOINT

The nature of competition, and especially that of the marketplace, is so subtle and complex that we cannot learn much from formal definitions. Connotations are essential to an understanding of competition. Accordingly, we will explore an analogy in some detail in the expectation that it will promote understanding of the competitive process and identification of competitors.

A nonbusiness illustration of competition

Every school of business pursues its goals in an environment in which other business schools are vying for the same prizes. Among the more important prizes sought are high-caliber students seeking the B.S. degree, promising candidates for the M.B.A. degree, highly qualified Ph.D. candidates, and participants in executive training programs. Beyond that, each school seeks teachers with a strong reputation in their fields and researchers and talented junior faculty; they want research grants and endowments; they look for good sites for their new buildings and executive training facilities; and possibly they want attractive consulting assignments for their faculty. It need scarcely be mentioned that these prizes are very scarce and that no school of business has as many of them as it would like to have.

The dean might regard all other business schools as a group that frustrates his goals. He might not distinguish the particular schools that keep him from the prizes he seeks; instead, he might simply think of himself as operating in a hostile environment peopled by nameless and faceless opponents. But he could adopt a more differentiated view and identify the schools that now possess the prizes that are available and particularly those he covets. If so, he would pay particular attention to the schools that were encroaching upon his school and appeared determined to separate it from the advantages it now possesses.

He might adopt a third course and conceptualize his environment as peopled by a large number of paired rivals. Each school of business would belong to as many pairs as there are other schools of business. To best achieve his school's goals vis-à-vis each of the other schools would call for different behavior on his part—which, of course, might not be possible. He can ignore most other schools because they do not seek or possess any of the prizes he cherishes. Against some rivals, he will mainly be a defender of advantages he possesses; against others he may be an aggressor; against still others he will defend some prizes while striving to win different prizes. He may sometimes cooperate with a pair rival to gain at the expense of some other school. This view of a business school's competition calls for a school-by-school analysis of the environment.

A fourth view of the environment is even more differentiated and complex. It presents each school of business as a member of a rival pair with each other school. Accordingly, the dean would recognize the existence of many rival pairs of which he is not a member. Nevertheless, his school may be directly affected by what happens to those pairs. If, for example, one school takes very aggressive actions against another, many other schools are likely to be injured much as bystanders at a riot are likely to be. Intense conflict between a pair of schools might injure many other schools, as by raising questions about the quality of education offered and the dedication and caliber of teachers. Consequently, the dean must remain alert to the possible outbreak of trouble in other dyads and, when possible, prevent or correct it. Or he may decide to stay out of markets where such outbreaks are likely to occur.

The most accurate view of market rivalry is the fourth, because a business school does indeed belong to many pairs of schools that seek the same prizes. Similarly, each school and pair of schools are potentially affected by what happens to other pairs of rival schools; that is to say, what each pair member does to deal with the other pair member will influence its market strength with respect to all other schools that seek the same prizes. To function successfully, a dean must be aware of many of those pairs even though he belongs to only a few of them. Also, he will want to manage those of which he is a member in recognition of the interrelationships among them.

The parallel between business schools and business firms is fairly direct. Both pursue similar goals; their goals are conflicting; they do not share equally in the prizes or benefits available; the prizes or benefits can be diverted from one to another school or firm; and some schools or firms are effective in winning certain prizes or benefits but ineffective in winning others. Some pursue advantages of one kind, whereas others focus primarily on different ones. Not all pursue their prizes or benefits in the same way—some are aggressive, whereas others rely mainly on openness, frankness, persistence, strategy, cunning, or manipulative behavior. Beyond those differences, each school or firm is more directly affected by a few others than by the large majority. They are therefore mainly concerned with their relations with the members of the pairs to which they belong.

This example of competition was selected from outside the field of business so that the reader might not be hampered by his present views. Actually, schools of business try to be income-producing and are strongly affected by the behavior of rival schools. If a dean were helped in planning the actions of his school by adopting the views of market rivalry that are sketched above, top executives would certainly find those views illuminating. The chief conclusion to which they lead is that a firm should view itself as related uniquely to many other firms; it should be concerned only with the firms that seek the same prizes that it desires (included will be firms in different industries in many cases); and it must monitor other pairs of firms that are vying for prizes similar to those it seeks, because their actions may indirectly affect its situation.

A working definition of market rivalry

The term "competition" confuses many people who are familiar with formal economic theory; for its technical and conventional meanings are so dissimilar. The term is almost indispensable to describe a condition in which several individuals or teams or organizations contest for some prize. Such contesting is common in markets that economists call oligopolistic or monopolistically competitive. Laymen and businessmen see competition whenever firms engage in advertising or other promotional activities, conduct research and development programs, or try to secure the services of strong distributors—no matter how much market power the individual firms possess. Although we will minimize the use of the term "competition," we will sometimes use it to denote the presence of firms that try to secure prizes to the detriment of rivals who would also like to possess them.

We will not employ the terminology of formal economics. By "market rivalry" we will mean a "condition of pressure experienced by business firms as they independently pursue particular prizes. The pressure stems from the presence and behavior of rivals who seek at least some of the same prizes. The degree of pressure varies with changes in the actions and capabilities of rivals, changes in the requirements of prize givers, and changes in the environment within which the rivalry occurs." *

Where market rivalry as so defined exists, individual firms are under pressure from other firms to use their resources efficiently, and they are also constrained from certain types of behavior by the presence of certain other firms. The severity of this pressure on any firm and the number and form of the constraints on the firm's activities vary according to the characteristics and behavior of rival firms. Executives responsible for managing competitive relationships must therefore understand and adapt to wide variations in the degree and character of market rivalry.

* Anthony O. Kelly, *Market Rivalry: An Entrant's Viewpoint* (unpublished doctoral dissertation, Columbia University, 1971), p. 63.

MARKET MODELS FOR PRICE-SETTERS

In the following section we will develop two views of modern markets that may help price-setters to conceptualize their problems. One of the models describes markets mainly by using the characteristics and behavior of sellers; the other builds its picture of markets around the behavior of customers.

The discussion of models applies only to market situations that are oligopolistic—that is, to markets in which only a few firms operate. Moreover, it applies to oligopolistic markets in which the firms' products are fairly close substitutes for one another, although they are not considered to be such by many customers. Little will be lost by these restrictions; for almost all marketing executives and price-setters are employed by firms in oligopolistic markets and offer products that only a few customers view equally.

An oligopolistic market defined

We will build a simplified view of an oligopolistic market by assuming sellers whose wares are acceptable to almost all customers for them, although each firm's output is not considered equally desirable by most customers. The market actions of each of these firms have some effect on one or more of the other firms, and often on all of them. In what way? Shall we assume a completely symmetrical relationship in which the effects of any one firm's actions are felt equally by all other firms? That condition could be diagramed as an equilateral triangle (see Fig. 5-1a). Also, is each firm affected as much by a rival's actions as that firm is affected by its actions? The first condition may be termed one of symmetry or equal impact, and the second might be called reciprocity or mutuality.

Both pure symmetry and pure reciprocity are absent from most real-life markets. In almost every oligopolistic market each firm is more affected by the actions of certain firms than others. Under such conditions, we say that each firm is closer to or more directly in competition with specific other firms than are still other firms. That notion can be shown by a simple diagram (Fig. 5-1b) of circles scattered irregularly. Firms A and B are in close competition, whereas Firms A and D are not; Firms C and B compete more directly than do Firms A and D; Firms C and D are in close competition, whereas Firms B and D are not.

Not only do firms in oligopolistic markets vary widely in their effect on one another, but those effects are not often reciprocal. Whereas Firm

Figure 5-1. Two models of an oligopolistic market.

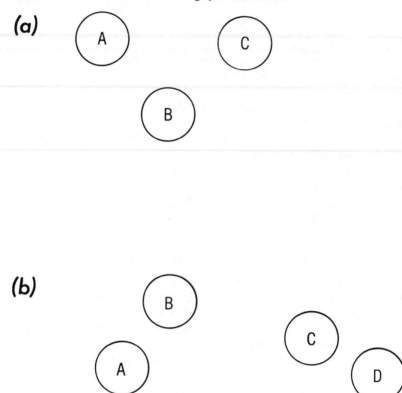

A may attract many customers from Firm D (Fig. 5-1b) by a 10 percent reduction, a similar price action by Firm D might attract, say, only 5 percent of A's customers. Put simply, Firm A's customers may be much more loyal than Firm D's. Accordingly, let us view an oligopolistic market as a series of dyads and describe the relationships that commonly exist between the members of the pairs. We will then examine the relationships found among the many dyads that operate in most oligopolistic markets.

A classification of dyads. As a first step we must distinguish pairs of firms that are interrelated from those that are not. By an interrelated pair, we mean two firms whose individual promotional efforts influence the other's sales. More specifically, a sizable price reduction or an increase in outlay for advertising, personal selling, customer service, product improvement, or retail distribution by one member of the pair reduces the sales of the other perceptibly. Now, as already indicated, the fact that one firm's promotional efforts strongly reduce the sales of the other firm does not mean that its own sales are similarly influenced by the activities of its pair member; the directness and strength of the interrelation are not the same in both directions.

There are many reasons why the relationships that exist among pairs of firms in an oligopolistic market need not be mutual or symmetrical. For example, it is not very difficult to imagine a powerful firm in an industry, say, the firm selling the most popular brand, increasing its advertising or lowering its price and having a very direct effect on almost all other firms. A small firm—which would be strongly affected by what the powerful firm would do—might make what is for it a major promotional move that would not perceptibly influence the powerful firm.

Another example of nonmutuality and assymetry can be suggested. One firm deals almost exclusively with loyal customers; they feel tightly linked to it because of past favors and the conviction that it offers the best value for them. The other member of the dyad deals only with customers that are nonloyal and careful searchers for best price. Whereas the first firm's actions might win many nonloyal customers away from the second firm, the second firm's promotional actions would have little effect on the first firm.

Now let us investigate dyads themselves by looking first at the nature of the two members and then at the nature of the relation between the members. Individual members of dyads can be described in the following terms:

1. Power—the ability to grow at the expense of the other. A firm's power mainly reflects its financial resources, management skills, reputation, distribution organization, location, personal ties and loyalties, information, and production cost advantage.
2. Market/competitive strategy. Is the firm destructive, aggressive, cooperative, or defensive? How ambitious are its growth goals? How strong is owner/director pressure for sales and profits?
3. Loyalty of its largest customers.

The relation between dyad members can be close or distant; that is, the effect of one firm's actions on the other may be strong or weak. In addition, the firms may be hostile or friendly, aggressive or cooperative. The relation between dyad members cannot be predicted accurately from a description of power, market strategy, and customers. It seems to depend on many subjective factors. By using the three dimensions—

power, market strategy, and customer loyalty—each member of a dyad can be compared with the other. That is, we can construct a profile of each dyadic relation such as the hypothetical one of Table 5-1. We sometimes find that one firm is dominant in a particular dyad, that in almost all relevant dimensions it is stronger than its partner. The other firm, then, is weak and vulnerable relative to the first. In a few dyads we find near-equality of the members in all dimensions listed. In still others, we find one firm strong in some dimensions but weak in others. The third type of relation is likely to be the most common one, but all three types are found in most markets.

The nature of the relation between members of a dyad would presumably be reflected in the effect each firm's actions have on the other firm and the actions it would take. For example, firms that strongly dominate dyad partners who are their closest rivals presumably would reflect their dominance in their marketing and pricing behavior. They could be expected to cash in on their power in one or more of the following ways:

☐ Achieve a substantial increase in sales, possibly at the expense of the rival.

☐ Obtain a higher price and profit margin than the weaker member of the dyad.

☐ Enjoy substantially lower marketing costs than the rival.

Table 5-1. Profile of a dyadic market relationship.

Dimensions	Relative Strengths *	
	Firm A	Firm B
Power		
Financial resources	100	65
Management skills	100	90
Reputation	100	95
Distribution organization	80	100
Location	100	100
Personal ties and loyalties	90	100
Information	100	90
Production cost advantage	100	95
Market strategy toward partner		
Degree of destructiveness	X	
Growth goals		X
Pressure for increased sales and profits		X
Loyalty of largest customers	90	100

* The numbers indicate degree of superiority or strength of the firm's advantage and the higher number is always 100. When no advantage is involved, as in market strategy, the entry X indicates which firm is most likely to attack the other.

☐ Impose a particular form of market behavior, such as price-followership, on the rival.

When the situation is one of strong dominance, the weaker member probably recognizes its weaknesses and is reconciled to enduring some important disadvantages. It will, of course, attempt to limit its losses.

When firms are equally strong overall and also equal in individual dimensions, both dyad members will probably seek to avoid significant changes in their market behavior and in market results lest they precipitate a self-defeating struggle. Their rough equality of power suggests that neither could win the struggle, so the penalties for conflict are extremely high and the rewards for avoiding conflict are great. When firms are essentially equal in power but each is substantially stronger than the other in certain dimensions, they apparently are willing to risk market disruption. Often, however, they do not assess their relative strength accurately; they tend to overvalue their strengths and undervalue their weaknesses.

These generalizations about the behavior of firms with respect to their dyad partners could be off the mark. Current research on market behavior does not employ dyadic analysis. The reader should therefore regard the broad statements as unsupported but reasonable hypotheses; even so, they may suggest ways in which this line of thinking might be developed. Marketing executives would do well to analyze the dyads that are found in their markets and search out the patterns in the behavior of their rivals. An understanding of those patterns would provide a strong base for forecasting their aggressive actions and would suggest their responses to the actions of a rival.

Description of all dyads to which a firm belongs. A high degree of diversity in the dyads of which an individual firm is a member is to be expected. A firm will dominate some dyads in almost all respects, be roughly equal in others, and be dominated in still others; in most it will enjoy points of superiority. The fortunes of any firm in an oligopolistic market would seem to depend mainly upon the proportion of its dyadic relationships that the firm dominates. We might, therefore, gain insight into the competitiveness of a market by finding the proportion of firms that dominate almost all of their dyad partners.

Description of all dyads in a market. Let us now try to describe all dyads in a market as they might be viewed by an executive responsible for pricing. We will look both at the dyads of which our firm is a member and the far larger number of which it is not. Our question is how all the dyads in an oligopolistic market are interrelated. That is, we want to know to what extent, how quickly, and under what circumstances the things that take place between members of one dyad alter the behavior of other dyads. Let us first record the obvious:

1. The actions by one firm in a dyad will affect virtually all other firms with which that firm is related; rarely can a firm take actions that influence only one of its dyad relationships.
2. The actions of one firm that strongly affect its dyad partners are likely to be transmitted in turn to their dyad partners. In that way the actions of one firm tend to spread throughout a market and affect even the firms with which it has no direct relation.

The market conditions in an oligopolistic situation can be understood from a description of the dyads that operate there. The crudest description would be the number of pairs that are related in the manner defined, but a better description is both possible and desirable. Let us examine the possibility of describing an oligopoly by characterizing the dyads that are found there. We can then judge whether the result is illuminating and provides a firm in the market with a useful guide for action.

Take as an example our price-setter for a TV manufacturer. We will assume for simplicity that only four firms constitute the industry. Firm 1 is the strongest in the industry; on almost all scores, it ranks first by far. Firm 3 is the weakest member of the industry, and Firm 4 is the second strongest. The situation is described in Table 5-2, but far more is indicated in that table than relative power of the firms.

The information presented in Table 5-2 provides the basis for constructing a sociometric picture of the total market; it also should illuminate each firm's market position and guide its market actions and, in particular, its price decisions. The table shows clearly that a firm must work out differentials between its price and the prices of all other dyad members. Since it may charge only one price for its offering, each firm must effect a compromise, so that its price will inevitably be better with respect to one rival than another.

An assessment of the dyad model of market rivalry. As sketched, the dyad view of a market is quite complex. It is far more so than the models currently employed by economic theorists, but is far less so than the model employed by most marketing executives who operate in oligopolistic markets. Marketing executives usually confront more than three rivals; they do not know many of the circumstances that we have assumed are known; and they must manage many variables other than price. A model of modern markets must also take into account the major elements in a

Table 5-2. A description of dyads.

Firms in Dyad	Degree of Closeness	Nature of Relationship	Dominant Member	Customer Loyalty	Closest Rival	Most Committed to Rapid Growth
1 2	Slight	Friendly	1	High Low	4 4	2
1 3	Moderate	Friendly	1	Moderate Low	4 2	1
1 4	Extreme	Hostile	1	Moderate Moderate	4 1	1
2 3	Moderate	Cool	2	Low Moderate	4 2	2
2 4	Extreme	Friendly	4	High High	4 1	4
3 4	Moderate	Hostile	4	Low High	2 1	4

marketing mix and not be confined to price alone. (This point will be covered presently.)

The main effect of the dyad model is to direct the pricing and marketing executive's attention to the many dissimilar interfirm relationships that compose a market; it warns against his viewing his firm as vying with similar firms that are symmetrically and reciprocally related to his own. In short, it directs him to ask, "What is the most appropriate price, personal sales, advertising, distribution, and service differential for me to establish between my offering and that of each other firm with which my firm is closely related?" It also suggests the characteristics of its pair members that should be considered in answering those questions. Each executive would presumably restrict his analysis to a manageable number of rivals—probably those he considers his closest ones.

An oligopolistic market based on customers

Here is another model of an oligopolistic market; it is based on customer responses. If we know that certain firms press and constrain one another, then we know something about their present and potential customers. Indeed, the behavior of customers, rather than that of firms, may create the market condition that we describe as competition. What then does a state of competition imply about customers in an oligopolistic market? First, for market rivalry to exist, customers must be willing to consider patronizing more than one firm. Second, competition exists only if the actions of one competitor can induce some customers to shift from another seller to himself. When the first condition obtains, the second obtains also, and the converse is true as well.

To set prices that are appropriate for an oligopolistic market, sellers must understand the reactions of potential customers as well as those of rival firms. If customers are extremely unlikely to alter their purchase behavior—that is, if all are intensely loyal to particular sources of supply—then competition is extremely weak. Conversely, if very small inducements will lead customers of one firm to buy from another, then the two firms are in close competition. Thus it is mainly the responsiveness of customers to actions by different sellers that creates a condition of market competition. It is because sellers are aware of customer responses that they respond as they do to the market moves of their rivals. Thus, to understand the nature and degree of rivalry in any market, we should know how many customers can be induced to shift their purchases to a different brand or to a different retailer and what will induce them to make the shift.

Let us now apply this line of reasoning specifically to price. We might say that firms are price-competitive when their customers switch in response to a modest price inducement and that price competition is low if a price reduction will attract few customers from a rival. In short, the degree of price competition in a market is to be judged by the degree of customer immunity to substantial price inducements. (Later we will discuss a technique for measuring, or at least conceptualizing, the degree of price competition.) The same line of thought can be applied to marketing instruments other than price. If, for example, a firm attracted many customers away from rivals by increasing its advertising, it could be described as advertising-competitive.

A price-setter might want to distinguish between individual regional markets—and customer subgroups—on the basis of the marketing instrument that is most effective in switching customers from one seller to another. Customers who are relatively indifferent to variations in price might be moved by modest changes in packaging, benefit claims, customer service, or guarantees. Although any market usually contains some customers who are sensitive to different marketing instruments, the marketing executive must be concerned with customers in the mass rather than individuals. When he views customers in the mass, he is likely to find significant differences from place to place and time to time in the factors to which most customers are responsive. When most customers are switchable primarily by nonprice factors, a price-setter will ordinarily seek a high price and use the proceeds to pay the cost of providing the difference in quality or service that the customers seek. Clearly, the proper role for price in a market depends upon the importance that customers attach to price, that is, the price difference that will induce them to give up their currently favored suppliers.

To describe the competitiveness of an entire market, or the competitive situation of an individual seller, it is necessary to describe the switchability of customers. A device particularly useful for a price-setter is to specify the differential in price that a customer would pay for his favored brand over each of the others. Table 5-3 is based on the device; it describes a simple hypothetical market by the switchability of customers under the inducement of price. A plus figure in the table means that the customer prefers the first of the paired brands sufficiently to pay that much more for it, and a minus number has the same significance for the second of the brands. A zero means indifference to brand, and an asterisk means refusal to buy one brand at any price.

For example, Customer 1 of Table 5-3 might be described as follows: He would be willing to patronize Firm A, B, or D, but he would not buy from Firm C. As for the other, he would be willing to pay $2 more for brand A than for brand B, $1 more for brand A than for brand D, and $1 more for brand D than for brand B. We could say that brands A, B, and D compete for his business or that they are in competition for his patronage.

Table 5-3, then, presents a hypothetical market viewed from the consumer side. Seven individuals' preferences among four brands are described. Each individual could be considered typical of, say, 1,000 customers, and so we have constructed a very simplified picture of a market

Table 5-3. Price differential structure for customers for an item sold by four firms.

Brands Involved	Reaction of Customer						
	1	2	3	4	5	6	7
A vs. B	+2	0	0	*	−2	−1	+1
A vs. C	*	0	−1	*	−2	−2	0
A vs. D	+1	0	*	*	0	0	−1
B vs. C	*	0	−1	0	0	−1	+1
B vs. D	−1	0	*	+1	−2	−1	0
C vs. D	*	0	*	−1	−2	+2	+2

NOTES: An asterisk indicates that the customer would not purchase from one member of the pair. A plus or minus sign indicates preference for the first or second member of a pair, respectively. A number is the dollar amount of price difference the customer will pay.

composed of 7,000 customers who are cultivated by four firms. From that information we could erect a demand schedule that would account for the distribution of customers among the four sellers with any assumed price for each brand. In the construction of Table 5-3 some difficult issues were faced:

☐ Are these differentials transitive? That is, if a customer prefers brand A to brand B and would be willing to pay a $2 premium for it and prefers brand A to brand C and would be willing to pay a $3 premium for it, should we expect him to prefer brand B to brand C and be willing to pay more for it?

☐ What is the relation between price differentials and switchability and brand loyalty? Is brand preference the same as brand loyalty? One answer is that a customer is loyal to a brand—that is, mainly buys that brand—when he is willing to pay substantially more for it than for other brands. A customer might be loyal to a brand that he does not prefer simply because it usually is cheaper than the others and offers better value, although at lower quality. In other words, brand preference has clear meaning only when the prices charged for different brands are known.

☐ Whereas we seem to be assuming that, given some price incentive, a buyer would be willing to switch brands, in some cases, a customer would not patronize a particular seller no matter how great a differential was offered. Given the possibility of very large differentials, this assumption is not too plausible.

Most of these vexing questions can be resolved if we make some realistic assumptions about the size of the price moves that sellers could make as a practical matter. For example, we will assume that no seller can afford a price reduction larger than $4, except for a very short time and for promotional purposes, because of the cost situation. We will also assume that no customer would pay a price premium larger than $5 for one brand over any other. Given those assumptions, certain customers are not switchable because no seller can afford to offer a sufficiently large price incentive.

We could assume a pattern of prices for the four firms in the market, including equality of price, and determine the number of customers that each firm would serve if those prices prevailed. For example, if prices were equal for all brands, Customer 1 would buy brand A and Customer 3 would buy brand C. We could also determine the effects on the number of customers served by each firm of particular changes in price by each seller, assuming no change in price by any other. By analyzing the switches in patronage brought about by various price changes, we could then forecast the responses of the individual firms on the assumption that each firm's management knew the brand preferences of all seven customer segments. Presumably, any firm that suffered a large decline in sales due to a rival's price change would be forced to respond in some manner. It need not match its rival's move, but it could cut price less or more than the rival did, or it might increase its advertising, customer service, or sales force.

Such a numerical analysis of our hypothetical example would be very laborious but would produce no new insights. It would show that each firm would be forced to balance three factors in arriving at price: (1) the effect of any change on its sales, assuming no change in the prices of rivals, (2) the response of rivals, given the number of customers it would win by changing price and the number of customers it would win from each of its rivals, and (3) the effects of changes in sales on costs of production.

This example has been carried far enough to establish the connection between customer valuations of different brands and the sales of each brand, given any set of price relations. It also shows that the effects of price changes depend on those customer valuations; the valuations determine the distribution of a sales in a market. The competitiveness of a market, then, appears to be determined quite as much by customer valuations of rival brands as by the efforts of sellers to win customers away from their rivals.

An assessment of the seller- and buyer-oriented models

Any business executive knows that his customers and rivals force him to operate efficiently. The loyalty and bargaining power of customers can create strong pressure on him as a seller; his rivals can deprive him of customers. Also, almost every executive regards at least certain of his rivals as distinct and particularly threatening; he does not lump all rivals into a single group that represents the enemy. What, then, might be gained from the models of competition we have discussed? If neither the buyer- nor the seller-oriented model offers important insights by itself, could some new understanding of price be derived from a combination of the two? Let us explore that possibility with our hypothetical TV set firm.

Our price-setter might construct a detailed profile of his firm's three to five main dyadic relations and describe his firm's relations with all of the others in the industry in more general terms. From that effort, which would be quite considerable, should emerge a structured and organized picture of his firm's market position relative to its rivals that would add considerably to his understanding of his firm's markets and thus help him conduct his pricing program.

Assume now that he combines his dyadic analysis with a customer analysis. To do so, he would add to the profiles he had prepared of his close rivals a few new elements: the number of large and important customers—they are *not* the same thing—the loyalty of each customer, and the customer's bargaining power, buying tactics, and bargaining skills. Once he had completed that analysis, he could characterize the customer situation in the entire industry by the switchability of customers in response to price changes.

Let us examine a few potential dyad-customer profiles to see what guidance they might offer a TV price-setter. By their nature they will include only relevant information; our interest is in whether that information is the *most valuable* that could be assembled for this purpose, whether it is worth the trouble of assembly, and whether it could be processed further to achieve greater insight.

The value of combining seller and customer models of market rivalry depends on whether the customers of any firm in a market are distinctly different from those of other firms and are not essentially a fairly representative cross section of all the customers in the market. On one level, the answer is clear: When dyad members are distant rivals, it is primarily because they do actually serve and seek to serve largely different customers but they are to be considered rivals to the degree that they try to win patronage from each other. Consequently, most dyad profiles would contain an account of a different group of potential customers. Just how great are the differences from dyad to dyad? Are sellers able to alter their market behavior to adjust to or exploit those differences?

Inasmuch as our purpose is to aid in setting price rather than to get to the very heart of the competitive process, we need not carry this discussion too much further. Several untied knots should be identified and some unresolved questions left sharply stated. First, it would appear that to be useful to an operating executive, a classification system for markets would incorporate a sizable number of dimensions and thus result in dozens of market types. Our discussion was limited to a single market type, a heterogeneous oligopoly. We found that the dyadic method of analyzing and describing a market from a single price-setter's viewpoint provided a basis for distinguishing among markets that are heterogeneous oligopolies. Second, the nature of market rivalry in any industry varies widely from firm to firm not only in intensity but also in the measures that must be employed to retain prizes and gain others. Market rivalry exhibits itself in myriad activities under diverse circumstances. No simple classification of markets or of types of competition will meet the needs of business executives, although they may convey some enlightenment to students.

Important questions are raised by a dyad analysis about the market behavior of different kinds of dyads. When is one firm clearly dominant? When are firms equal in all particulars? When are firms equal overall but markedly different in individual characteristics? Is there no consistent pattern, or does the pattern become consistent only when the learning process is taken into account? What significance to the price-setter could be attached to a lack of consistent patterns?

THE ESTABLISHMENT OF PRICE VIS-À-VIS RIVALS

The foregoing discussion of alternative conceptions of market competition has prepared the ground for a discussion of setting price in the presence of rival firms. A price-setter performs two fairly distinct tasks when he takes account of rivals. The first is to identify the rivals with which he will be concerned in arriving at price; the second is to establish a differential between his price and each rival's price. To do the second, he would usually benefit from an explicit substrategy.

Identification of rivals

By a competitor an executive usually means a firm whose market actions influence the price charged or the level of sales attained by his firm. Of course, a rival's influence can vary greatly in degree; thus we must distinguish between close competitors, substantial competitors, and distant competitors. A price-setter will want to take account of all rivals that significantly influence his firm's price or sales.

A competitor, as we define it, affects its rival in several ways: it mainly constrains its rival's actions and feasible options. When a close competitor charges a given price, a firm has the following main choices: It can charge a price similar to its competitor's price; it can charge significantly more than the competitor charges and accept a relatively small volume of sales; or it can charge substantially less than the competitor charges and hope to divert sales volume from the competitor without provoking retaliatory action. The fact that a firm charges a given price does not necessarily require that its close rivals charge the same price. A firm usually possesses several feasible price options and a far greater number of marketing mix options. To explain why that is so, it would be helpful to describe oligopoly markets in which sellers have virtually no feasible price or marketing mix options.

Rivals viewed from the standpoint of price alone. If you are responsible for pricing on behalf of a firm, what firms are your competitors? What other firms' prices should you take into account in setting price for your firm? As already indicated, one firm's prices can influence another's in three possible ways. In one sense, however, each firm, and not a rival, sets its own prices; each firm is a master of its actions—provided it is prepared to accept the consequences. But the presence of rivals does determine to a large degree what those consequences are. And although a firm is free to charge what it wishes, the presence of rivals will lead it to do different things than it would in their absence.

In addition, a rival has the power to determine the relation between your prices and his. For example, he can prevent you from underselling him by always matching your price and by announcing his intention to keep on doing so. If you decide to charge more than he charges, he can frustrate your plan by raising his prices when you raise yours. In sum, although you can determine what price you will charge, you cannot determine the differential between your price and your rival's.

The influence of one firm's price on a rival firm. Conceptually, we can give fairly precise meaning to the effect that one firm has on another. One firm affects another and is a rival to it to the extent that a reduction in its prices significantly reduces the other firm's sales. It is not a price rival if a change in its price has virtually no effect on the sales of the others. The ratio of the percent change in the amount of sales of one firm in response to a given percent price change by a possible rival provides a numerical measurement of the price competition between the two. Technically this ratio is termed the cross-elasticity of demand.

No particular value of the ratio represents a competitive relation between firms. Clearly a ratio of zero would denote the absence of competition, but the ratio at which competition could be said to exist must be arbitrary. Competition varies in degree over a very wide range; one firm's price changes may affect the unit sales of another so slightly that anyone would say the two do not compete. The significance of the cross-elasticity of demand in any market relates primarily to the likelihood, speed, and nature of the retaliation to its market moves that a firm might expect. When the cross-elasticity of demand is high, retaliation is swift and usually in kind.

Cross-elasticity of demand is very difficult to measure and apply. In most cases a marketing executive cannot forecast how specific changes in price or other marketing actions by another firm will affect his own sales. We hear a great deal of talk about the effects of competitors' price actions from salesmen and even directly from customers, but the precise relation between one firm's price changes and another's sales is highly problematic. Some customers actually do stop buying, when, say, a rival lowers price, but an executive can't know whether they are waiting for his firm to lower price or, in effect, pressing his firm toward a price reduction. Sometimes they shift their patronage for a while but return to the fold after finding the price-cutter a less satisfactory supplier. Conversely, some customers are slow to shift patronage to the price-cutter because they hold sizable inventories; they will shift, but only after a while.

Just how many customers have been lost through normal attrition and how many because of a rival's price cut is almost indeterminable in any specific case, even after the fact. Nevertheless, almost every marketing executive does form an opinion of the effect of a rivals' price changes on his firm's sales. Whether that impression is correct or mistaken, it determines how his firm will behave. If not all marketing executives in a firm have the same impression, incidentally, the firm is unlikely to pursue a consistent policy.

The identification of rivals based on buyers' characteristics. Another method that a price-setter might use to identify his rivals is based on the hypothesis that customers who intend to make a purchase will examine the wares of only selected suppliers. Household consumers, for example, usually consider only selected retail stores and particular brands of an item; this phenomenon is so well recognized that it has been given the name "evoked sets." A family considering the purchase of a household appliance may decide to shop for it at their favorite department store and at a particular discount store that they have patronized in the past. Ordinarily they will either purchase the appliance at one of those two places or not buy it at all. Another family may be willing to consider three brands of the appliance and will shop for it at the most accessible stores or at the stores they usually patronize or at a store in which they are making some other purchase. To the second family the store is a secondary consideration and the emphasis is on obtaining one of the preferred brands; to the first, the reverse is true. A third family may decide which brands they wish to consider and also decide to make the purchase at one of their two favorite retail stores.

What firms are competitors in the three situations described? In the first instance, the only brands competing for patronage are those carried by the two preferred stores. The brands carried by the second store would not even have received consideration if the family had made its purchase in the first store they visited. The family who decided to consider only three brands of the appliance might be said to place those three manufacturers in competition for their business. Other manufacturers presumably have tried to win their favor through advertising and other merchandising efforts. We might therefore identify the firms whose wares are in the running at different stages of the purchase, with many being given consideration in early stages and only a few achieving a position of preference at the last stage. The third family have formed strong preferences for both brands and stores, so the brands in competition are those the family have decided they might purchase if their favorite stores carry them. A price-setter usually is wise to adopt the standpoint of buyers in identifying rivals. It is the buyers who, consciously or unconsciously, compare the prices and quality of offerings, and it is their decisions about what and where to purchase that are the main concern of sellers.

Strategy development vis-à-vis rivals

A firm's goals relative to its present and potential rivals include a variety of desired ends that can be divided into two broad sets. The goals of one set are related to the general industry environment: the firms operating— their financial and marketing strengths and their aggressiveness—and the traditions, values, and expectations of executives in the industry. An example of the latter is the presence of price leadership or even geographic market sharing or a widespread belief that one should leave the other fellow's customers alone. The institutional counterpart is the trade association or the committee established by government or by the industry. A firm's prices can have an important effect on some of these environmental features. For example, low prices might speed the exit from and discourage the entry of firms into a market; predatory pricing by one or more firms might make a trade association relatively ineffectual.

The goals of the second set relate more to current market behavior than to industry environment. They can be separated into four efforts: (1) to gain desired ends at the expense of rival firms, (2) to hold desired prizes away from rivals, (3) to avoid conflict with rivals in certain spheres or even cooperate actively with rivals, and (4) to learn from rivals. All four efforts have implications for a firm's price behavior. Involved is a determination about which firms can be fed upon, which must be fended off, with which it is possible and desirable to be friendly, and from which to try to learn. And once that determination has been made, the

SELECTED SUBOBJECTIVES RELATED TO RIVALS

1. Feed-off rivals.
   a. Offer preferential terms to the most valued customers of rivals to lure them away.
   b. Offer preferential treatment to strong resellers to lure them away from rivals.
   c. Achieve excellence—give both ultimate customers and resellers more of what they value.
   d. Identify the most vulnerable rivals and concentrate on taking away the customer segments and resellers they now serve and use.
   e. Attract their most talented executives by offering high compensation or challenging opportunities.
2. Fend-off rivals.
   a. Lock up the executives, valuable customers, and resellers you now control.
      (1) Whenever possible, use long-term contracts with them.
      (2) Acquire a part ownership in reseller organizations when possible.
      (3) Develop strong personal ties.
      (4) Try to limit alternatives available to them.
      (5) Load up customers with heavy inventories of your product.
   b. Maintain secrecy about the things you do very efficiently.
   c. Do not reveal identity of your most valuable customers, executives, resellers.
3. Friend-with rivals.
   a. Develop close personal contacts between top executives in your firm and theirs.
   b. Explain whenever possible that all rivals lose from direct conflict with others of roughly equal strength.
   c. Establish industrywide cooperative arrangements for:
      (1) Research and development.
      (2) Data gathering.
      (3) Dealing with government agencies.
      (4) Public relations.
   d. Be quick to offer assistance to rival in distress to establish principle of cooperation and to earn right to reciprocity.
   e. Develop institutional arrangements such as trade associations, industry committees, and trade journals.
4. Learn-from rivals.
   a. Become informed about what the most progressive of them are doing.
      (1) Monitor their product changes, their marketing programs, their personnel policies, and the like.
      (2) Foster personal contacts among your executives and theirs.
      (3) Cultivate close friends among your customers so that they can report on what rivals are offering.
   b. Develop skills in doing what they are doing well.
      (1) Acquire resources skilled in copying products and programs.
      (2) Hire away some of their employees.
   c. Study sources that might reveal what your rivals are planning.
      (1) Records of court cases

Figure 5-2. Goal hierarchy designed to highlight rival-related subgoals.

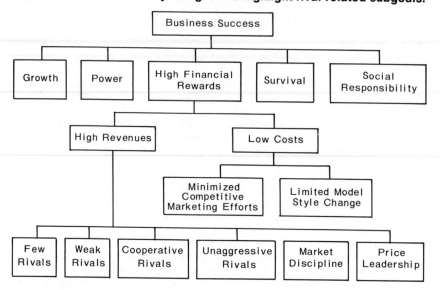

marketing executive would be wise to formulate strategies for gaining at the expense of his firm's rivals, holding onto the prizes he has, developing a cooperative relationship with other firms, and learning from them quickly and inexpensively. Thus we see that strategies vis-à-vis rivals are both defensive and offensive, both cooperative and instructive. Figure 5-2 presents a hierarchy of objectives designed to highlight the subobjectives a firm might pursue relative to rivals. The more complete set of Selected Subobjectives Related to Rivals is oriented around the goals of feeding off, fending off, friending with, and learning from rivals.

Strategic competitive logics

Dr. A. O. Kelly has developed a list of what he calls competitive substrategies, which he divides into initiatory and response substrategies. Initiatory strategies are of two broad types: precedence (being the first to take action) and preemption (taking action that excludes rivals). Precedence may give the initiator a lead that is difficult to reverse, because he may have gained customer loyalty before the second firm has followed his lead. Also, the initiator, if he introduces a new product, may eventually find his brand name used to designate the product itself, as Frigidaire, Kleenex, and Jello are often used. Also, the initiator of action may gain substantial profit before he is followed.

Precedence can be employed to catch rivals off guard, and it can be combined with such a heavy commitment of resources that it may succeed by demonstrating superb competence. In the particular case of the initiator of price changes, many believe that customer gratitude for a price reduction goes mainly to the firm that initiated the decline even as the blame for an increase in price falls mainly on the firm that made it first.

Preemption generally takes place when the first firm to take an action somehow makes it impossible for others to follow. For example, a seller offering a price cut in conjunction with a long-term contract can tie up most of the business in a market before a rival is able to develop a similar offer. According to Dr. Kelly, firms achieve preemption in three ways: (1) The most concentrated offensive, which calls for a very rapid and extensive action before rivals even fully realize what is happening; (2) Brand proliferation, which occurs whenever a firm shuts out rivals by introducing self-competing brands, possibly at quite different prices, to capture so much of an existing market that other firms would not find it attractive to enter the market or remain in it; and (3) Overexpansion, which is intended to intimidate rivals by creating excess capacity. In the case of price, a very large price reduction might have the same preemptive effect—other firms might feel wholly incapable of meeting it and may not even try.

What response strategies have been identified? Kelly names three: imitation, reprisal, and exploitation. Imitation is of two varieties: identical matching and dominating. The first amounts to me-tooism; the second to going the initiator one better, as in offering deeper price cuts. Reprisal also can take two broad forms: riposte and saturation. The riposte is a quick response in the hope of striking a vulnerable spot of the initiator and perhaps causing him to rescind his action; saturation is a massive dominating move that literally swamps the initiator's move.

Exploitation as a strategy is based on the notion that the initiator is vulnerable and that his points of vulnerability can be exploited by an alert firm. One form of exploitative response behavior is to capitalize on what the initiator has done, as by intervening in a sales discussion just before the sale is closed and stealing the customer by making a better offer. Another form, called contrasting, consists in doing the very opposite of what the initiator does, thereby implying that he was wrong and simultaneously enjoying great visibility.*

The marketing strategies that a firm might adopt toward rivals can

* Adapted from A. O. Kelly, *Market Rivalry: An Entrant's Viewpoint*, an unpublished dissertation at Columbia University, 1971.

be summarized by the following list, each item of which is followed by mutually exclusive alternatives. A wide variety of strategies can be sketched by circling one alternative in each set. Like the competitive substrategies assembled by Dr. Kelly, the resulting strategies are relatively general and high level, although many of them could be employed in pursuit of the Selected Subobjectives Related to Rivals.

- ☐ Attitude toward rivals: no holds barred, constrained aggressiveness, live and let live, cooperative.
- ☐ Time orientation: present, future.
- ☐ Attitude toward market share: determined to gain one, intent on retaining current one, willing to lose current one gradually.
- ☐ Ethics: law-abiding, not law-abiding.

ESTABLISHING PRICE DIFFERENTIALS VIS-À-VIS RIVALS

A price-setter's chief task is to establish suitable price differentials between his price and the prices of rivals. If he assumes that ultimate customers will rate his offering against the whole field, much as Consumers Union rates the quality of different brands, he will try to find a price position for his firm relative to all firms in the industry. His assumption, however, is contrary to considerable evidence that suggests that each buyer actively screens only a limited sector of a market and even then relies mainly on general impressions rather than detailed information and an understanding of specific price patterns. We can, then, distinguish the whole-field approach from rival-by-rival analysis, and the two will be discussed separately in general terms. The following section applies the general concepts developed here to the TV set illustration.

Price differentials vis-à-vis all rivals collectively

If a price-setter assumes that his customers will rate his brand's price against virtually all other brands, he will select a position for his price in the broad array of offerings that conveys the target image the firm has selected for itself. Indeed, many firms define their marketing strategy specifically in terms of relative price: "We're the most expensive brand." "Our brand is medium-priced." "We want customers to see us as offering high quality at medium prices."

Two general goals might be achieved by price-setters in establishing price differentials relative to all rival brands. First, they seek a price that helps to communicate the general quality image they have selected. Second, they employ price as a balancing device. These uses of price will be discussed in turn.

Price as a means of communication. Price communicates to most customers more than information about the seller's monetary demands: it says something about quality, reliability, and the nature of the people who use the product. Many customers use price as a clue to attributes of the product itself, the service offered, the reputation of the firm that produces the item, and the socioeconomic status of users. The aspects of price that communicate most are (1) relative price, (2) frequency of price promotions, and (3) emphasis on price in advertising and window displays and on packages and in-store signs.

Accordingly, a price-setter will want to learn to speak the language of price fluently. He will want to know how various subgroups of customers perceive and interpret at least the three basic aspects of price. Specifically, he might want to know how to attract customers who wish assurance that his firm will provide high quality, unusual styling, and full service. Sellers who claim that their brand offers exceptional value strongly suggest they have exercised economies in an effort to keep the price down. Conversely, sellers who place emphasis on the excellence of the products or services they offer are not in a position to claim very low price.

Firms generally attract an unrepresentative group of customers because, as sellers, they behave in an unrepresentative manner. They make promises that attract customers who believe their promises rather than those of rivals. In some markets it is impossible to distinguish among sellers' promises—every seller promises everything. Typically, individual sellers feature distinctive benefits and make special claims that appeal far more to some customers than to others and thus account for the mix of buyers served by any firm. The price-setter, to the extent that he is skillful, will communicate with price in ways that invite the patronage of certain kinds of customers while alienating others.

The use of price as a communications device is particularly appropriate in the design or composition of an offering. It provides a line of thinking that helps a seller decide what to offer; it is less useful once the firm has already locked itself in on all scores other than price.

Price as a balancing device. A price-setter can view his task to be that of making his offering attractive to the particular number of customers to whom his firm has decided to sell. That means he will examine the firm's offering and compare it with other offerings. At this point he will take his firm's offering as the given and ask what number of buyers he could attract at different prices. To make those estimates, he must decide how various types of customers evaluate alternative offerings—that is, what benefits they seek and what weight they attach to each. With those carefully considered estimates he can then construct a demand schedule, which will indicate the quantity he expects to sell at different prices. Table 5-3 presents hypothetical information of the type on which such an analysis would presumably rest.

In designing an offering, a firm's product planner must consider the responses of different types of customers to the different features that might be incorporated into the product and how many units with different combinations of features would be sold. Such an approach permits a seller to decide into what kind of an offering he should become "locked." When an executive employs this approach *in advance*, he is compelled to forecast the offerings of rivals—not often an easy task. Most important, he must assess the impact of differences in his offerings on buyers' choices. With that done, he will ask what might be accomplished with price to achieve different volumes of sales. Thereupon he or some colleague will compute the profit implications of each outcome, while taking into account rivals' responses. The attainment of a large sales increase would ordinarily alert an executive to the probability of a speedy and strong response from rivals. In thinking through these issues in an effort to design an offering or set a price, an executive must make many judgments on little evidence and therefore cannot feel very confident of his conclusions.

Setting price differentials for each rival

Most of the reasoning that was discussed in the preceding section applies to the process by which a price-setter might best establish a differential between his price and that of any single rival. The price charged by the two members of a dyad communicates something about the similarity of the firms. A firm can set price with the purpose of offsetting the other firm's advantages in, say, quality or service—that is, trying to balance his offering with that of his rival.

Size of the differential

One important issue arises in the use of price as a balancing device: should price be set at a point that makes a firm's offering just equal to its dyad partner's in the view of its desired customers? The answer is clear. If it succeeded in making the two offerings equally attractive, it would enjoy only a 50-50 chance of winning the patronage of those customers. To increase his firm's expected sales, the price-setter must create a gap between his offering and his rival's. The wider the gap, the greater his chance of attracting customers. But the greater his power to attract customers, the greater the probability that his dyad partner will narrow the gap.

What general principles would help a price-setter think his way through this key issue of setting price vis-à-vis rivals? The first may be termed "failure through excessive success" or "cut off the dog's tail a little piece at a time." The second is to favor measures that take a little from each of many rivals and avoid those that have an impact primarily on a single firm. These principles require elucidation.

Failure through excessive success. When a firm takes some measure, say, a product redesign, that increases its sales sharply, it may find itself in trouble. Unless the great sales increase comes at the expense of many rivals, one or more of the rivals must have sustained a heavy sales loss. Such losses may be so damaging that they must be countered. The counteractions may bring the distribution of patronage back close to the initial one but on terms less advantageous to all sellers. When many rivals contribute to the rise in the successful firm's sales, no counteraction need occur, especially when the shift of market shares takes place in a growth market so that few firms suffer a drop in absolute sales when their market shares decline.

Underlying failure through excessive success is a central powerful pressure that operates on almost all managements. They feel obliged to resist any substantial decline in volume almost without regard to the profit implications of such resistance. Firms organize their production, purchasing, and financial plans around a target sales volume. Many act toward market share as if they had a religious duty to maintain and extend it. Consequently, extreme and irrational behavior by rivals may be precipitated by imposing a sharp sales decline upon them.

These principles suggest the great importance of adopting a dyad viewpoint when evaluating potential market moves. Only one severely affected rival is needed to precipitate sharp counteraction. And the initial market move now augmented by the counteraction virtually insures that other dyad members will be injured and feel impelled to take strong countermeasures that undo the gains of the company that was initially successful.

The principles advanced to explain when, whether, and how rivals respond to a firm's move to increase its market share significantly are extremely simple and not altogether convincing. One would expect far

more sophisticated thinking than a stubborn determination to maintain
market share regardless of cost. In particular, the following factors are
likely to be considered by the management of a firm that is being hurt or
feels threatened by a rival's market move. First, is the effect of the move
likely to be enduring or temporary? Does the aggressor firm possess the
resources needed to sustain its advantage? Second, do I have under development some measure that—if I wait—will permit me to regain what
I will have lost? Third, have I the resources to counter the aggressor's
move and will he intensify his efforts if I take countermeasures? Fourth,
what actions will other rivals take if I do and if I don't counter his
aggressive actions?

THE HYPOTHETICAL TV SET PRICING ILLUSTRATION

We are now prepared to resume our discussion of our price-setter for a
TV manufacturer who is reviewing an inherited price structure. Specifically, we will consider how he would identify his rivals and establish a
differential between his price and theirs.

The identification of rivals

It is far from simple for a manufacturer to identify his rivals, because he
usually operates in literally hundreds of geographic markets. In each of
them the relative strengths of the different brands differ considerably.
Also, the various producers vie for different prizes * both nationally and
in individual markets; for example, they seek strong distributors in some
markets, mass retailers in others, strong servicemen in still others. Certainly a price-setter must view this country as a set of quite dissimilar
submarkets and cannot react to each other TV set producer on the basis
of its average performance in all markets.

TV set manufacturers do not behave in an identical fashion in all
markets, but they cannot behave differently in each one. To apply that
notion most particularly in the field of pricing, the price-setter would
want to find a price position relative to other producers that was effective
in general—that is, in most markets—and then adjust price in the markets that are quite different.

To have diverse prices in individual markets is not at all unusual in

---

* The concept of various prizes as the goals of market competition was developed by A. O.
Kelly, op. cit.

many lines of business. In package goods markets, for example, price promotions are scheduled at different times in different places. Thus we find a 25-cents-off promotion for brand X coffee in, say, twelve cities during March and in another eight cities during April, possibly including two that received the promotion in March. In some cities where brand X is sold there might be no promotion at all during that year. Brand Y coffee might similarly be promoted in groups of cities, but usually not concurrently with a brand X promotion in any market. Such price promotions made direct price comparisons among different brands of many consumers' products difficult, but it is nevertheless possible to describe one brand as being higher or lower in price than another. Price promotions are only one device by which manufacturers try to adapt to the special conditions prevailing in a market.

The task of adjusting price in individual markets for a product that is sold nationally is enormous and involves very high costs and not insubstantial risks. Individuals who are thoroughly informed about individual markets and are highly skilled in pricing are required to administer flexible pricing arrangements. In addition, vexing legal problems arise when a firm departs from uniform price in all markets, and, simply on the basis of economy, an executive may be obliged to treat markets as if they were the same when he knows them to be moderately different. Thus, in setting price our price-setter will presumably concentrate his efforts on the few TV set manufacturers that he considers his firm's chief rivals in most markets. They will be the firms that seek to sell to the same kinds of ultimate customers and to the same retailers as his firm does.

It is not always easy to identify a firm's rivals on the basis of common knowledge or personal observation. Many manufacturers of major appliances do not know very much about the retailers to whom their distributors sell or about the kinds of ultimate customers to whom their retailers sell. Of course, the ultimate customers and retailers to whom their brand is sold may not be distinctive in any way; in that event, they may consider all other brands of TV sets equally close rivals.

Our price-setter will presumably want to examine information available in-house to learn which are his firm's closest competitors. In its absence he may request that it be collected for his purpose. The information that would best meet his needs includes:

☐ Data on the brands that his potential ultimate customers consider buying.
☐ Data on prevailing brand preferences.

- ☐ Retail customer statements to salesmen about different brands of TV sets.
- ☐ Shifts in the brand preferences of ultimate customers, including brand-switching data if the product is one that is purchased frequently.
- ☐ Other brands that are carried by retailers that sell his brand.
- ☐ Which brands replaced his when a retailer dropped his—and which brands were displaced by his.

Regrettably, such information is rarely consistent or unambiguous. Especially is that so when the data are not processed in a manner that takes explicit account of (1) the types of ultimate customers and retailers whose views and actions have been recorded and (2) the geographic area in which the research has been conducted. The chief errors in interpreting such data are reduced by having someone who is very familiar with an individual area analyze the results for that area.

The establishment of price

Let us assume that in one way or another our price-setter has identified three rival manufacturers that compete most directly and actively with his firm for given types of ultimate customer and retailer. How might he best proceed to appraise the prevailing general relation between his firm's price and the price charged by each of the three rivals? He would, as indicated, recognize his ability to vary price in isolated markets, but he would know that any shift in his list price would alter his price relationship with all of his rivals. Let us say he finds that his firm's list price to distributors and its suggested list prices to retailers and ultimate customers are higher than those of every other TV manufacturer that sells nationally and could be considered a close competitor. Would such a condition signal the existence of a price problem?

Indicators of a mistaken price. Clearly, if the firm's sales were far below those of the preceding year, if its market share had slipped markedly, and if all this had followed a shift in the firm's prices relative to those of its rivals, the price-setter might well suspect that the firm's prices were out of line. But if the firm's prices were not much above its standard costs—*full* costs at a fairly high level of output—he might question his diagnosis. He might, for example, decide that his problem resulted from the firm's relatively inefficient manufacturing operations.

If the firm's sales, market share, and profits had advanced even though or because its prices were above those of rival firms, the price-setter could hardly conclude that his firm's prices were out of line with those of its rivals. Of course, his firm might have prospered even more at higher or lower prices. In short, the prices charged by any firm relative to its rivals' prices cannot in themselves establish the existence or non-existence of a pricing problem.

The facts assumed—that the firm's prices are clearly above or below those of particular rivals—are both extreme and very simple. A TV manufacturer's line includes many models, only some of which can be considered directly comparable with those offered by rivals. For comparable models, a manufacturer is likely to be relatively high on some and relatively low on others. Although one could construct a weighted average of the prices on comparable models in the lines of different manufacturers, such a computation could not be considered the same as either customers' or retailers' perceptions.

Some firms routinely price their offerings with specific reference to a particular rival's similar items. In such instances, the relation between the list prices of the two firms is apparent to those who are responsible for price-setting on behalf of all major manufacturers and who usually call the attention of their distributors and, through them, of their retailers to the price relation. Also, a general impression usually is formed by members of an industry about the relative prices of different manufacturers and tends to endure long after the underlying reality has changed; misperceptions of price relationships may be almost as common among rivals as among ultimate customers. * It is not easy for individuals to perceive prices, price relationships, and patterns of price change in most markets because of the great mass and ambiguity of information.

Let us assume that our TV price-setter has concluded (1) that his firm's prices are generally very slightly higher than those of the single firm that he considers the closest rival, (2) its prices are generally perceived by most of the trade to be slightly lower than that firm's—that is, his firm enjoys a better price reputation than it deserves, (3) his firm's prices are moderately lower than those of the firm that he regards as the second closest rival, (4) the price relationship is accurately perceived both by customers and by the trade, and (5) the third closest rival charges prices equal to his firm's and his top management believes that this rival directly imitates his firm's prices. Those assumptions can be expressed in Table 5-4 by using index numbers to describe actual prices and perceived prices.

* See F. E. Brown and A. R. Oxenfeldt, *Misperceptions of Economic Phenomena.* New York: Sperr & Douth, 1973.

Table 5-4. The price position of Company A vis-à-vis its rivals. (Company A = 100)

Rivals Arranged in Order of Closeness	Sales, $ millions	Actual Prices (Weighted Average of Compet- ing Models)	Price Perceptions	
			The Trade	Ultimate Customers
Company X	110	97	101	103
Company Y	140	110	110	110
Company Z	80	100	100	100

We are now ready to seek a more thorough answer to the question: what should our hypothetical price-setter regard as a wrong price? The following issues arise in answering that question.

☐ Should he not be more concerned with price perceptions than with price realities? What factors explain the divergence of the two; that is, what might a firm do to achieve a better price image than it deserves?

☐ What differential in price should he seek to establish between his firm's perceived prices and those of Company X? Of Company Y? (Company Z presumably would continue to imitate his company's prices.) That is, what factors should determine the optimum price differential?

☐ How important is price in accounting for Company A's relations with its rivals? Do factors other than price figure more prominently in accounting for the relative success of individual brands? For example, can Company A more readily tolerate a shift of, say, 10 percent in price differentials than an equivalent shift of advertising or product-planning efforts?

☐ Is the relation between Company A's prices and those of its rivals more important at the retailer or the ultimate-customer level? Is that true of relations with all of its rivals, or would the answer vary from rival to rival?

These issues are complex and will be discussed in turn.

Price perceptions versus price realities. Pricing skill can perhaps be demonstrated most directly in a firm's achieving a better price image in the eyes of ultimate customers and resellers than it deserves. Deficiency of pricing skill may result in a firm being viewed as charging more than it does. At least as much as its actual prices, the prices that affect a firm's fortunes are those that customers perceive. To be more specific, it is the stores that customers shop first that largely form customer impressions of prices in general. Generally, customers have no reliable knowledge of the prices that most stores are charging for the particular items for which they are shopping.

Once they are in a store that they believe offers good value, most customers may be largely insensitive to price considerations. On the one hand, they may assume that other stores are charging more for the brands they are considering than the store they are in. On the other hand, the actual prices that the store they are in is charging for different models of their preferred brand are likely to affect their behavior much more than the prior impressions of the related price of different brands.

For example, they might have had the impression that brand A was more expensive than brand X when they set out to purchase a TV set and, upon starting to examine different brands, might have looked more closely at models of brand X. At some stage, customers typically will look at other brands. Ordinarily, retail salesmen will encourage them to do so. Most customers need to reassure themselves that they have made a wise selection, which ordinarily means that they have examined alternatives. When they do examine a brand that they expected to be more costly than their favored brand, they could misperceive its price to confirm their strong convictions about the relative price position of the two brands. In the main, customers can be expected to compare the features of the two brands that are most salient for them and form a new assessment of the relative price and values of those particular brands and models and for that particular store. If this accurately depicts the reactions of most customers, then advance price impressions are at least as important as price realities for products that embody many dimensions some of which are technical and mysterious to the customer.

What determines a particular brand's *perceived* price position relative to other brands? It appears that the most important single determinant is not the currently prevailing price, but past prices. Beyond the past price reality, other factors often have the effect of distorting most customers' price impressions. Advertising, packaging and the store environment can—although they need not—influence customers' impressions of the value embodied in a brand and even in particular models of that brand. For example, it is widely believed that the top-priced item in a line offers greatest luxury, but at a premium, and that the bottom item in a product line offers poor value because the manufacturer cut all possible corners in order to hold price to a minimum. Another widespread view is that the promotional model offers the best value if the customer is not too concerned with cosmetic factors. Whatever the particular conviction, customers have been found to incorporate a goodly amount of attitudinal content in their perception of price.

Horizontal differentials. These are the factors that determine the optimal price differentials among prices of rival firms:

☐ Equality with rival's prices would be expected to make sense only in the unlikely event that nonprice aspects of offerings are themselves manifestly equal—a difficult state to imagine.

☐ Each member of a dyad has considerable power to determine how large a differential will exist between the prices of the dyad members. As indicated earlier, a firm need not tolerate the price differential sought by its rival.

☐ The price differential likely to prevail between dyad members is one that meets the desires of both members more or less equally.

☐ The differential established will endure only if both firms prosper or suffer financially roughly to the same extent. If their fortunes diverge substantially, some of the differentials between themselves and their dyad partners—in price, promotional effort, and the like—typically will be altered by the firm whose fortunes suffered most.

We observed earlier that members of a dyad—whether by design, out of necessity, or because of the play of market forces—will arrive at a whole set of differentials that maintains the relative market position of the two members or that results in gentle erosion rather than a dramatic shift in relative position. Accordingly, a firm that might gain considerably in customer favor would be wise to raise price and achieve higher profit margins while averting a gain in market share large enough to provoke the retaliation of particular rivals. (It would not fear retaliation if its gain was at the expense of many rivals and therefore injured no one rival markedly.) By doing so, the firm would gain higher profits— perhaps an improved quality status—and still not reduce its rival's sales volume below the rival's expectations. The stronger firm would be more profitable but not bigger and would not injure its rival directly if it applied that general rule.

A firm's price differential vis-à-vis a particular rival affects the amount of patronage it would draw from that rival; the larger the differential in its favor (the lower its price) the larger its share of the two firms' combined sales. Similarly, and almost in contradiction, a price-setter should recognize the relation between his price differential relative to another firm and the probability that the other firm will take steps to reduce that differential.

Nonprice factors and the establishment of price differentials. Many marketing factors were not taken into account in our hypothetical example; we spoke almost exclusively about price. We should ask about the best marketing mix for our TV price-setter to adopt vis-à-vis each dyad-partner rather than the best price. To determine what marketing mix would be appropriate, the price-setter must understand not only the responses of those rivals but also, and more particularly, the responses of the potential and present customers of his own and related firms.

To work toward the best marketing mix for his firm to adopt vis-à-vis each dyad partner, the price-setter would proceed in stages. He would first describe the prevailing marketing mix for each partner and determine the division of customers or, better still, of patronage that results from those marketing mixes. Then he must ask how the present customers of all rival firms would respond to the many attractive and feasible changes that his firm might consider and how their rivals would react. That question relates to both customer and rival responsiveness; ordinarily, if customers are highly responsive, sellers who are affected by a change in their customers' behavior will be forced to act.

This analysis parallels the form of analysis described in the preceding chapter: the price-setter starts with the prevailing situation and explores the likely effects of the most attractive actions that he considers feasible. If no change seems attractive, he has already arrived at the best solution.

What then are the symptoms of a marketing mix that is defective vis-à-vis a particular rival? Say a firm is spending too much on some marketing effort and not deriving attractive rewards (added patronage) from those expenditures, how could it find that out? How would a seller find out that potential customers did not value the things he was offering as much as he supposed or that they were not much impressed by what he was claiming? If the customers he hoped to win were tightly tied to their present suppliers and would switch to another only for very large inducements, how could he learn that was so?

Let us now consider the reverse situation, one in which a firm was spending too little on its marketing efforts. That would mean it could attract a considerable number of customers away from one or more rivals by a relatively small added expenditure. And if it were to make that relatively small expenditure, its actions would not be matched—and thus offset and countered—by the rivals who were affected. Ordinarily, that would mean that the small outlay by one seller would draw away patronage from many other rivals so that no one of them would feel significantly affected. If they did feel a strong effect, they presumably would neutralize it by a small expenditure. How could a marketing executive recognize such a situation?

By changing the marketing mix, one seller might influence his dyad partners in many different ways. For one thing his partners, if they sell in many markets, are likely to have varied reactions from place to place. Sellers can often take actions that are confined to a few markets. They may also take actions that are directed mainly at a select subgroup of their rivals' customers, apart from region. The subgroup may be members of a particular ethnic group or readers of a particular medium for example.

THE COMPOSITION AND EVALUATION
OF A MARKETING MIX

The ultimate customer or retailer seeks many benefits from a purchase. Accordingly, he will evaluate different brands—perhaps thoroughly, perhaps carelessly—according to multiple criteria. Those criteria would not have equal weight and they might be regarded as interdependent. The evaluation process is almost always performed unconsciously by customers, and so might be carried out very imperfectly. Table 5-5 presents the manner in which a customer could accurately appraise two brands. What is involved is an analysis and processing of a series of differentials.

Let us assume that we are concerned with the evaluations of an ultimate customer who will base his decision on seven characteristics of the competing brands. We indicate in Table 5-5 the hypothetical characteristics, the weights the customer assigns to them (for simplicity, we assume that he considers them to be independent), and his assessment of the extent to which the two brands in question have them.

The system of Table 5-5 represents a simple rating scheme. It incor-

Table 5-5. Criteria for evaluating a TV set.

Characteristic	Assigned Weight	Presence of Characteristics in		Net Score	
		Brand A	Brand B	Brand A	Brand B
Sharpness of picture	0.25	100	90	25	22.5
Clarity of sound	0.12	100	105	12	12.6
Ease of tuning	0.10	100	100	10	10
Durability	0.08	100	90	8	7.2
Ease of service	0.08	100	110	8	8.8
Appearance	0.15	100	80	15	12
Price	0.22	100	105	22	23.1
				100	96.2

porates the customer's values (the list of characteristics and the weights assigned to each) and his view of their features (the estimated extent to which each brand possesses the characteristic). The system outlined presumably is the one that a customer would want to employ if he were prepared to devote full time and care to making an evaluation. Possibly his subconscious carries out a similar process.

In this hypothetical example, the customer would prefer brand A over brand B by a slight margin. Presumably, if all associated circumstances were equal, he would buy brand A. Given brand A's slight margin of superiority, the price-setter could not expect the customer to spend much time in searching for brand A or be willing to shop in retail stores he did not trust or like to get it. In short, the greater the margin of difference between rival brands, the greater the effort a buyer could be expected to make to obtain it.

In the example of Table 5-5 price is assumed to be somewhat less important than sharpness of picture in influencing customer choice. That must be exceedingly common; a price-setter can do his firm much harm if he exaggerates the importance that the ultimate customer or retailer attributes to price. Although price may be crucial for him, since it represents his main job responsibility, the price-setter must adopt the customer's viewpoint in carrying out that responsibility.

One important question remains for discussion: Should the price-setter be mainly concerned with establishing price for the ultimate customer or for the retailer to the extent that the interests of the two conflict? In the case of TV sets, the problem is not very difficult; for the power of the retailer to influence customer choice of TV sets has been well documented. In the case of most other products, the choice is not so clear or easy; the customer cannot be influenced very much by retailers in the selection of most products that he purchases frequently.

In this discussion of marketing mixes, as contrasted with price, we were forced to be sketchy because a full treatment would extend an already overlong discussion. What is said about marketing mixes might be said about price: Some sellers can create a margin of superiority over rivals, which is equivalent to a price differential in their favor, of varying amounts. The larger the amount the greater will be the share of the total sales obtained by all together but the greater also will be the likelihood that the rivals will take actions that would reduce that margin of superiority. The most commonly used means to increase the appeal of an otherwise unappealing offering is a price inducement. A price-setter needs great skill to balance the conflicting consequences of a widening differential between his firm's price and that of its rivals.

SUMMARY AND CONCLUSIONS

A firm's price can be conceived of as a set of (horizontal) differentials—that is, differences between what it charges and what rival firms charge for their most similar offerings. These price differentials must be related to differences in customer preferences for competing brands, which in turn often reflect variations in the benefits that customers perceive in them. Rival firms need not charge identical prices for very similar items; the discovery of the optimum horizontal differentials is perhaps the most crucial task of the price-setter. This task is enormously complicated, for a firm is a member of at least several and often many dyads. If a price-setter charges the best price vis-à-vis one rival, he will be charging a mistaken price relative to another rival. Thus, he usually must seek out a compromise horizontal differential—one that is best for none of his dyad relationships but acceptable for all.

What makes pricing vis-à-vis rivals so crucial is that errors can be terribly costly. A price move that provokes rivals to strong undesired retaliation can devastate a firm's earnings and create a market condition that is difficult to reverse. Conversely, price actions that contribute to an orderly, disciplined, and responsive market will make a major contribution to a firm's profits, stability, and survival.

6

Pricing Products in Their Prime

RESELLERS

RESELLERS ARE THE MOST IMPORTANT single factor in the success of many U.S. companies. A manufacturer that accounts for, say, 30 percent of the total sales of a product in one regional market may account for only 0.5 percent in another. Yet in both markets the manufacturer sells the same brand, relies on the same national advertising, and carries out the same marketing policies. The difference in sales success is probably due to differences in the caliber of that manufacturer's resellers in the two markets, rather than differences in customer preference.

If resellers are to be effective, a manufacturer must win their support and loyalty. To do so, he must enable them to earn sizable rewards from selling his brand. That means the price resellers charge must exceed the price they pay by an attractive amount; reseller profits are very directly related to the difference between the two prices. The manufacturer is able to influence both of the prices and therefore the difference.

How manufacturers influence reseller prices

Although a manufacturer cannot dictate the prices charged by independent distributors and retailers, he can sometimes influence them strongly and directly. For example, he can "suggest" reseller prices, he can mark a price on his merchandise (but resellers can use their own price labels), and he may even advertise a price directly to the ultimate customer.

A manufacturer often exerts an indirect influence on price. For example, he can usually help his resellers command attractive prices by (1) giving distributors an exclusive right to handle his brand in a specific area and thus freeing them from the competition of others who sell the same brand—though not from firms that sell rival brands, (2) refusing to sell to price-cutters who might reduce profit margins to the point where resellers find it unprofitable to carry his brand, (3) extending various forms of assistance to the distributor, such as market research information, access to computer services, and marketing advice, that contribute to greater profitability.

Beyond his direct and indirect influences on the prices obtained by his resellers, the manufacturer also determines the price he will charge his resellers. In these ways, he determines the resellers' profit margin to a greater or lesser degree. If he enables resellers to earn a large margin, he will win their support and loyalty as a general rule.

The manufacturer's goals in price-setting

A manufacturer needs the support of resellers to attain his own profits and related objectives. Accordingly, in affecting reseller prices, manufacturers are pursuing their own profitability while attempting to provide attractive profits for their resellers. Those goals clearly conflict, and usually one or the other party is forced to accept less than he wants.

More than attractive unit profit margins, manufacturers set price to achieve a high volume of sales. They want to earn their profit margin on a large volume and have the cost advantages that usually accompany the production of a large output. If they allowed high margins of profit per unit for resellers and took high unit profits for themselves, both they and the resellers would be at a disadvantage, because fewer units could be sold at those prices. Manufacturers must make the price to the ultimate customer attractive enough to meet their sales volume goals, even while they make it profitable for resellers to carry and promote their brand. Thus, in setting price to resellers, the manufacturer ordinarily seeks to:

☐ Provide an attractive profit for all *efficient* participants in his distribution system and thus induce them to carry his brands.
☐ Provide an incentive for each participant to support his line to the extent desired.
☐ Permit efficient participants in his distribution system to compete on roughly equal terms with other resellers—both those who offer the same brand and those who offer rival brands. He

must not appear to favor one type of reseller over other resellers of his own brand, if they compete with one another.

☐ Avoid prosecution under the Robinson-Patman Act, which prohibits price discrimination when it injures competition or competitors.

☐ Keep the price of the item to the ultimate customer at a minimum, consistent with the other objectives.

The simultaneous attainment of these five goals calls for great juggling skill on the part of the manufacturer and generally some compromises. Almost invariably, to meet the demands of one type of reseller a manufacturer will be forced to accept less for himself or put another type of reseller at some disadvantage.

DESIGN OF A PRICE STRUCTURE

Some manufacturers simply sell their wares to their resellers, doing so without concerning themselves about what happens next. They may pursue that policy on the ground that their customers know what prices to charge the ultimate customers far better than they do. Manufacturers who lack the power to influence reseller prices adopt that policy out of necessity, but others do so by choice.

Many manufacturers, and especially those who have the market power to influence strongly the prices charged by their resellers, are deeply involved in suggesting the prices to be charged for their products all along the vertical chain between their factories and the ultimate customers. As already indicated, some manufacturers have strong market power in that respect. Most, however, have only modest power to establish reseller prices directly but nevertheless exercise strong influence by persuasion and the respect they command.

We will discuss now the circumstances in which a manufacturer can influence the prices charged by his resellers and also those in which he is wise to do so. After that we will consider what a manufacturer should do when he sets prices for all resellers who handle his product.

When can a manufacturer influence the prices charged by his resellers? Only a manufacturer whose brand influences customer choice can control reseller prices on the basis of power. The brand need not be very popular, but it must be valued by a group of consumers. Manufacturers who can determine reseller prices must find resellers who are willing to charge those prices instead of selling other brands whose prices they

could determine without outside influence. Few resellers would accept
an infringement on their ability to set prices if the brand offered no advantage over the alternatives.

However, not all resellers put a high value on the power to set price
under ordinary circumstances. They often sell so many different products that they welcome guidance from the manufacturer as to what price
to charge. But almost always, unusual situations arise—an unforeseen
need for cash, a heavy accumulation of inventories due to an unexpected
sharp decline in demand—that put pressure on the reseller to alter price
to the possible disadvantage of the manufacturer. If individual resellers
are permitted to meet such special needs in that way, they can make the
sale of a product unattractive a large part of the time for most of the
resellers upon whom the manufacturer depends for the resale of his
product. They will therefore have little incentive to carry or actively
promote the product.

What is a price structure? In its simplest sense, a price structure consists of prices (usually "suggested" prices) to be charged by the different
firms that sell a manufacturer's line of products. Ordinarily that means it
consists of suggested prices for distributors and retailers along with any
special discounts, overrides, and special financial arrangements on the
sale of a particular line of products. Table 6-1 presents a sample price
structure for a manufacturer of television sets. Presently, we will examine it closely to explain the separate elements it contains and the purposes they serve. Before that, it would be useful to understand the origin
of the term "price structure."

"Price structure" embodies an illuminating metaphor; it likens the
design of viable pricing arrangements for resellers to the construction of
a building. Both call for a careful putting together of separate pieces to
produce a structure that can survive the stresses that may be placed upon
it. To design a strong building efficiently calls for much forethought and
foreknowledge—the development of blueprints and the application of
certain engineering principles. The same requirements hold for a price
structure.

Several conditions usually must be met if the parts that compose a
structure are to be strong enough for their function. In the case of a
building, the structural units must be of the right size and quality. In the
case of a price structure, the chief structural units are margins and discounts for the various parties who handle a particular brand of product;
they too must be of the right size and quality if the price structure is to
be strong.

The strength of a structure is also related to its complexity: as a gen-

Table 6-1. Sample price structure for TV sets.

Model Description	Suggested Retail Price	Minimum Retail	Distrib- utor Cost	Retailer Cost	Factory Co-op Con- tribution
18 in. diagonal, 180 sq. in., walnut-grained plastic	$329.95	$269	$227	$256	$3.40
18 in. diagonal, 180 sq. in., AFT, timer, walnut-grained plastic	$349	$289	$241	$272	$3.60
18 in. diagonal, 180 sq. in., AFT, transformer, walnut-vinyl-clad metal	$369	$309	$248	$287	$3.72
23 in. diagonal, 295 sq. in., AFT, transformer, walnut-vinyl-clad metal	$499.95	$429	$325	$370	$4.87
23 in. diagonal, 295 sq. in., AFT, transformer, grained maple on wood	$529.95	$459	$338	$384	$5.07

The pricing formulas of "less 4 percent" and "less 4 percent and 3 percent" apply where applicable (as explained below) on all models listed except color television. Color television prices, below sheet prices, are based on quantities purchased and fall into three categories:

Annual Volume	Price Formula	Commission Rate
0 to $5,000	Sheet	7%
$5,000 to $30,000	Sheet less 4%	5%
$30,000 and over	Sheet less 4% less 3%	3%

eral rule, the more complicated the less strong. The complexity of both price structures and buildings varies with the number and dissimilarity of the parts that compose the total structure. A large building consisting of unbroken walls is relatively easy to design and construct and will ordinarily be strong; similarly, a price structure composed only of small independent retailers who buy from a single distributor is usually easy to design and will be strong. However, when structural members of different size and quality must be combined in unusual shapes, both ease of design and strength are compromised.

Most structures are designed to endure. In the case of a price structure, the actual prices themselves are not expected to remain unchanged for long; but the price relationships expressed in margins and discounts should not change much, and the parties who comprise the manufacturer's distribution system are expected to remain in the system for a substantial period. The price structure is expected to bring that result about by making the relationship of the various parties harmonious and profitable. Survival of such a relationship requires each party to be effective. The retailers, for example, must perform capably if the distributors and manufacturer are to achieve a large sales volume, and the manufacturer must provide attractive merchandise at reasonable prices. All in all, the relationship of the parties who make up a distribution system is one of high mutual dependence; and in his design of a price structure, a manufacturer must try to make that fragile relationship mutually advantageous so that it will endure.

Principles of price structure design

The analogy between a price structure and a building implies that certain engineering principles dictate how a structure should be erected and specify the conditions that must be met if the structure is to be sturdy. If the price structure is to contribute to the achievement of an enduring and efficient distribution system,

1. Each efficient reseller must obtain unit profit margins in excess of unit operating costs on an attractive volume of sales.
2. Each class of reseller margins should vary in rough proportion to the cost of the functions the reseller performs.
3. At all points in the vertical chain, prices charged must be in line with those charged for comparable rival brands.
4. Special distribution arrangements—variations in functions performed or departures from the usual flow of merchandise—should be accompanied by corresponding variations in financial arrangements.
5. Margins allowed to any type of reseller must conform to the conventional percentage norms unless a very strong case can be made for departing from those norms.
6. Variations in margins on individual models and styles of a line are permissible and expected. They must, however, vary around the conventional margin for the trade.
7. A price structure should contain offerings at the chief price points when such price points exist.
8. A manufacturer's price structure must reflect variations in the attractiveness of his individual product offerings.

These principles, admittedly, are broad and loose. An "attractive volume of sales" is not a precise concept. Functions that are roughly proportional in cost to the margin allowed is also an imprecise notion, as is that of "prices in line with those charged for comparable rival brands." Some increase in the precision of these terms is possible, even though they cannot be made completely precise. An attempt will be made to clarify their meaning.

Each efficient reseller must obtain unit profit margins in excess of unit operating costs on an attractive volume of sales. Here we are dealing with vertical differentials, the differences between prices paid and prices received by resellers. Such differentials must be in line with reseller unit operating costs or the resellers will not long remain within the distribution system. This principle is particularly difficult to apply because a reseller's sales volume is affected by the price that he charges, and so are his operating costs per unit; for most resellers' total operating costs are virtually unaffected by variations in sales volume. In other words, a reseller might be allowed a fairly low margin (vertical differential) and still operate quite profitably if he achieves a high sales volume. Conversely, with a much larger margin that kept his sales volume low he might operate at a loss.

Some vexing questions arise in connection with the measurement of "unit operating costs." Whatever his true unit operating costs might be, what matters most to the reseller is what he believes them to be. Since most distributors carry many different lines of product and often represent several different manufacturers, their nonmerchandise costs for items or product lines cannot be compared with any accuracy. Almost all of their sales costs are common and can be allocated to individual items only on some arbitrary basis. Understandably, manufacturers and resellers often hold different views as to the proper way to compute costs, and resellers generally hold views that result in higher unit operating costs than manufacturers consider valid.

Differences in reseller costs have four main causes, which have a decidedly different significance to the manufacturer. First, some resellers are far more efficient than others; second, some resellers support the sales of the lines they carry very vigorously—they offer better service, do more sales promotion, employ better salesmen, and cultivate the hinterland better than the average reseller; third, the companion lines carried by resellers often influence their operating costs; and fourth, some resellers face very intensive competition for business in their markets and incur heavy costs in combatting their rivals. Whereas a manufacturer would not willingly subsidize the inefficiency of his resellers (unless he could not attract more efficient ones), he usually would feel obliged to cover costs incurred to promote his products and combat competitors.

Even when a reseller's high costs result from apparent inefficiency, a manufacturer sometimes faces a serious dilemma. Firms that do not keep good records, manage inventories well, or store and move goods at low costs are often highly imaginative merchandisers. Many manufacturers would prefer such resellers to those who were outstanding on cost control but weak in attracting customers.

Thus our engineering principle that margins should be related to operating costs remains quite ambiguous after close inspection. What costs? Whose costs? One thing is clear. Both legal considerations and the need to deal equitably with all firms within his system dictate that a manufacturer treat in the same way all firms performing the same functions in the same market. This last point is central to the design of pricing arrangements, so central that it need *not* be included among our engineering principles. To include it would be much like instructing someone to take account of gravitational forces in the design of a building.

Each class of reseller margins should vary in rough proportion to the functions the reseller performs. This principle implies a key question: should margins be related to functions, costs, or both? Few manufacturers possess the power to establish margins to suit their own taste, views of equity, or calculations of reseller costs. If resellers perform valuable functions for the manufacturer at very low cost to themselves, they usually will be able to command highly profitable margins. Bargaining power, as much as costs, determines a particular reseller's margin.

But what are the dimensions by which a price-setter could usefully classify resellers? The most common basis of classification is by function performed for the manufacturer, along with the class of customer with whom the reseller deals. Many manufacturers ask these questions about a reseller:

Does he hold inventories?

Does he make purchases in large or small quantities?

Does he provide repair services?

Does he extend credit to his customers?

Does he deliver?

Does he help train his customers' salesmen?

At all points in the vertical chain, prices must be in line with those charged for comparable rival brands. Manufacturers must not put their resellers at a disadvantage relative to their rivals. The closest rivals, of course, are other resellers who sell the same brand in the same area; accordingly, some manufacturers limit the number of resellers who carry their brand. They frequently give distributors exclusive rights in a specified territory, and the distributors, in turn, often limit the number of retailers who carry particular brands. A very few retailers have exclusive rights in an entire community.

The problem of protecting resellers against rivals carrying the same brand is greatest when some retailers buy a particular brand from the distributor and others buy it directly from the manufacturer. If retailers who buy direct are also heavy advertisers, enjoy strong buyer acceptance, and sell at low prices, the other retailers usually face the choice of appearing to overcharge or handling the item at a loss. The biggest price structure problems faced by many manufacturers and distributors are of this type.

A price structure must withstand the onslaughts of rival brands. When he sets suggested retail prices or prices to retailers, the manufacturer must take full account of rivals' prices and rivals' responses to the prices he sets. He need not charge what they do or less than they do, but he must take their price into account along with whatever he knows about consumer brand preference, the services offered by the different brands, convenience factors, and the like. Clearly, he cannot make it impossible for his resellers to achieve an attractive sales volume by requiring them to charge high prices. Conversely, he need not press their margins too low in an effort to insure them—and himself—a high volume.

The relation between the prices charged by resellers and the prices of different brands at the same level can be described as horizontal differentials. These differentials must be kept within tolerable limits; that is, they should yield tolerable volumes of sales and acceptable amounts of total profit. Retailers will often handle rival brands. Even then the price on each brand should not place that brand at a clear disadvantage or the retailer will not be willing to devote space and working capital to it.

Interestingly, a horizontal differential that is tolerable in Milwaukee may be quite out of line in Atlanta. A brand that is very popular in one city may be out of favor in another. The prices established for the brand should, to the extent possible, take such regional differences into account.

Special distribution arrangements should be accompanied by corresponding variations in financial arrangements. As will be explained in the following section, many manufacturers work out special arrangements to adapt to the capabilities and resources of unusual resellers.

They will perform certain functions themselves in some cases and have the resellers perform them in others. A distribution system wherein all distributors and retailers perform the same functions and receive the same discounts and margins is the exception.

Differences in the functions of resellers are usually associated with the differences in costs to the reseller, manufacturer, or distributor, and price structure will generally reflect those differences. The manufacturer will not necessarily adjust margins and discounts to reflect cost differences precisely, partly because the differences are difficult to measure in any specific case and partly because they vary substantially from case to case. Mainly he seeks a result that will be acceptable to the parties involved and appears to be equitable to other members of his distribution system.

A hypothetical example might clarify the point. Some retailers want to carry an item and could produce attractive sales volume for the manufacturer and distributor but are unable to provide the necessary repair service. The distributor may then arrange with another retailer to perform the repair service for all the retailers. Ordinarily, he would charge the nonrepairing retailers for the service to be rendered by the retailer who did the repair work for the group. Such special arrangements are not ordinarily written into a manufacturer's price structure; they are usually treated on a case-by-case basis rather than governed by general rules.

Margins allowed to any type of reseller must conform to the conventional percentage norms unless a very strong case can be made for departing from those norms. In most trades, resellers have come to regard some particular percentage margin as normal, fair, and proper. They may not obtain that margin on most of the items they sell; even when it is indeed a typical margin, they may not receive it all of the time. Often they will be offered extra large margins on selected items or be asked to accept a below-average margin on promotional items. But although the conventional margin may not be an economic reality in the marketplace, it may nevertheless strongly influence the reaction of resellers to the lines they are offered. Failure of a reseller to be "allowed" the conventional margin may create major resentment that results in resellers giving limited sales support to a brand. As a general rule, therefore, a manufacturer is unwise to rely upon resellers who receive what they consider inadequate compensation for their services.

Variations in margins on individual models and styles of a line are permissible and expected. They must, however, vary around the conventional margin for the trade. Most manufacturers offer many models and styles within any line of product. They usually include one or more items whose main purpose is to increase traffic for retailers. Such promotional items are generally the lowest priced in the line and yield relatively low margins of profit for the manufacturer and for all types of reseller. Resellers are willing to accept items that do not contribute satisfactory profits because they will usually try to limit the sale of the items and because they benefit from the store traffic that promotional items create.

Manufacturers usually offset the low margins on promotional items by offering items with higher-than-conventional margins; usually such items offer special and luxury features. For example, the cost to the reseller of special extras on major appliances is usually about one-third the amount by which the extras increase the suggested resale price, whereas his usual margin is less than one-half the difference.

A price structure should contain offerings at the chief price points, when such price points exist. Price points are found only at the retail level; they represent the prices at which customers have become accustomed to find offerings. They are sometimes described as conventional prices.

Price points are particularly interesting in that very few customers actually make purchases at them; they serve primarily as points of reference for retailers and customers alike. Retailers use them as the basis for describing the amount of discount they offer; consumers regard them as the usual prices even though they do not pay them. With the spread of price discounting, price points have eroded almost completely. Also, inflationary forces in recent years have weakened customer impressions that items are available at particular price points.

A manufacturer's price structure must reflect variations in the attractiveness of his individual product offerings. Prices have little meaning apart from the goods or services to which they attach. Visible differences in the quality of offerings must be associated with differences in price. To maintain a particular kind of price structure—with price points separated by, say, $20—a firm may have to design offerings to match by adding offerings at parts of its line and discontinuing other offerings. Also, it can adapt its price structure by adding items at the high- or low-price end to adjust to shifts in demand.

MAIN VARIETIES OF RESELLER ARRANGEMENTS

Price structures should meet the pricing problems and exploit the opportunities of a manufacturer as they are reflected by the reselling arrangements in the industry. Although reselling arrangements vary widely from trade to trade, the chief factors that influence the design of a price structure are the number of steps in the reseller structure, the similarity or dissimilarity of the firms at each level, and the relative bargaining power of the resellers on the different levels.

Steps in the structure and their effect on price

In size and complexity, a manufacturer's price structure will usually parallel his distribution structure. If it is composed of many levels and subgroups of firms at each level, it will be highly complex. A simple reselling system requires only a simple price structure.

In the traditional reselling system, the producer sells to a distributor who sells to a retailer who sells to the ultimate customer. This system involves three sellers and it has three steps. When the producer sells directly to the ultimate customer, the system has only one seller and one step. Certain distribution systems include more than three steps and the two-step system of manufacturer to retailer to customer is quite common.

A product increases in price as it passes from one step in a reselling system to the next: the distributor pays less than the retailer who pays less than the ultimate customer. The difference between what each reseller pays and receives is intended to defray his operating costs and yield a profit. Under those circumstances customers have an incentive to jump over one step to buy at a lower price. Some retailers, especially large ones, buy directly from the manufacturer at essentially the same price that distributors pay, and some individuals buy certain items at wholesale.

Ordinarily when customers jump over a level of resellers, they forgo certain services they value. They may lose return privileges, get little help from sales personnel, do without credit accommodation, be forced to buy larger quantities, and so on. However, many customers prize the savings in price much more than the benefits they forgo. That is especially true of resellers who gain a strong competitive advantage by buying at a low price and offering their customers a lower price. Every price structure is designed with the threat of jump-overs in mind.

To hamper jump-overs the manufacturer must describe the customers who are entitled to buy at the various prices. Usually they are defined by their functions. As with almost everything, some borderline cases exist and some cheating occurs; but if such cases are a tiny minority, the general price structure need not be threatened. On the other hand, when the functions of resellers are not easily determined, the borderline cases and cheats become so numerous that the manufacturer cannot influence the prices charged by anyone but himself.

Similarity of firms at each level

The number of steps in the reseller structure is only one influence on a price structure. The similarity or diversity of the firms at each level is at least equally important. At any level, some resellers can generate far larger sales volumes than others. For that reason they will be highly prized by the manufacturer and consequently will possess strong bargaining power. That is to say, the manufacturer would be willing to give them preferential terms rather than lose their patronage, and frequently he is forced to do so. Major differences in bargaining power are usually manifested by differences in price, although legal constraints limit those differences somewhat.

As already indicated, a manufacturer or distributor will sometimes sell his product to a reseller who cannot perform all of the functions usually required of him. Since his inability to fulfill some functions increases the expenses of other resellers, some adjustment is made by reducing the margin or increasing the price to the reseller who performs less than the usual services. When the number of such resellers is large, the differences in price are included in the price structure.

Large differences in size of purchases by resellers usually give rise to variations in the prices charged. The large customer is characteristically offered quantity discounts. Quantity discounts to distributors are an intrinsic part of the price structure that a manufacturer will erect. Sometimes the manufacturer also suggests the quantity discounts that his distributor should extend to retailers, although those are beyond his direct control.

Relative bargaining power of resellers

Because resellers differ widely in bargaining power and in the skill and daring with which they use it, a manufacturer will generally design a price structure that takes bargaining power into account. Usually that means preferential advantages to the resellers who can produce large volumes of sales and have very attractive alternate sources of supply. Manufacturers who have established a strong customer preference for their brands, on the other hand, will exercise their market power to limit the special advantages of large-volume sellers.

Problems are created in an entire industry by the fact that manufacturers whose brands are weak are forced to offer sizable inducements to large-volume sellers. Large retailers are generally permitted to buy direct, that is, to jump over. Manufacturers of strong brands are subjected to strong pressures by large retailers to offer similar privileges. Retailers who are skillful bargainers sometimes succeed.

Variations in operating efficiency

Any manufacturer's distribution system will include resellers at every level who differ substantially in efficiency and market position. As a result, a margin that is attractive to one firm is not enough to cover the operating costs of another. What is competitively tolerable to one distributor or retailer is decidedly intolerable to another. Such individual differences constitute a core problem for manufacturers in the design of a reseller system. Much of the problem results from manufacturer inability to identify the difficulties and assess their magnitude. Also, prevailing notions of equity lead the most favored and efficient to expect equal—if not favored—treatment.

Interrelated nature of a price structure

We've already stressed the importance of vertical relationships: that the price obtained at each level should permit profitable operation if a firm operates efficiently, and that each of the resellers in a single manufacturer's system should be able to survive in competition with the others. That means mainly that retailers who buy from a distributor can achieve substantial sales in the face of competition from the retailers of the same brand who buy direct from the manufacturer. Similarly, a manufacturer's horizontal price relationships must be such that resellers of his brand can compete on equal terms with resellers of rival brands.

Let us change one factor, a reseller's price. Specifically, we will assume that the margin allowed to retailers who buy brand B from independent distributors is too low. That being so, the retailers who buy brand B from distributors fare badly in competition with those who buy direct from the factory. They also find themselves at a disadvantage relative to retailers of brands A and C—both those who buy direct from the manufacturers and those who buy from distributors. Consequently, retailers begin to drop brand B, and both the distributors and the manufacturer begin to experience low sales volume and probably high costs. The distributors then press for higher margins to defray their higher operating costs per unit and thus aggravate the problem.

This example illustrates the most common difficulties in the design of a price structure. The problems that result from too high or too low a margin for distributors, rather than retailers, would be similar and no less drastic. An error anywhere in a structure usually gives rise to problems at other points in the structure.

PRICE STRATEGY RELATED TO RESELLERS

We have already explored the development of substrategies that would guide, inform, and constrain price decisions as marketing executives aim to achieve customer- and rival-related goals. We will now seek strategic notions that would help a price-setter build an effective price structure. These notions usually revolve around subobjectives and hopefully incorporate some ingenious actions that would lead to their achievement by efficient means.

Figure 6-1. Benefits a manufacturer might obtain from resellers.

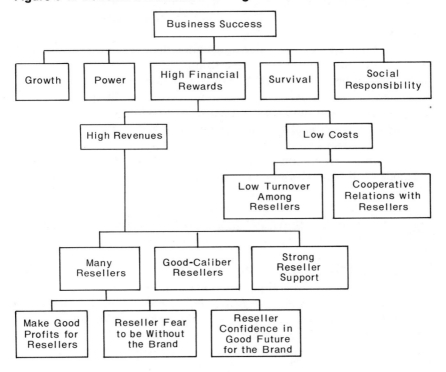

To identify promising subobjectives for strategy development, we must develop a hierarchy of objectives for the firm. However, the hierarchy will be different in each case; for it should be designed specifically to highlight goals of a particular type. In this case, then, we require a hierarchy to highlight the benefits that a manufacturer might obtain from resellers. Such a hierarchy is presented in Figure 6-1. It indicates some vital subobjectives that would be suitable starting points for marketing and pricing substrategies that relate to resellers. A larger number is presented in Selected Subobjectives Related to Resellers.

The TV set revisited

With the price-engineering principles as background, we can return to our price-setter for a TV manufacturer. He has inherited a price structure and wants to evaluate its suitability from the standpoint of his distributors and retailers, that is, its effects on the number and caliber of the resellers who carry his line and the sales support they give it. As suggested earlier, a price structure must realistically reflect an industry's system of distribution and the bargaining power of those who compose it. Accordingly, let us sketch distribution arrangements in the TV industry.

Most TV sets are sold by manufacturers to independent distributors who handle only one brand of television and who, in turn, sell to retailers who usually sell several brands to ultimate customers. This three-step distribution system might account for about 60 percent of an average appliance manufacturer's total sales. In addition, most TV manufacturers will sell approximately one-fifth of their output to manufacturer-owned distributors—so-called factory branches—who sell to retailers who resell to the ultimate customer. Beyond those two main methods of distribution, most manufacturers sell direct to large national chains of appliance stores, discount houses, and department stores. Sometimes they do so in cooperation with their distributors; that is, they will share the sales efforts and profits with local distributors. Finally, many manufacturers sell directly to a small handful of large mass retailers, the house accounts.

It should be emphasized that individual TV manufacturers depart radically from these general patterns. For example, some manufacturers sell to no retailers directly, no matter how large. Some have developed several subsystems that take account of the differences in sales arrangements. Different selling arrangements often involve different flows of merchandise and of cash. In some cases, the manufacturer will deliver

---

SELECTED SUBOBJECTIVES RELATED TO RESELLERS

1. Secure broad exposure of product to potential customers.
   a. Offer financial incentives for resellers in form of wide margins.
   b. Offer resellers assistance such as financing, managerial services and inventory keeping.
   c. Create strong consumer preference for the brand and thus exert pressure on resellers to carry it lest they would seem to be low-quality stores.
   d. Minimize reseller risks due to price reductions and sudden decline of demand.
2. Obtain strong sales support from resellers.
   a. Have them invest their own funds in advertising, perhaps through co-op advertising plan.
   b. Obtain disproportionate amount of space in resellers' display space.
   c. Obtain disproportionate space for signs.
   d. Obtain disproportionate space in catalogs, store, on shelves.
   e. Have resellers develop a specialized sales force to sell your product.
   f. Have reseller salesmen give disproportionate time to your product.
3. Induce resellers to drop rival lines, especially those that are strongest competitors.
4. Induce resellers to hold in stock more items in your line.
5. Have resellers carry larger inventories of each item in your line.
6. Have resellers offer good service on your product, especially in the event it does not function well.
7. Obtain fast and reliable market research information from resellers.
8. Obtain useful suggestions from resellers.
9. Have resellers provide a pool of manpower suitable for employment, especially for such positions as regional salesmen and managers of factory branches.
10. Have resellers carry out and transmit your policies to customers.
11. Contribute to cost reduction.
    a. Induce resellers to place orders at convenient time—generally early in season.
    b. Induce resellers to pay bills without frequent urging.
    c. Have resellers perform repairs and minor adjustments without involving factory.
    d. Have resellers accept delivery at convenient times and in amounts that are economical for the factory.
    e. Induce resellers to process orders and returns in an efficient way for the factory.

---

his products to the distributor who delivers to the retailer; in other cases, he will deliver directly to the retailer even though the purchase was made from a distributor. The manufacturer may deliver to a central warehouse owned by a large retail chain or to its individual stores. On occasion, the manufacturer will deliver direct from his local warehouse to ultimate customers who bought the product from retailers who in turn bought the product from a distributor. The timing of payment tends to vary with the delivery arrangements.

These different distribution arrangements and flows of merchandise are usually associated with differences in the costs, risks, and control of the manufacturer. They often are associated with differences in prices also. In part the differences in price simply reflect cost differences; often they are intended to encourage distributors to adopt one distribution arrangement over the others; for they better meet the manufacturer's needs.

Our price-setter's evaluation of his firm's price structure would parallel analyses described earlier. He would consider the consequences of altering the vertical—and therefore the horizontal—reseller margins on (1) the number of resellers who would carry his line and (2) their caliber —that is, ability to produce a consistently large volume of sales for the manufacturer at a reasonable price to him. He would make a separate analysis for each level of reseller and each major class of firm at each level. He would examine the margins allowed to independent distributors, factory-owned distributors, retailers who buy from distributors, and retailers who buy direct from the manufacturer. For each type of reseller he would (1) appraise the vertical differential (compare operating costs with margins allowed) and (2) appraise the horizontal differential (assess the competitive advantages of the firm's prices relative to its major rivals).

Such an appraisal entails mainly a forecast of the effects of raising or lowering the margins allowed to a particular type of reseller. Specifically, it involves answers to the following questions:

☐ How would actual price charged by that reseller and others be affected by the change in margin? (Suggested prices are not to be confused with actual prices.)
☐ How would the number of resellers who carry the brand be altered?
☐ What kinds of resellers would be attracted by the change? What kinds would be lost as a result of the change?
☐ What amount of sales effort would be given the brand by the different types of reseller as a result of different levels of margin?

Several spheres might be affected by a change in margin, so the price-setter would systematically appraise each one. He might organize his appraisal in some such way as Table 6-2. Some effects of a change in reseller margin may be beneficial, but the change might also have adverse effects. The price-setter would presumably first estimate the many

Table 6-2. Impact of potential changes in distributor margins.

Potential Changes	+3%	+2%	+1%	−1	−2	−3
1. Number of good distributors in big cities that would:						
Drop the line.						
Give added sales support.						
Give less sales support.						
2. Number of mediocre distributors in big cities that would:						
Drop the line.						
Give added sales support.						
Give less sales support.						
3. Number of good distributors in small cities that would:						
Drop the line.						
Give added sales support.						
Give less sales support.						
4. Number of mediocre distributors in small cities that would:						
Drop the line.						
Give added sales support						
Give less sales support.						
5. Effect on factory branch profits						
6. Effect on transshipping						

consequences of altering margins by different amounts and then assess the net impact of each change. He could change more than the average margin; he could also alter the margins allowed on individual models in the line with or without a change in the average.

The analysis implies questions: Can price-setters forecast the effects of shifting margins? What might they do to establish these functional relationships so that they might accurately appraise the effects of any proposed change in margins? Few price specialists claim they can forecast the full effects of changes in suggested margins. They recognize that the effects will vary and that substantial differences are to be expected from market to market. Also, the average or overall reactions of resellers—and their rivals—to changes in the margins of any manufacturer are not predictable because behavior in many trades is quite inconsistent. However, price specialists can do some things that should improve their ability to forecast. They can:

☐ Review past experience of their firm and other firms with actions similar to the one under consideration.

☐ Establish panels of resellers and discuss their reactions to the contemplated action.

☐ Conduct a test of the change in selected markets.

These measures are not always available or feasible, and they cannot be expected to produce accurate indicators of the effects to be expected. Still, they can usually add information that would improve a price-setter's estimates. However, the price-setter must accept the fact that his estimates will almost certainly be mistaken and monitor the results of his actions or take corrective action when it is required.

SYMPTOMS OF A DEFECTIVE PRICE STRUCTURE

A price-setter usually cannot tell whether his price structure is about as good (that is, achieves his firm's goals as well) as can be expected realistically. If opportunities existed to increase his profits by increasing the margins on certain models, the price-setter would not usually receive clear signals of their existence. On the other hand, he usually will get loud—but often misleading—signals of major price structure problems. He must therefore sift through the evidence reaching him that suggests his margins are wrong to find cases deserving close study and possible change. The symptoms of a defective price structure consist mainly of complaints by resellers that they are being injured competitively or making little or no profit because of existing margins. The most serious complaint is that a whole class of resellers cannot sell reasonable quantities of merchandise because its members are being undersold on the same brand by resellers who jump over one level of distribution.

If the manufacturer has evidence that the complaining retailers' purchases from the distributor are down while the purchases of the jump-overs are soaring, he knows that he has a serious problem. He must fear that the complaining resellers will drop his line altogether, which will cost him the sales volume he had enjoyed from that source. He might hope to rearrange the margins to reduce the advantage enjoyed by the jump-over retailers so that both types of reseller are economically viable. However, he might actually achieve higher sales and profits if he consciously favors one type of reseller over the other. Specifically, he may be prepared to give up the patronage of the very large retailers who buy direct from him to protect the small retailers who, collectively, sell more, sell more consistently, are more loyal, and exert less pressure for price reductions. Conversely, he may favor the large mass-merchandisers because they can generate large sales volumes and can hold their own against the mass-merchandisers who carry rival brands.

Complaints by his resellers that they are being undersold by rival brands are another symptom of possible defects in a manufacturer's price structure. Some complaints, of course, may come from resellers who are not effective or imaginative. Most manufacturers receive many such complaints even when their prices and margins are, if anything, defective in the opposite direction. Still, the complaints must be listened to and evaluated. The clearest symptom of a defective price structure is an increase in the number of resellers who drop the line. Although some turnover among resellers apparently is inevitable, a sudden loss of resellers who are of good quality should make the price-setter drop all else and reexamine his margins. In particular, he will want to communicate with some of the resellers he has lost.

A manufacturer's drop in market share may or may not reflect a defect in his price structure. Generally, the identity of the firms whose share of market has increased would suggest whether defective margins or other factors caused the apparent trouble. Accordingly, in appraising his inherited price structure, our TV price-setter would be wise to communicate with the firm's regional sales managers, study written complaints, and analyze turnover among retailers and independent distributors. He might also establish panels of resellers of different types and meet with them periodically—perhaps in the company of other marketing executives—to discover defects in his price structure at the earliest possible time. He would want to examine data describing their operating costs as well as listen to their broad-brush estimates.

The management of short-term price changes

A price structure may appear to be quite satisfactory but still have many defects. The prices incorporated in the structure, which is composed mainly of "suggested prices," serve mainly as starting points. Many changes in price are made from those starting points. The position of a brand depends as much on such price changes as it does on the initial suggested prices.

Short-period changes may be initiated by the manufacturer, distributor, or retailer; sometimes all three will join forces to create a particularly attractive price promotion. Often one of the three will change his price to meet a problem of his own. The situation that gives rise to most price reductions by a reseller is an unbalanced inventory. A reseller who accumulates large numbers of one or more models will usually reduce the price of those models in the hope of stimulating their sale. When the inventory imbalance has been corrected, the price reduction usually is withdrawn.

Sometimes a reseller changes most though not all of his prices to combat a general sales decline. The sales drop may result from a rival's promotion that gave retailers a financial incentive to push the promoted brand. If the price reduction was passed along to the ultimate customer, the attraction of the low price to the consumer diverted business to that brand and lowered sales of other brands correspondingly.

Price changes on only a few models are most common, but promotions of a whole line do occur at least in selected markets. Accordingly, individual prices change fairly frequently from the suggested list price. Someone—it need not be the one who establishes price for the firm—must monitor the market to learn what price moves are taking place and decide whether to initiate such moves himself.

The effect of short-period price adjustments on the sales of certain manufacturers can hardly be exaggerated. A manufacturer could offer his distributors and retailers margins as attractive as those given by other manufacturers—give his resellers merchandise of good quality, provide national advertising, good repair, warranty, and so on—and still sell relatively little because of faulty short-term prices. He may be the victim of various developments. Several rival manufacturers or distributors may be promoting particular models that have been backing up in inventory. Under those circumstances, sales by the manufacturer in question of models similar to those promoted by the other companies will decline sharply. (A strong promotion on one model usually affects sales of several rival models, and even others in the same line.)

To remain fully informed about such price developments would make enormous demands on a price-setter that he could not hope to meet. He cannot know enough about what is happening to the price of individual models in all geographic markets to counter every rival's moves that should be opposed. He must rely on distributors to learn of the price actions by rivals in their markets and to take suitable action. Hopefully his distributors know far better than he when they would be wise to do nothing but wait for the price-cutter to dispose of excess inventory. He would usually like to get his prices back up as soon as possible and earn customary margins.

A price-setter cannot evaluate conditions in most individual geographic markets and determine the extent to which his price structure is suitable. He may be compelled to base his assessment on the average relationships—the typical horizontal and vertical differentials—incorporated in the price structure. In addition, he would want to assess the responsiveness of his firm—in particular the salesmen who call mainly on distributors and very large retailers and his own associates at headquarters—to shifting local conditions. Do they give distributors all the advice and help that they might give in their own self-interest? Do they give that help quickly and equitably? An affirmative answer to those questions is required, and so is an effective price structure if the firm's distribution system is to prevail in the face of its competition.

SUMMARY AND CONCLUSIONS

A price structure is mainly designed to create an enduring reselling system for a manufacturer's wares. To do so, it must take account of the relative strength of demand for the brand, the operating costs of different types of resellers, and the diverse selling arrangements employed by the manufacturer.

Given the numerous constraints on him, as well as variations in circumstances both within and without his distribution system, the manufacturer must expect points of weakness to develop from time to time in many markets.

Mainly, a price structure combines vertical and horizontal price differentials that must be viable in the face of operating costs and competitive circumstances. A good price structure can be effective only if it is combined with great flexibility so that the manufacturer and his distributors can adapt quickly to changes in local market conditions.

7

Reconciling
the Optimum Prices

IN THE THREE PRECEDING CHAPTERS we discussed a single aspect of pricing decisions for products in their prime. Chapter by chapter, we reasoned our way through to the price that should be set with respect to each of the three key parties to the pricing process. We explored the benefits that a firm might gain from the main parties to the business process together with the effects on each of those parties of changes in price. More particularly, our discussion was largely organized around a consequence net that described the tangible and intangible effects of price changes on each party to the business process.

We must expect the best price for, say, ultimate customers to be inappropriate for rivals and resellers, and the price that is best for rivals and resellers probably would be unsatisfactory for ultimate customers. How, then, can a price-setter find the best of the best prices? Or must he find yet another price that would be best when all three parties to the business process are considered?

OPTIMUM PRICES

If the best price for all three parties combined were different from the three best prices for the separate parties, by what route would a price-setter find this new price? What should he do after he has identified three prices for his product, each different from the others, that are best for particular parties to the pricing process? Recall that these prices would be part of a mix of marketing tools that was designed to achieve maximum synergy. Either the price-setter must test the three to find the best of them or find a compromise price that is different from all three but within the range that they define.

It surely is disappointing to learn that, after he has come this far in his price analysis, the price-setter still has some distance to travel before he arrives at his price decision. But as we shall see, the analyses already described will have cleared the ground for the balance of the price-setter's trip to his destination. Two methods of proceeding are available to him. First, he could test each of the three optimum prices for its suitability to the other two parties while recognizing that he probably needs to find a fourth compromise price. Second, he could build a price from scratch. In using the first method, he will test the suitability of the prices for the other parties to the process that appears best for a single party. In starting from scratch, he makes his price decision without regard to the present price. Although the second approach is different from that we discussed in the preceding four chapters, the analyses discussed earlier will provide the chief data inputs that it requires.

Earlier in our comparison of price with other marketing tools we argued strongly that, whatever else he does about price, a price-setter must do at least the following:

1. Take account of the separate parties to the pricing process and not simply develop a price suitable to one of them.
2. Treat price as one of a large bundle of marketing tools that is used in combination and design a mix that achieves synergy.
3. Set a price that is both dictated and constrained by the firm's general objectives and by its long-run marketing strategy.
4. Consider his decision costs as the floor for price. (The concept of decision costs is developed later in the chapter.)

If these four elements, and the subelements that they imply, are not considered by the price-setter, he almost certainly will set a wrong price. Both methods to be described for finding the best price for all parties to the pricing process should be judged by whether or not they meet these requirements.

The testing of optimum prices

The mode of analysis presented in the preceding three chapters may be described as a testing of incremental changes from the prevailing price; a price-setter will almost always find the prevailing price to be a reasonable starting point when pricing products in their prime. The approach now to be considered extends the incremental analysis that is central to economic theory to take account of the many effects of price changes, beyond changes in unit sales, and the interaction of price with other marketing instruments. To conduct such an analysis, a price-setter must guesstimate the tangible and intangible and the soon and late effects of a series of price changes. That conclusion is inescapable; a forecast of all significant consequences of charging other feasible prices must underlie every price recommendation.

To test the suitability of an optimum price for one party to the pricing process for the other parties, the price-setter must forecast the effects of changes from the prevailing price. He can also employ that method to seek a compromise price. To do so, he lists the effects of selected price changes on all parties to the process and assesses the net benefit or injury that would result.

For example, assume that a price-setter for a TV manufacturer has conducted the analyses described in the preceding chapters. Assume, further, that he has concluded that the best price for the focal item* in his line is $299 with respect to ultimate customers, $279.95 with respect to rivals, and $319 with respect to resellers. He would already have worked out the effects of a $299 price vis-à-vis ultimate cutomers; that is, he would have recorded his estimates of the sales and unit costs that he expects. From his earlier analysis, he probably also knows what the $299 price means with respect to rivals and resellers. That is, he knows what kinds of resellers he will gain and lose if the price is $299 rather than $319, the optimum for resellers, and the amount of sales support he can hope to get from them.

Now he will look at the effects of a $319 price, the preference of resellers. He will be able to identify the many different consequences of that price compared with a $299 price. He will record that so much of a decrease in sales is to be expected in the near term and a different amount in the long term, so much of an increase in production and marketing costs, some rise in reseller support that could be obtained, a shift in brand image, and possibly a resistance on the part of his firm's salesmen to call on price-sensitive customers.

Having listed those differences in consequences of a $299 price and

---

* A focal item is the offering in a product line that a price-setter treats as a base from which differentials are computed. Ordinarily it is the most widely advertised and sold item in the line. A price-setter usually simplifies his task enormously by establishing price for a focal item and then determining differentials for the others.

a $319 price, the price-setter will place a value on each consequence. That is, he will translate the nonfinancial effects of the price differences into monetary terms: How much is it worth to get or avoid the expected change in brand image? Since the effects will occur at different times and present income is more valuable than future income, he should express the differences in current dollars, the present value of their expected net benefit. To do so he will estimate the dollar value of all of the benefits and costs of the two prices and then compute the net benefits of each price. (Each sum will be adjusted for the time value of money to its present value.) By that process, he will decide which price offers the best combination of benefits.

Let us say that as a result of this analysis he favors a price of $289 over any other feasible price he might charge. He has then found the best compromise price. At this stage he should test more prices than he tested in arriving at his three optima. Knowing that he would be employing this testing process, he probably would not test a very large number of prices to determine each of the three optimums.

Thus, to test any price or price change, the price-setter first identifies the effects on the different parties affected, places values on the effects, and translates the values into present equivalents. He then compares the price with alternatives to find the one that yields the greatest net benefits. In his original analyses, he will have identified the effects of price changes on the different parties and determined the functional relationship between price changes and those effects; he will thus have accumulated the basic data he requires for the testing process.

In concept, the process is simple enough; in practice, the price-setter faces very difficult estimates. He must take account of special circumstances and make adjustments for the interdependence of the different marketing tools used by his firm.

Building a price from scratch

If a product is in its prime, a price-setter need only evaluate and adjust its existing price to arrive at a price decision. Nevertheless, he will gain important benefits if he sets price without using the prevailing price as his starting point. In other words, he should also employ a nonincremental approach, at least from time to time. He should challenge all past assumptions and strategies and consciously seek new and better ones; he should identify shifts in the resources and capabilities of all firms; and he should take account of significant developments in the environment.

As has been said, price has far more consequences than immediate financial revenues and costs through its effect on sales volume. It is an instrument of marketing policy and must be constrained and directed by that policy. And like most other business decisions, price decisions should be influenced by a superstructure of thoughts that represent directives and constraints. The thoughts include (1) the owners' desires regarding the business(es) in which the firm will engage, (2) the philosophy and credo of the chief owners and top executives, (3) the kinds of customers to whom the owners wish to sell, (4) the strategies that management wishes to employ, (5) the objectives pursued and the weights attached to them, (6) top management's assessments of its own resources and capabilities and those of rival firms, and (7) the target-brand image that top management seeks to create. One way or another these thoughts or determinations should affect the decisions reached about price and related marketing instruments. But relatively little has been said about any of them up to this point, except for substrategies. We need not discuss how these or implied choices should be made. They are not made by the price-setter; they are handed down to him. But we emphasize that the price-setter should inform himself about them and use them in a particular sequence.

We shall now examine a series of steps by which a price-setter might best arrive at price if he were to start from scratch. Our main purpose is to indicate how a firm's objectives, strategies, policies, resources, brand image, and philosophy should influence a pricing decision. The rationale underlying these steps will be discussed when it is not self-evident.

The seven items listed earlier as directives to and constraints on the price-setter are not always clearly stated; also, they are not usually developed as elements in a tightly interrelated bundle of ideas. Indeed, some of them are not stated explicitly and are interpreted differently by individual executives. The price-setter's first task is to learn the constraints and directives that should influence his price decisions and then take them into account in a manner that accords them their proper influence on price. Not infrequently he must either raise questions or make explicit assumptions that will force his superiors to take a stand on issues that they have overlooked or attempted to avoid.

Stratagems for pricing offerings from scratch

The price-setter is not much concerned about the business(es) in which the owners and top management want to engage; he is usually assigned the job of pricing a specific line of products that the owners intend to offer as long as it yields attractive profits. He is, however, affected by the other items in the list of seven and should deal with them in a sequence that insures their consistency and that gives him maximum guidance in carrying out the next step. That process is a modification of what is called the multi-stage approach to pricing.*

Step 1. Identify the different types of customer that the firm is trying to cultivate.
(a) Design a separate distribution system to attract and serve dissimilar customer segments effectively, when-ever that is feasible or desirable.
(b) Determine the margins for resellers composing each of the distribution systems, along with the special costs that the firm incurs to sell through those systems.

Step 2. Describe two or more sets of circumstances under which the item is to be offered to the ultimate customer. That is, select the retail environment most conducive to the attraction of traffic and the creation of customer desire and willingness to buy.
(a) Indicate the kinds and amount of service that should be provided, at retail, to the customer.
(b) Define the kind of sales support desired from retailers.
(c) Determine the price or range of prices at which the item should be offered for sale. Base the determination on an explicit assessment of customer sensitivity to differences in price.
(d) Determine appropriate differentials between items in the product line (models, sizes, product features, and so on).

Step 3. Develop a profile of the firm's closest rivals. Identify the in-dividual prizes that are sought from them and those that they will seek from the firm.

Step 4. For each set of circumstances identified in step 2, estimate the outcomes relevant to the attainment of the firm's objec-tives. Specifically,
(a) Estimate the level of sales anticipated at the desired range of prices. (If the range is wide, the sales should be estimated at the top, middle, and bottom of the range.) Also, account should be taken of the timing of the sales.

* See A. R. Oxenfeldt, "Multi-Stage Approach to Pricing," *Harvard Business Review*, July–August 1960, pp. 125-133.

(b) Estimate the cost for the full line of offering as well as the cost of the individual offerings.

(c) If changes in the product line would accompany different selling arrangements, indicate those differences and estimate their cost.

Step 5. Develop a cost floor for the focal item in the line under each set of circumstances. The cost floor represents the unit cost to the manufacturer to make the item available—production costs—plus the estimated unavoidable unit marketing costs. Both are based on the assumption he will continue to produce his other offerings. The cost estimates should be adjusted to take account of different target levels of sales.

Step 6. Establish a price ceiling for the focal item under each set of circumstances. Take account of quality differences among the rival offerings, both real and perceived. Drop items if their price ceilings do not exceed their combined production and marketing cost, plus profit, under the corresponding set of circumstances.

Step 7. Establish differentials among the items in the full line of offerings that represent prices that the quality and feature differences can command. By reference to cost information insure that items that do not cover their costs directly or indirectly are not included in the line. An item can cover its cost indirectly by stimulating sales of other items through a building of traffic or by creating quality acceptance for the entire line.

Step 8. Starting with the price ceiling for the focal item, explore the effects (on sales now and in the future) of reducing price midway to the cost floor and perhaps at several other intervals. Spell out in detail the expected consequences of the different prices—their effects on the different parties and at different times. Place a current value on the consequences, and determine which price would be most advantageous under the different sets of selling circumstances.

These eight steps incorporate a number of fundamental marketing stratagems as well as some basic concepts related specifically to pricing. The most important of them are:

Market segmentation—recognition of significant differences among customers in the benefits they seek and their responsiveness to different actions that sellers might take to spur sales.

Backward reasoning—designing a distribution system by defining
the circumstances at the very end of the distribution chain,
usually at the retail level, and working backward step by step to
create those circumstances.

Demand interdependence.

Incrementalism in the computation of costs and benefits.

Team pricing.

Market strategy based on analysis of market segments and the
strengths and weaknesses of the organization and its rivals.

The computation of costs for pricing purposes

Businessmen compute costs for two main purposes: (1) to help them to
perform their custodial functions (reporting to owners and tax authorities
and attempting to uncover dishonesty and inefficiency) and (2) for decision-making purposes. Cost data help management perform its custodial
functions, for they serve as cost standards for internal control purposes
and provide inputs for the firm's periodic accounting statements. Cost
data are directly or indirectly employed in the valuation of assets and the
measurement of profits.

Costs are also an inescapable ingredient of all decisions. If decisions
involved no costs, management would have no reason to oppose them; if
they involved no benefits they would be rejected out of hand. Accordingly, the very important and powerful concept termed decision costs
has emerged. Decision costs are those that would result from making the
decision under consideration and taking the actions it implies. They
should be compared with the benefits that would result from the action;
they are the estimated additions to a firm's total costs that would result
from making the particular decision while doing what was otherwise
planned.

Decision costs represent forecasts, for the decision will be executed
in the future. They are therefore subject to some uncertainty. They are
also highly situational; they require that account be taken of any special
circumstances surrounding the decision. Accordingly, one could speak of
the decision costs of adding a particular item to the firm's line of products, of dropping a specific item, of shifting the plant location, of changing a mode of delivery. These illustrations of decision costs are easy to
grasp and apply; for the action under consideration is easily described
and its costs can be readily visualized. But the concept of decision costs
is not clearly and easily stated as it applies to pricing. What, then, is the
decision for which costs in a price decision are computed? What related
decisions should be distinguished?

It would appear that a price-setting decision comes down to "What price should we charge for our model X652 next year?" The next question is "What actions would be required to carry out that decision?" To turn that question into a specific decision whose cost might be computed, it is necessary to consider a specific price decision for model X652. Is it to raise price by 5 percent, lower it by 10 percent, or what? To compute the cost of a price decision, it is necessary to state those questions very specifically. We will accordingly reword our hypothetical price decision as follows: "Should we raise the price of model X652 by 5 percent next year and do the things we generally do when we raise price?"

With those guides, computing the cost of a specific price decision might appear to be straightforward enough. However, several reasonable interpretations of the price decision are possible; they differ from one another in assuming different alternative actions. More specifically, the cost of a price decision must mean something like this: "What would it cost me *extra* to do this (about price) rather than to do nothing?" Cost computations imply comparisons, but price decisions often do not involve clear alternatives. Let us examine alternative interpretations of this hypothetical price decision for model X652:

1. Leave price where it currently is or charge some specific other price. In other respects—that is, in advertising, personal selling efforts, and so on—do just what is being done now.
2. Drop the model altogether and continue to offer the rest of the line.
3. Drop the whole line of which this model is a part. Otherwise, offer all other lines that are currently offered.

Let us examine what is involved in estimating the cost of the three alternatives. The first implies that it relates solely to price demands and does not have a bearing on what the firm will offer for sale. The firm will continue to offer model X652 and all other models no matter what decision is made about the price of X652 at this time. The actions required to implement this alternative might include the following.

The printing and distribution of new price lists.
Announcements and explanations of the price change to the company's salesmen.
The re-marking of prices on merchandise.
Reprogramming of computers to incorporate the new prices for invoicing and inventory valuation.

Changing the output of model X652 and of any other models whose sales would be affected by a 5 percent increase in the price of this model.

Changing the firm's marketing efforts to sell model X652 if such changes would be made.

The cost of this decision would involve the following computations:

1. An estimate of the total costs that the firm would incur if the price were not changed and an estimate of its total costs if the price of model X652 were raised by 5 percent. The second total would include the six items listed above.
2. A determination of the difference between the two totals, which represents the cost of the specific price decision. That cost must then be compared with the added revenues that the firm would obtain as a result of the decision. The comparison would reveal the net effect of the decision to raise the price of model X652 by 5 percent.

Let us now turn to the second alternative, which has the price-setter facing the choice of offering model X652 at the best price he can obtain for it or dropping it from the line. Accordingly, it has him thinking, "If the firm continues to sell this model, I would recommend that we charge 5 percent more for it. Should I recommend that we continue with it at the higher price, or would we be better off to drop it?" The cost of that price decision represents the amount that the firm must spend to offer model X652 for sale and also offer all other items in its line as compared with the cost of continuing to offer all other items than that one.

Although this interpretation seems strained, it represents the cost floor for most price decisions. A price decision usually is best viewed as a decision to offer an item for sale at some price, rather than stop offering it. The actions required to carry out such a decision include all of those listed in connection with the first alternative. That is, it includes the costs that must be incurred to change the price plus the production and marketing costs that the firm would save if the item were dropped from the line. That total will exceed the costs of a price change while continuing to offer the model for sale. It would be compared with the benefits of that decision—the revenue that the firm would derive from that item beyond what it would earn if the item were dropped—to determine whether the item should be offered for sale at that price.

The third alternative is extreme; it is to either produce the entire line of TV sets or drop it, model X652 along with all the others. Model

X652, that is, would be considered necessary to the whole product line. Consequently it would be assigned a share of the costs common to the line because those costs would be eliminated if the entire line were dropped.

If these are the different costs that a price-setter wants to measure, how does he get the data he requires? Are the data ready-made and available from the firm's regular accounting records, or must they be custom-made? If the latter, what are the proper calculations? What pitfalls must be guarded against? To whom should the price-setter go for help in processing cost data for his own purposes? Some of those questions can be answered easily; others are highly complex and controversial. Here are some partial answers:

1. The relevant cost figure—the decision cost for model X652—is not ready-made; it must be produced to order to take account of the special circumstances of the particular situation. The special circumstances might include the amount of excess production capacity, the availability of labor, the state of employee morale, and the firm's inventories of raw materials and components.

2. The required computations must be based on all of the significant consequences to the firm of the cash outlays involved in offering the item as compared with the cash outlays involved in alternative actions. The consequences should include those of both the near and the far future.

3. The pitfalls in computing decision costs are largely conceptual. Specifically, executives often shift from estimating decision costs to thinking about custodial costs and tend to ignore opportunity costs—the uses of their limited resources that they are forgoing.

4. A price-setter should regard the task of calculating the costs of a price decision as a joint effort with the accounting department, rather than a task that he could or should assume or that he could delegate to the accounting department.

Programmed costs

One category of cost causes particular concern. These are programmed or optional costs which are not to be considered as part of the decision cost. Programmed costs are those that need not be incurred to make the product available or even to remain in business; rather they are incurred in the expectation that they will add to *net* revenue. Typical of such costs are outlays for advertising, marketing research, sales training, and new machines to replace less efficient ones. Such outlays could be described as investments by an operating firm to capitalize on opportunities to increase net profit. They could also be viewed as outlays for special projects rather than costs of making the product available. The important point in any event is that they are not required to make the product available to the customer and do not result from the decision to produce and sell it.

Programmed costs look like any other costs on the firm's books; few firms handle them differently from other costs on their accounting statements. Consequently, decision makers have great difficulty in separating them from other costs. Let us examine a borderline case to clarify the problem and indicate the importance of the distinction.

A firm is earning a tolerable level of profits and its advertising director recommends the launching of a major new effort to capitalize on a theme that he believes will make the firm more distinctive and its product more unique. When asked how the firm will be compensated for its added advertising outlays, the advertising director says, "Out of a combination of increased sales volume and higher prices." He elaborates by saying that he believes the firm would be wise to retain its present prices for a while but should raise them in four months when the new models of the product are introduced. He estimates that sales will rise about 15 percent as a result of the advertising program and the sales increase will return almost 60 percent of the added advertising cost. The higher prices that the firm will charge thereafter will return far more than the 40 percent of the program's cost not covered out of higher volume.

What is especially interesting about this example is that the cost of the advertising program is to be incurred with the intention of increasing price. Does that mean the cost of the program became part of the cost of that product for purposes of making a price decision? Or would it be more accurate to say that the cost of the advertising was the cost to the firm of the price increase? The firm did *not* increase price to cover the cost of advertising; it increased its advertising in order to raise price. If a management decided that it wanted to increase price and adopted an increased budget for such things as advertising, customer service, and added salesmen in order to make a higher price viable, those costs would surely be considered part of that marketing program and that price decision. On the other hand, it could not consider those added marketing costs as the costs of making that item available that must be included in its cost floor. What can a price-setter draw out of this somewhat involved discussion that would be of help? The following propositions should cover most situations:

1. Estimate the reduction in costs that would occur if the product

were dropped. Costs that would not be changed clearly cannot be said to be costs of making the product available.

2. If dropping the product would lead the firm to reduce particular outlays, the question that still remains is whether those costs are needed to make the product available. If the product could be sold in sufficient volume to support itself even without a given outlay for, say, advertising, then advertising is not a cost of making the product available but is instead an investment in a special project to capitalize on the firm's opportunities to expand its profits by increasing the demand for the product. In that case, the cost of the price decision for the product would include no advertising cost. The price floor—the minimum price that could be considered seriously—would then include no advertising ingredient.

3. When programmed costs are incurred to permit a price increase, the price increase is the benefit that the firm obtains as a result of the advertising program, and not the penalty it must pay to make that program possible. In short, the added costs do not require a price increase.

As suggested at several points, the difficulties of computing the costs of a price decision, or the cost of making a particular product available while continuing to offer all other present items, arise from dissimilar costs that look the same on the company's books. Most of a firm's outlays are absolutely required. If the firm is to remain in business, it must pay its salesmen's commissions, do a minimum of communicating with its potential customers through price lists, catalogs, and so on, and perhaps inform resellers of its presence if it is to persuade them to handle its brand. Those outlays are truly costs of the decision to offer the product and therefore of the pricing decision. They would be included in the cost floor because by dropping the product the firm could eliminate the costs. All other costs associated with the product must be considered optional and so need not be included in the cost of the product for the price decision.

Hopefully these observations on how to compute a price floor will put the price-setter on guard against accepting the cost calculations that happen to be available to answer the question, "How much does this product cost?" Only by answering the question, "What would we do if we didn't make this product available?" can he, or anyone else, estimate the costs that result from the decision to offer a product for sale. But even then the estimation of the decision cost of a pricing decision remains complex and leaves room for controversy.

PRODUCT LINE PRICING

Another important set of issues that was raised by the earlier description of pricing from scratch revolves around product line pricing. These issues include (1) interdependent demand and (2) team pricing. The first is a widespread market situation that price-setters must recognize when it exists. The second represents one important strategy for exploiting a condition of interdependent demand.

Interdependent demand takes many forms that are important to a price-setter. It exists when there is a connection between the sales and price of his product and those of substitute and complementary products sold by other firms. Substitute products are competing products, and what was said earlier about rivals and competitive products applies to substitute products as well as to different brands of the same product. Our concern here is with substitute and complementary products sold by the price-setter's own firm. How should such products affect price decisions from scratch?

If a firm sells products that are substitutes for one another, that could make an important difference to a price-setter. For example, a price-setter could greatly increase the sale of a single product in his line by lowering its price and might even create the appearance of having increased the profitability of that product greatly. But if that sales increase came almost entirely at the expense of another item in his firm's line (that is, another model of the same product), then the decision to lower that item's price was badly mistaken. What the firm may have gained on the one item could have been more than offset by its losses on the other. Thus when firms sell close substitutes, a price decision can be evaluated only by considering its effects on all items in the line.

Similarly, a price reduction that increases the sales of one product and then leads almost directly to increased sales of a related product— one that is said to be complementary—should be evaluated by taking account of both the direct and indirect effects. Whereas the drop in price could seem mistaken if it were judged by its effect on the profitability of the item the price of which was lowered, it might appear otherwise if the increased sales of the complementary product were considered. Thus, when interdependent demand exists—and it does exist a very large part of the time—price-setters face particularly complicated problems: they must look at *all* of the effects of their price actions.

We will confine our discussion of pricing in the face of interdependent demand to substitute products, and then only of a particular kind:

when very close direct substitutes are offered by the price-setter's own firm.* They are the other TV sets if he is setting the price of a single set; they are other package styles and grinds of coffee if he is setting the price of a particular package of a particular grind; they are other classes of airline service if he is pricing a particular class of air service. He knows that the closest substitute for his brand of TV set model X652 is his own model X752, which has the same chassis but a slightly different cabinet. He may sell a customer one of the two, but almost never will he sell that customer both models at the same time. The sale of one virtually precludes the sale of the other to the same customer.

If model X652 yields a higher profit than model X752, the price-setter wants to do what he can to foster the sale of X652. So when he is selling close substitutes, a price-setter will try to increase the attractiveness to customers—and maybe to salesmen—of the higher-profit item. Contrariwise, he might adopt the strategy of setting price in a manner that would make all models in his line equally profitable. Then he would be indifferent as to which model the customer bought. If he were to adopt that strategy, his price decision would be greatly simplified. He would need only to establish the desired margin of profit and add it to the cost of every item in his line.

As will be explained later, an equal profit strategy is *not* likely to be a maximum profit strategy. Although it might be desirable for certain purposes to have all models in the line equally profitable—and might even appear to be more "equitable"—customers usually are more responsive to price changes on certain items than on others. And the price-setter generally sets price with two different short-term objectives in mind. One is to lure a customer to the site or purchase; the other is to induce him to make a purchase. Therefore, the prices of different items in a product line should build a high volume of traffic and also large volume of sales, preferably of the items in the line that yield the highest profit. To achieve those twin goals, the price-setter usually must:

1. Attract attention with a low-price and low-profit offering, and thus build traffic.
2. Give the customer a reason for not buying the low-priced offering.
3. Persuade the customer to buy another—and relatively high-price, high-profit—item in the line.

* For a much more exhaustive discussion of this issue by this author, see "Product Line Pricing," *Harvard Business Review*, July–August 1966, pp. 137–144.

4. Make the item of (3) appear to be good value, mainly by including other items in the line that are particularly expensive.
5. Make the firm that offers the line appear to be progressive, reputable, and well established.

The term "team pricing" has been applied to a strategy that pursues these goals. Team pricing can be employed if the starting point is incremental analysis, prevailing prices, or scratch. The core concept of team pricing is that each item in a product line should have a particular mission that is established in association with the missions of the other items in the line. A planned assignment of missions to all items in the line has a greater collective impact on customer purchases than the sum of individual impacts of items viewed as self-contained and autonomous could have. Team pricing aims to derive maximum profit from the full line, rather than from individual items. The profit that each item contributes when the firm obtains maximum profit from the line as a whole usually is less than its own maximum potential contribution to profit.

Influence of objectives, strategies, and policies

Now that we have supplied two essential parts of the price-setter's kit of conceptual tools, we can return to the discussion of pricing from scratch. We have already seen that many elements—objectives, philosophies, strategies, brand images, and so on—must be combined in this approach to pricing. Next we should ask whether and how those considerations enter into the incremental analysis that has been described in the preceding four chapters.

In the first place, if the price-setter found that a price he was considering had consequences that ran contrary to the firm's philosophy or credo, he presumably would reject those prices. Also, he would consider only actions that were consistent with the firm's target image and marketing strategy.

In the second place, he would evaluate the outcomes of different prices (marketing programs) on the basis of the firm's goals and needs. The value of any consequence would depend on the firm's objectives and their relative importance. It is in this valuation process that top management's directives and constraints affect the decisions of its subordinates.

One feature of the approach described in this and preceding chapters that causes particular difficulties is the combining of price with other marketing instruments. It has been stressed repeatedly that price changes usually should be combined with adjustments in advertising, personal sales, and promotional arrangements, as well as changes in product, customer service, and so on. To discuss such adjustments will not help much. Little can be said in general terms about the joint effects of marketing instruments; at best, we might reach tentative conclusions about particular combinations of marketing actions under specific market circumstances. One general conclusion can be advanced with considerable confidence about the use of marketing instruments in combination. It is that their joint effects are rarely equal to the sum of their parts. A skilled price-setter will learn, usually by trial and error, what combinations of marketing tools and particular price changes are best in given market environments.

SUMMARY

The most promising price from the standpoint of an individual party to the business process usually will not be best for all of the parties involved. However, the analysis performed to find that price will usually provide most of the data required to find the best price. To find the best price, the responsible price-setter would conduct an analysis very similar to the one by which he made his initial price determinations. That is, he would identify the effects of changes in price, place a value on each effect, and compare the values.

From time to time, a price-setter should think his way through to a price decision without regard to the prevailing price. He should take explicit account of the firm's ultimate goals, business philosophy, marketing strategy, target brand image, and the like. In setting price in that way he will make use of the data developed in finding the best price for each separate party to the business process. Also, he will ordinarily use incremental analysis to compare feasible attractive prices suggested by the constraints and directives set down by top management.

8

New Product Pricing

MOST FACTORS THAT CONCERN a pricing executive at various stages in a product's life cycle are basically similar: He must take account of the responses of ultimate customers, resellers, rivals, and even his colleagues; he must be concerned with product costs; and he must take into account the demands of government. Given these basic similarities, the price-setter can be expected to apply the same methods during each stage of a product's life cycle. Accordingly, in this chapter the many concepts and tools discussed in earlier chapters will be adapted to the special problems faced in pricing new products.

CLASSIFICATION OF NEW PRODUCTS

Newness is a matter of degree. Strictly defined, a new product is one that embodies an entirely new concept; nothing like it has ever been offered to the consumer before. As thus defined, a new product would create demand; wholly new consumer appetites would be whetted by it.

The author gratefully acknowledges the assistance he received from Laird Scott Miller in the preparation of this chapter.

In the present culture, with its huge population of products and services, few things meet that definition. Firms rarely offer a product that even remotely approaches that degree of newness. A new product *for a firm* usually means that the firm is offering something for the first time that other firms have been selling for some time. But even when the firm is the first to offer it, a product usually promises consumers benefits that they currently obtain in other ways but in a novel manner.

Those extremes identify two different pricing problems. The first can be most aptly described as new *product* pricing, whereas the second can best be described as new *producer* pricing. Unfortunately, many products do not fit neatly into either category. The TV set can again be used to illustrate the concept under discussion. In 1946, the TV set was considered a new product, even though television was not so new. About 10,000 sets had been sold in the United States prior to World War II. More important, television was never *completely* new in the demand sense in that it created new wants or appetites. People of that era had enjoyed home entertainment by listening to the radio—entertainment that offered programs similar to those possible on television. Drama, news, comedy, sports events, and musical variety were radio staples. Also, people looked to motion pictures for visual entertainment similar to that later provided in television. Therefore, although the technology of television was new and audiovisual entertainment in the home also was new, the existence of closely related entertainment made television far from unique.

The definition of a new product may have little operational significance for a price-setter, but the relative newness of a product strongly affects the manner in which a price-setter approaches his task. The key differences between a new and a prime product is the *degree* (as opposed to the *kind*) of *uncertainty* affecting the key variables involved in establishing an appropriate product price. The newer the product the greater the uncertainty associated with the key variables. The price-setter must be able to adapt his usual pricing tools to this extreme uncertainty. Much more useful than a definition is a classification system that separates new products into significantly different types for pricing purposes. To develop such a system, it is necessary to identify the characteristics of new items that are particularly relevant to pricing decisions. Any product will embody some unique characteristics, particularly in the wants it satisfies and the benefits it offers, but some dimensions can be used to describe virtually every product and also have some pricing implications. The following are some of the more important questions about new products that a price-setter should ask.

☐ Is it a different way of meeting án existing need or does it meet a new need?

☐ Is its producer protected against competition?

☐ Does it pose difficult problems of learning for the customer or are the methods of use and the benefits offered almost obvious?

☐ Is it a big-ticket item or does it involve a small expenditure?

☐ Would its failure result in heavy losses or costs apart from its own cost?

☐ Is the technology on which it is based quite mature or still developing? If the latter, how rapidly?

☐ Would its use make users heavily dependent upon one source of supply?

☐ Are there any serious doubts about whether it can deliver the benefits promised?

These questions are relevant in three ways: (1) They indicate the importance of considerations other than price that will influence potential customers for new products and therefore the relative unimportance of price as a sales determinant in many cases. (2) They suggest the speed with which other firms will enter the market and the market power of those firms. (3) They suggest the degree of risk that the manufacturer and resellers assume if they offer the new item.

Another basis for classifying new products that may have even more significance for price decisions is the position of the new product among the firm's offerings. That is, does the firm offer only the new product or is the new product only one of many offerings? Does the firm now offer products that are designed to meet the same need and that can be expected to decrease in sales as the sale of the new product increases? Will the new product probably expand the sale of other products in the firm's present line? In developing a classification of new products for pricing purposes, both the characteristics of the product itself and the product's place in the firm's offerings must be considered. That the possibilities are very numerous can be seen by circling one of the mutually exclusive alternatives in each item in the following list:

1. Nature of the concept: radically new, fairly new, familiar.
2. Exclusivity: protected, not protected.
3. Expected contribution to firm's goals: total (the only product produced), intermediate (moderate source of revenue), slight (minor source of revenue).
4. Effect on sale of firm's other products: none (as when the product is the only one produced), big, small.

PRICING AND UNCERTAINTY

In pricing both new and prime products, considerable uncertainty always exists about the correctness of the judgments made in reaching a pricing decision. In pricing both kinds of products uncertainty results mainly from an inability to predict the effects of price differences that is usually only partly due to the absence of information. In the case of a wholly new product, the lack of information is particularly severe. No historical data are available to indicate how changes in the firm's marketing actions will affect consumer purchases or rivals' actions. Furthermore, executives making decisions about the new product have virtually no personal or subjective information that relates specifically to the product.

On the other hand, products in their prime have a historical record, however incomplete, that permits inferences about the sensitivity of sales to changes in price and other variables such as product design, packaging, weight of advertising, and advertising themes. Also, many executives will have accumulated considerable subjective data. They will remember how resellers responded when informed about a pending price change, how the economic environment seemed to influence consumer attitudes to price changes, and the like. Consequently, when an executive alters the price of a mature product, he will usually have considerable objective and subjective information at his disposal, even though it will always be more meager and less accurate than he desires. More important still, he will have the prevailing price for that item—one that has been exposed to real-life market forces—as a starting point.

The dearth of objective (quantitative) and subjective (qualitative) information to assist in pricing new products has two important implications. First, even though relevant subjective information is scanty, initial pricing decisions for a new product often must rest primarily on such data in the virtual absence of objective data. Quantitative data generally could be obtained from market tests and market surveys, but for reasons to be discussed later, such data usually have only modest value.

A second important implication of the dearth of relevant information is that a pricing executive should insure that information systems that will yield timely information for future price decisions are set up for new products. In other words, two phases of new product pricing can be distinguished: (1) the establishment of the initial new product price and (2) the subsequent revision of the initial price to adjust to actual market conditions. The second phase is probably the more critical of the two for the long-term success of the new product.

We will now explore methods of establishing the initial price for a new product while recognizing that the first and perhaps most vital price decision for a new product is management's determination that the product will produce profits in line with its profit goals.

IS THE NEW PRODUCT ECONOMICALLY VIABLE?

A price-setter's expertise ordinarily is required to help forecast the profitability of a new product. He must make his contribution to the forecast even before the product has assumed its final form and while alternative channels of distribution are under active consideration. Given the unknowns about what the firm will do, it is logically impossible to forecast what customers will do. That fact notwithstanding, managements press to terminate research and development projects that lack promise in order to avoid unnecessary expense; they push forward their highly promising projects and possibly even spend much more than the minimum necessary in order to save time. In most cases, the chief determinant of a project's profit promise depends upon the price that ultimate customers will pay for the product in quantities that would support an enterprise. (What customers will pay for a product has little significance unless it is associated with the quantities they will purchase.)

Someone usually is required to assess the economic viability of a project at different stages of development. In many firms, that assessment is made by the individual—not infrequently an engineer—who is in charge of the project. The project manager requires access to the persons who are most familiar with conditions of demand so that his estimate of the item's ultimate price will be as valid as the firm can make; ordinarily those who are responsible for setting price on the firm's present products should be consulted. In estimating the price that a new product will command, the following questions must be considered along with the estimated costs of further development.

☐ What different product or service features might be offered to customers?
☐ What positive benefits would the offering yield to different subgroups of customers? What disadvantages would each subgroup perceive in the different versions of the offering?

☐ What would each version of the offering cost if different levels and scales of output and the likelihood of technological developments were taken into account?

☐ What would be the costs of marketing the different versions of the product through different channels of distribution?

☐ How much of each version of the offering would be sold at prices that would cover all production and marketing costs plus a minimum acceptable return for the producer?

It need scarcely be stated that every one of these questions is enormously difficult to answer while a product is undergoing development; they are even quite difficult when a product is in its prime. Still, a firm must do the best it can while taking account of the high cost and low accuracy of data that might be collected. In general, its pricing specialists can be particularly helpful, even if they are responsible for very different kinds of product than the new one. They must rely mainly on guesswork to make those determinations and inevitably will make many errors as a result. Of course, even more errors would be made if persons who had no expertise in pricing were to forecast prices or if every project that was started were carried through to conclusion without periodic reevaluation.

SETTING THE INITIAL PRICE FOR A NEW PRODUCT

In setting the initial price for a new product the pricing executive will want to consider (1) the relevant customer segments, (2) the often diverse demands of ultimate customers, (3) the impact of price upon the actions of present and future rivals, (4) cost conditions, and (5) appropriate distribution channel strategies. Furthermore, the price-setter must take account of the impact of price on his unit costs and on the sales of the other products in the firm's line. Given the many variables that he must consider and the uncertain impact of price on each of the elements individually and in combination, he badly needs a systematic means for setting the initial price. His need for an orderly procedure is far greater with new than with established products.

A systematic approach to new product pricing

Those responsible for introducing a new product usually make many interrelated decisions extending over a substantial period. They start with the decision to explore the profitability of a new offering; they may then select product features for the new offering, choose suitable packaging, design distribution channels, select basic marketing strategies, and establish margins for distributors and retailers. Subsequently, in most cases, they make decisions about price, advertising themes, promotions, customer service, packaging, guarantees, and the like.

As already explained, most managements periodically review their decisions to continue developmental work on new products. The reviews involve estimates of costs, prices, and sales, though they need not be careful, let alone written. Thus management usually explores cost and demand conditions for a new item some time prior to the actual product launch. It also will consider alternative distribution arrangements, sales appeals, and product features. As the actual launch approaches, many alternatives will have been discarded as unsuitable and others will have emerged as promising. And all the while the executives responsible for the new item will be accumulating opinions and scraps of information, receiving suggestions, formulating hypotheses about what will work, and thinking about how to make the item more salable. Those ingredients form the chief basis on which management's early decisions regarding the new product will be based. Some managements also conduct market research at an early stage in new product development, but ordinarily the research pertains to product performance and involves use testing. At that stage, little reliable information about the effect of different prices on sales, brand image, salesmen's calls, resellers' sales efforts, and so on could be obtained no matter what method of research was employed.

The selection of the product version to be offered. Almost every new product can be offered in a variety of forms each of which represents a different mix of benefits and presumably has a different best price. How might executives select among the alternative versions? In comparing several new product options, a product planner usually faces the following situation: one option is more costly than the others but is also more highly prized by customers than the others. If he were to charge the same price for all, he would sell much more of the preferred version, but his costs would be higher also. To estimate the relative profitability of each version, he must consider a series of alternative prices for *each* version. Version 1 might be more profitable than, say, version 2 if a high price were charged for both but less profitable if a lower price were charged for version 1. To select among alternative product versions thus involves two steps. First, the most profitable price for each version—that is, its own most profitable price—must be determined. Second, the most profitable outcomes of the different versions must be compared and the one that yields the highest return must be selected. The process is very difficult because management has so little information about the product on which to base its forecasts. Also, the version of a product most profitable in the early stages might not be the one that would be most profitable a few years, or even months, later.

Despite these difficulties, executives responsible for the selection of a product version will do well to employ a systematic approach similar to that suggested here. Specifically, the product planner should prepare, for each product version, a cost and sales schedule that indicates the firm's estimated total sales and margins costs at different levels of price. From such a schedule, he would select the most profitable price for the period to which the schedule applies. He would compare the product options and select the most lucrative one.

Table 8-1 presents hypothetical data for three versions of a new product that a marketing executive considers the best alternatives available to his firm. For each product option, three retail prices have been considered (presumably those that look most attractive), as well as three reseller margins for distributors and retailers combined. Although these data are not offered as realistic, they do express the following usual relationships:

1. The higher the price for a given product option the lower the sales.
2. The greater the margin to resellers the greater the sales at a given price.
3. The greater the sales the lower the unit production costs.

Observe that no allowance for marketing costs has been included. The implicit assumption is that marketing costs would not vary with either the price charged, the margins allowed, or the product option offered. That assumption may not be realistic, but it involves no error in principle and simplifies the calculations, which are already cumbersome.

Given these many assumptions, Table 8-1 shows that the second product option is superior to the first because it would make a greater contribution to the firm's total net revenue if it were sold at $375 at retail and if distributors and retailers combined were allowed a margin of $125, which would represent a pull-through or customer-oriented strategy. At that price and with those margins, the firm would sell 23,000 units and obtain a total net contribution to profits and overhead of $690,000.

Interestingly, at this stage management is making vital price analyses but not any price decisions. By the time it actually introduces the new product, its estimates are likely to have changed substantially. It

Table 8-1. Data for three versions of a new product.

Product Version (1)	Retail Price (2)	Est. Sales to Ult. Customers (3)	Distrib. and Retailers Margin (4)	Response of Rivals (5)	Est. Unit Costs at Corres. Volume (6)	Est. Unit Revenues, Gross (2 – 4) (7)	Unit Profit Contrib. (7–6) (8)	Total Profit Contrib. (8×3) (9)
Option 1	$300	20,000	$100	Firm A would	$175	$200	$25	$500,000
		22,000	120	reduce its	160	180	20	440,000
		25,000	140	retail price	150	160	10	250,000
	320	18,000	107	No change	185	213	28	504,000
		19,000	125	in rivals'	180	195	15	285,000
		20,000	145	prices	175	175	0	0
	335	15,000	112	No change	200	223	23	345,000
		16,500	130	in rivals'	190	205	15	247,500
		18,000	150	prices	185	185	0	0
Option 2	375	23,000	125	No change	220	250	30	690,000
	390	25,000	150	No change	210	225	15	375,000
	410	28,000	175	No change	200	200	0	
Option 3	450							
	470							
	485							

will usually charge a quite different price than the one thought to be most profitable at this stage of product introduction.

How to initiate the process of price determination. As was stressed repeatedly in earlier chapters, the price-setter seeks a price that meets his goals vis-à-vis the ultimate customer, his resellers, and his rivals—and probably others as well. The best price for one of the three might be unsuitable for the other two. We must assume that a price-setter cannot find a price for a new product that is suitable to all interested parties simultaneously. Instead, he must usually assess the suitability of a price to each party to the pricing process one at a time. For example, as developed in preceding chapters, he may seek the best price to charge on the assumption that he need only be concerned with ultimate customers. He can then repeat the process but now consider only resellers and again take account only of rivals.

At what point should a price-setter begin this step-by-step process? Usually, the best point depends upon the firm's basic marketing strategy. If the firm assumes the burden of winning the patronage of the ultimate customer—that is, if it adopts a customer-oriented or a pull strategy—the price-setter will usually be wise to seek the best price for ultimate customers first. If the firm relies heavily on resellers to gain customers for the new product—that is, if it adopts a push or reseller-oriented strategy—the price-setter will be wise to start by establishing the best price for resellers. To select between those strategies, management will presumably ask the following kinds of questions about its new offerings:

- ☐ Will other firms be able to offer competitive products in the near future?
- ☐ Will this product be known to and sought out by a large segment of the public without active support from retailers?
- ☐ Will production cost conditions allow the product to develop a mass demand if the margins paid to resellers can be held down?
- ☐ Can strong nonprice appeals be developed for this product after rivals appear?

Once he had determined price for the selected party, the price-setter would then adjust it to meet the constraints imposed by the other factors.

Now let us apply this line of reasoning to the TV set example. The price of TV sets could be set quite low in an effort to create strong consumer demand and thus reduce manufacturer reliance on resellers to make strong sales efforts on behalf of the sets. The consumer demand thus created might pull the product through the channels of distribution and induce large numbers of resellers to carry and expose it. On the other hand, by setting a price that provided large margins for resellers, the TV set producers might create powerful incentives for resellers to find customers for the product. In the latter case, the resellers might generate a very high level of demand and would push the product through the distribution channels.

To be even more specific about the early days of the television industry, we can well imagine that manufacturers feared that receivers would be so expensive that only the rich would be able to afford them. Limited ownership of TV sets would also mean that television would not become an influential advertising medium and the profitability of telecasting would be small. Also, the quality of programming would be so poor that the demand for sets would be adversely affected. On the basis of such reasoning, it is understandable that TV set manufacturers would try to keep the price of TV sets to the ultimate customer as low as practicable—partly by limiting reseller margins—while making strenuous efforts to develop strong consumer demand. They were so successful with that policy that diverse and strange resellers—garages and beauty parlors among them—sold TV sets even though the margins offered to resellers were relatively modest.

We have thus explained why a firm introducing TV sets into the market might elect a customer-oriented strategy. Now we must explain how a price-setter could find a price that would enable that strategy to work effectively.

New product pricing and the ultimate customer

What are the characteristics of a best price for a new product that implements a pull-through, customer-oriented strategy? In general we know that the aim is to keep prices relatively low so that sales will be high despite a lack of strong support from resellers. (The price must, however, be high enough to induce many resellers to carry the item.) To find that best price, the price-setter must forecast customer response to price. He must, for example, take account of the possible psychological barriers to price that might affect purchases. For example, most families of modest income might have been induced to pay up to $300 for a TV set that was then unproved, was known to involve frequent costly repairs, and delivered a mediocre reproduction of rather poor programs but would have backed away from purchase in large numbers if prices had been above that amount.

Apart from possible psychological quirks and barriers, the price-setter would mainly want to estimate sales at different prices, a task that is difficult for products in their prime and vastly more difficult for new products. It was explained earlier that in dealing with prime products he can draw upon a plethora of data related to a mature product and often has had extensive personal experience as well. Furthermore, he has a market-tested prevailing price to use as a starting point for his price analysis. Specifically, he can and should explore the effects of increases and decreases in the prevailing price, the approach employed in earlier chapters.

A price-setter for a new product also requires a realistic price to use as a starting point for a similar type of analysis. If his firm has adopted a customer-oriented pull strategy, he will mainly be guided in his selection of a starting price by his view of customer purchases at different prices, combined with knowledge of production costs at different levels of output. More precisely, he will try to inform himself about the responsiveness of customers to changes in price and the effect on unit costs of changes in output.

Accurate information about customer response to different prices is virtually unobtainable for new products, as has been stressed. One way to obtain useful information is to ask potential customers what products they regard as equivalent in value to the new product. Such a search for a comparative value could be conducted very informally and unscientifically or fairly formally and scientifically. If in the former manner, employees of the firm and friends of the price-setter could be shown a prototype of several versions of the new product under consideration and be asked to identify existing products that they consider comparable in value. As a check, they could be asked to place a value on the prototype in dollars and answer questions about specific products. They could also be asked to indicate the features they value particularly as well as their misgivings about the product. If it were desirable to gather more reliable information, a random sample in one or more of the planned test markets could be taken. In either case, the price-setter would seek to derive a starting point from the data collected as well as try to establish the range of prices that ultimate customers would pay.

The kind of data described would help the price-setter to assess the sensitivity of particular subgroups of potential customers to changes in the price of each prototype. By using his starting price, he would estimate the number of persons who would consider purchasing the product at different prices. He might adjust the hypothetical price up and down by 5 percent increments and estimate how the respondents' attitudes toward purchasing the product would change.

Another way to help price-setters during the introductory stage of a new product's life has been found useful by Gabor and Granger, two British economists who specialize in price research for near-new products. A near-new product is one that is new to the firm offering it for sale and also relatively new on the market. Gabor and Granger question respondents about the highest and the lowest price they would be willing to pay for the product. They have found, as did the French sociologist and market researcher Jean Stoetzel, that most people can readily state the upper limit to what any product is worth to them and can easily indicate a price below which they would not expect the product to perform satisfactorily. The British economists suggest that knowledge of the upper and lower acceptable prices provides useful data for persons who are responsible for price-setting, especially if that knowledge is combined with information about what the person paid for his last purchase in that product class.

The highest and lowest prices that potential customers would pay could establish a range of acceptable prices for a relatively new product. However, a price-setter will often be more interested in reseller views of the highest and lowest acceptable prices than he will in those of potential customers. Moreover, that range appears to be very wide, so that it leaves the price-setter with the difficult task of finding the specific price to charge.*

Let us now consider what a price-setter would do if his firm employed a cost-oriented strategy. Rather than consider the responses of ultimate customers to different prices to arrive at his starting price, he would estimate the production and marketing costs of the versions of the product under consideration and take account of the effect of different levels and scales of production as best he could. He would then test those prices—again crudely and cheaply—in the manner just described. Next he would adjust the best prices, if necessary, to reflect any constraints introduced by resellers, rivals, and costs. Those adjustments will be discussed below. Once he had made adjustments for the other factors,

* It would be particularly interesting to know how great are the differences in individual customer valuations—both on the high and the low side—and how much and how rapidly individuals' price valuations change after a product has been introduced and sold in at least modest quantity. For a description of this method of price research, see Andre Gabor and C. W. J. Granger, "The Pricing of New Products," *Scientific Business*, August 1965, pp. 3–12.

he would be ready to use an actual test market to evaluate the price. Depending on the resources available, he might be able to test several attractive versions of the product.

Test marketing as a source of demand information. The potential contribution of formal test market research in establishing the initial selling price of a new product deserves a few comments. Test market studies clearly can provide important objective data, but the results obtained are subject to very important limitations.*

The strengths and weaknesses of test market studies can be illuminated if we return to the TV set example and consider some of its critical limitations.

First, a firm usually cannot afford to test many attractive alternative product benefit mixes but must limit its tests to those considered best on an intuitive basis. Management may select poor product concepts, in which case the price-setter might develop a price for an inferior offering, one that may not be attractive to the public for nonprice reasons.

Second, and related to the first, resources may not be available to test more than one or two alternative prices for each product version. In Table 8-1 data were developed for three different product variations, each of which was assumed to be offered at three different possible prices. Each of these should be tested if possible.

Third, even if resources are available to test all variations, the real difficulties arise in finding enough market locations to test all nine alternatives under similar and comparable market conditions.

Fourth, since it will probably be necessary to market the product nationally at a uniform price, it would be desirable to test each variation of the product under different market conditions in order to account for geographical diversity. But even under the most ideal conditions, it is too much to expect that the test market research will provide such information.

Fifth, most market environments are dynamic, and unless the test market is timed to allow the shortest possible interval between testing and actual product introduction, the data may be somewhat obsolete.

Sixth, and possibly most important, because any marketing mix element can strongly affect the purchase response of ultimate customers, the role of price in public acceptance or rejection of a new product in a test market situation rarely is clear. Hence the objective test market data

---

* For a discussion of their limitations, see E. J. Davis, "The Validity of Test Marketing," *Commentary*, July 1965, pp. 166–175; F. Stanton, "What Is Wrong with Test Marketing?" *Journal of Marketing*, April 1967, pp. 43–44.

must be interpreted—that is, judgments have to be made—if the data are to help in the selection of the best variation of the new product, including its price.

Seventh, a market test indicates customer responses to the new product while the product is still quite novel and unfamiliar, that is, when the risk that it will not function as promised is greatest and its benefits are most difficult to assess. The testers are not able to simulate the condition in which many people know the product very well and can assess its value to them quite confidently.

Eighth, competitors may tamper with and disrupt a market during a test and thus invalidate the results.

Finally, market tests are usually focused primarily on consumer responses to the new product and can gather few data about reseller and rival manufacturer viewpoints and behavior.

Even though severe limitations affect the use of test market data, such information can have great value. The test market offers the only real market experience with the new product that management will have prior to actual introduction of the product. Much intuitive, quasi-scientific analysis will have taken place prior to that time, and each member of the management decision-making team will have made some important intuitive judgments. But test market data will provide the first real-life data base for all concerned. In subsequent decisions about the actual benefit mix to use with the new product, the test market data provide a common basis for management. They should help to create a consensus where otherwise there would be none, but the flaws in the data are likely to be major.

From the price-setter's point of view, test markets provide at least a crude measure of the appropriateness of the prices tested. If sales in the test markets are near the levels expected, the price-setter can have some—but still not a great deal of—confidence in his choice of price. If sales are either much lower or higher, he will have good reason to reevaluate his price decision even if nonprice factors may have caused the unexpected sales results. It cannot be emphasized too strongly that a firm cannot rely very heavily, let alone wholly, on test market studies to arrive at a best price. A great deal of logic and guessing underlies the decision of what options to test, and many subjective judgments must underlie the interpretations placed on the often bewildering results of market tests of prices for new products.

Market surveys as a source of information about new products. Skilled questioning of appropriate people often yields extremely valuable information. Much can usually be learned by exposing potential customers to samples of the new product, discussing the rationale of the product with them, and calling their attention to the various situations in which they might use the product.

The chief pitfalls in market surveys designed to determine the value that potential customers will place on a new product in a real-life situation are almost self-evident. Primarily, no one can replicate in an interview situation, no matter how skillfully planned and conducted, the customer attitudes toward, knowledge of, and desire for a new product that will actually develop. The sheer passage of time has effects that alter the influence of attitudes on behavior. Also, market surveys cannot simulate accurately the purchase situation, which is usually a retail setting in which the establishment and its personnel may strongly affect customer attitudes and behavior. Despite these and other important pitfalls, questionnaire surveys, whether in person, by telephone, or in writing, do help to fill what otherwise is a near-vacuum of information about the demand for a new and unfamiliar product.

Even when firms conduct no formal market surveys, their managements usually do collect demand information informally and unprofessionally. Members of families, employees, friends, and some near-strangers are questioned to get reactions to a new product. It would be hard to imagine executives who would rely wholly on their own assessment of potential customer valuations. Unfortunately, they often solicit information from highly unrepresentative persons and in ways that are calculated to confirm their personal views.

As suggested, market surveys are particularly valuable sources of demand information when used in conjunction with market tests. They help to explain why customers actually behave as they do, as well as indicate their perceptions, interpretations, and evaluations under real-life market circumstances.

Time phases of new products

The introductory period. New products that embody novel or highly unfamiliar concepts are usually slow to win a following, especially if they require purchasers to make a substantial outlay. Ultimate customers understandably would like a new product to develop a track record before they place a large bet on it. Manufacturers try to overcome the reluctance of people to buy new products by offering special inducements; they want to speed up the diffusion process. The usual inducements are a combination of low price—effective for only a limited, and often specified, period—and specially easy return privileges.

By those measures a producer shows his confidence that the first purchasers will be pleased and expects that they will help directly and indirectly to stimulate demand for the new product. In addition, the measures are reassuring to potential customers—they greatly reduce the risk of loss. The more rapid the acceptance of the new product, the sooner the manufacturer can gain production economies from producing a large volume. Thus what he may give away in the form of price inducements and easy-return arrangements, he may easily recover from production economies.

The pricing problems peculiar to the introductory period of a new product's life are these: Should a special price incentive be offered? How large a price incentive should be offered? To whom? For how long? Should resellers be asked to share the cost of the incentive? If so, how much of it? Under what circumstances? A fairly simple notion provides the conceptual basis for answering all of these questions. It is that such incentives represent investments designed to speed up and increase demand—or, which is much the same thing, can be considered substitutes for advertising outlays. Underlying that is a more complex and central notion: the initial price of a new product is only one event in what will hopefully be a long and fruitful life. That one event must be treated as one of a large number of related events and should be conducted and evaluated by its effect on the product's entire life. More to the point, it is almost always wrong to set price on a new item with a limited time horizon in view, as when the price of the item is set to put it in the black by the end of a year and a half.

Product youth and ultimate-customer response. The first price set for a new product is almost certain to be wrong. Hopefully, the size and direction of the error will become clear fairly soon after the product has been introduced, although the early market experience of a new product is frequently very bewildering. The price is likely to find favor with customers in certain areas and with particular characteristics and win no following elsewhere or find favor only with the groups that were expected to constitute its chief patrons anyway. Such developments should ordinarily lead a price-setter to revise his forecasts and alter the price.

Beyond errors that reveal themselves as the product gains market exposure, important price decisions may be required for the young product as different types and numbers of customers become its heaviest purchasers. Shifts from reliance on sales primarily to consumer pioneers, then to experimental consumers, and ultimately to conservative-follower consumers may call for price adjustments. Certainly a price-setter must be on-the-ready to adapt prices to major market changes.

Up to this point we have considered steps by which a price-setter might determine the best price for a new product from the standpoint of the ultimate customer. We are now ready to consider in some detail the concepts that might help a price-setter take account of resellers in setting price for a new product and then discuss the problem of potential competition.

RESELLERS AND NEW PRODUCT PRICING

We are concerned with the price of a product that embodies an out-of-the-ordinary concept and has undergone no severe reality test. Some people involved in the project will have great confidence in the profitability of the product for both producers and resellers, but most reasonable people must feel considerable doubt; after all, there is no solid experience on which anyone can base a confident judgment. Under those circumstances, a firm that devotes resources to the production or resale of the product risks financial loss in the form of either out-of-pocket expenses or forgone opportunities to take on other items. Also, the producer faces fairly distinct reseller problems in launching the new product as opposed to the problems with resellers during the product's early life. Accordingly, we will discuss the problems of the introduction phase and early life separately.

Pricing a new product: reseller considerations

The manufacturer of a new product requires far more sales support from middlemen during the introductory period than after the product has become widely known and accepted. He must usually pay for that sales support; his task is to obtain it in the amount and form that will best serve his firm's long-run interest and at minimum cost. Generally, that means that he must select his types of reseller and then select individual resellers of the types through which he plans to market his product. He will recognize that arrangements during the introductory phase will strongly influence relations thereafter.

When a manufacturer elects to distribute through a particular type of distributor, he does so because he wishes to have his product sold by the retailers on whom that distributor ordinarily calls. By asking—or allowing—particular types of reseller to handle his new product, the manufacturer agrees to accept the traditional margins. He may, however, create, by mutual agreement, special conditions during the period of the product's introduction. On the one hand, he may allow the reseller wider-than-usual margins to obtain heavy sales support when the new items need it most, or he may try to persuade his resellers to accept substantially less than their usual margins in an effort to attract many early users by a low price. In the second case it is assumed by both manufacturer and reseller that once the item has received a trial by many customers and a demand has been created for repurchase, resellers will obtain their regular margins. They are being asked to invest in the creation of an attractive new market for themselves—and for the manufacturer. Their willingness to do so often depends on whether they have been promised some degree of exclusiveness. And the manufacturer's willingness to offer reseller exclusiveness will vary with the assessment of the importance of widespread availability of the item relative to the value of reseller sales support.

Sometimes the special needs of new product introduction are met by an introductory price for a limited time. That price usually includes less than the regular margins for manufacturer, distributor, and retailer. It is offered on selected models—the ones the manufacturer believes will attract the early buyers of new products. Other models carry the usual reseller margins. At some point the introductory price must be withdrawn and the price increased, at the cost of a predictable fall of sales for some time and even some customer resentment.

Introductory prices often are financed entirely by the manufacturer. The resellers are allowed their usual margins; in exceptional cases they obtain even higher margins to elicit special sales efforts on their part. A common example of introductory price financed by the manufacturer is the coupon that returns to the customer a sizable amount of the purchase price of a newly introduced product. Manufacturers of new industrial products sometimes go direct to potential customers with an offer to have them use a product at a very low price in exchange for testing it under actual production conditions.

What is common and crucial to the introduction stage is that the new product must be exposed to potential customers, be tested under real-life use conditions, and win a following. That process is generally described as winning product acceptance, and it consists primarily of the dissemination of information, the changing of attitudes, and the making available of a new product to potential customers. For obvious reasons, manufacturers hope to win acceptance for their new products long before other firms can reap the profits from a market they developed.

Pricing a new product for its youth

Once a product becomes very familiar to all resellers and most consumers, it is no longer new. A substantial body of experience will have accumulated and will have greatly reduced the uncertainty of firms that became involved in its distribution. Many potential customers will know pretty well what they will get if they purchase it. In most cases, however, a large number of potential customers will remain poorly informed and unconvinced. They have never bought or tried the product. Some persons who tried it did not use it properly or may have received a unit that was defective. In short, the early youth of a new product is usually a time when the manufacturer continues to require active sales support from his resellers. At such times resellers will begin to receive financial rewards and gain a solid basis for assessing the future rewards they can anticipate from the product.

During the introductory stage, resellers of a promising product may be motivated by the desire to convince the manufacturer that they will produce a large sales volume for him. They may therefore give greater sales effort to the product than the current rewards justify in the belief that they are building a market for themselves that will endure for a long time.

Of course, if the new product is really very similar to products that have been on the market, the periods of introduction and early youth may be so brief as to appear not to exist. Still, some time, information, attitude change, and persuasion are needed before the new product's precise relationship to the old ones becomes known to all who are concerned.

COMPETITIVE CONSIDERATIONS IN NEW PRODUCT PRICING

The pricing of a new product might be viewed as a battle for spoils with enemies that are not yet on the scene, but that would place overriding emphasis on using price as a weapon to discourage other firms from offering the product for sale when the competition would be very damaging. Sometimes, of course, the firm is protected against competitors by patents, high costs of entry, large economies of scale, a secret production process, or the like. Usually, however, rivals are a major threat to the sustained profitability of a new product; indeed, they sometimes appear in large numbers even before the firm has begun to make a profit on the new product and make subsequent profits modest or less.

Professor Joel Dean has identified penetration pricing and skimming as the most logical policies (we might describe them as strategies) for producers of new products. The first, sometimes termed stay-out pricing, is defined as charging low prices as the principal instrument for penetrating mass markets early while simultaneously discouraging others from entering the market. The low-price pattern applies to long- rather than short-run profits; for time is usually needed to realize the volume potentialities of new markets. Two main conditions are propitious for a penetration price policy: (1) a high responsiveness of customers to price reductions, that is, high price-elasticity of demand, and (2) production costs that decline substantially with increases in volume of output.

A pricing strategy akin to penetration pricing has been highly publicized recently among business executives. It is ordinarily described, unrevealingly, as the experience curve, and it is associated with the Boston Consulting Group and its head, Bruce Henderson. The strategy combines a series of notions to support the conclusion that firms should seek steady increases in market share and attain market dominance. In doing so they will increase both their scale and level of operation and, it is argued, consequently realize lower production costs than rivals and earn attractive profits at low and steadily declining prices.

Some firms employ and appear to be well-served by the experience curve strategy, although it is not necessarily better than all alternatives. It is perhaps edifying to consider an almost diametrically opposite strategy, that of demand creation. In that strategy demand is regarded as largely a result of seller promotional effort, including product design, customer service, image building, and sales support. A high marketing cost strategy may enable a firm to gain the enduring support of the best distributors and retailers and also a strong and lasting preference for its brand that gives it a market dominance far more difficult for rivals to overcome than a dominance based on low cost and price. Even with low production cost, a firm can charge low prices only if it also accepts a low margin of profit, which is not an appealing prospect for most companies.

A skimming price strategy is defined as a policy of high initial prices that skim the cream of demand; price is lowered only as short-run competition forces it down. The strategy is most appropriate when (1) price elasticity of demand is low, (2) entrants are not an immediate threat, or (3) the entry of new firms cannot be prevented.

Underlying the choice between the penetration and skimming price strategies is the very reasonable assumption that the number of new firms is very sensitive to the profits, and therefore to the prices, in a trade. Not only does that assumption appear reasonable, but considerable evidence confirms it in *extreme* cases. Highly lucrative markets attract new producers—witness the whole field of pharmaceuticals and clothing fads. Unprofitable and unpromising products are not likely to attract new producers, but, as explained earlier, an outside producer cannot usually judge confidently the profitability or prospective profits of a product. Although profits and entry of firms into a market might be expected to be related, would there be any difference in the number and timing of entries into a business if the established firms were averaging a 16 percent return on investment rather than a 12 percent one or a 34 percent return rather than a 22 percent one?

Firms contemplating entry into a market probably are far more concerned with future costs and prices—that is, future profits—than with current conditions. They recognize that many firms devote the first years of a product's life to building a market; they would not consider the current profitability of a new product to be an indication of the profits that would become available in the future, especially if the product were really new. In other words, the number, size, and market power of entrants into a new market are affected by many factors that may be more determining than price and current profits. Among them are the reputed efficiency of the first producer and his reputation for aggressiveness against new rivals, the costs and risks of entry, and the naturalness of the item for strong firms that would almost certainly enter the market.

The pricing of TV sets when they were a new product

How might a price-setter for a new manufacturer of TV sets in, say, early 1946 have approached his task? We will assume that the firm, which had been a major producer of home and automobile radios, decided to offer five models in two different screen sizes: two table models and three consoles. If the price-setter were first to search out the floor and ceiling for price, he would compute a figure, based on decision costs, below which he would not set price. He might conclude that a quickening in customer acceptance of TV sets would justify the sacrifice of some current revenue. (As explained below, the value of speeding the adoption of TV sets by a given time might be roughly calculable.)

The difficulties of estimating the cost of TV sets under the hypothetical circumstances are enormous. First, it is not even clear what cost figure is relevant. Is it the cost actually incurred, including the set-up and shake-down costs? Is it the cost that will be incurred this year? This month? Or is it the cost that will be incurred after the firm has reached its "regular" mode of operation? In other words, should top management treat the extraordinary costs of getting into production on a new item with a somewhat unfamiliar technology and heavy but unpredictable marketing costs as the costs of launching a business that are to be amortized over the long-run future of the firm rather than defrayed during the current period?

It could be argued that present and near-term costs are largely irrelevant except to the extent that they indicate the costs that will be incurred in the future. That position holds that top management should regard itself as creating a business as well as offering a product for sale. Its perspective should be the life of the enterprise rather than the current fiscal period, unless poor (accounting) performance during the near term would jeopardize owner/director support for the enterprise. The price at which a new item is introduced will surely affect speed of acceptance, especially when the initial outlay is large and repair and malfunction costs might be major. To compute costs in a way that would charge present consumers with the extraordinary costs of launching an enterprise might insure failure. When those costs are very high, marketing executives are able to see that they must be recovered by returns over the life of the enterprise; otherwise, sales would be almost nil. When launching costs might be recovered quickly, marketing executives sometimes mistakenly adopt the attitude that they should be recovered almost immediately.

As suggested earlier, an executive might estimate the financial benefits his firm would obtain through speeding the adoption of a new product by formulating the problem in the following terms: what different sales results might the firm purchase for the new item and how much would each one cost? He might, for example, draw schedules of sales and costs that would be realized if the firm were to *start with* different prices. With the highest of, say, three prices (one that would cover all launch costs in a year), the firm would attain some given level of sales, unit production costs, unit marketing costs, and so on. In the following period, it would enjoy lower production and marketing costs and presumably would charge a different price. Management would again estimate its sales and costs at that different price and pick a price for the third year. That line of thinking would produce a schedule of estimated outcomes and the cost of obtaining them. A major ingredient of the initial price decision would be opportunity costs—the difference between the net profit earned and what would have been earned if another price had been charged.

The executive could repeat the process for, say, three different prices that reflected different views of the cost floor. He would have con-

structed three different demand and cost streams that could be contrasted and evaluated in the light of the firm's objectives. Usually, if it
started by charging a high price, the firm would end up with a low net
gain at the very start and throughout the period—at least relative to alternative and lower starting prices.

It certainly is not suggested that a firm's costs are irrelevant to its
pricing decision. Conversely, it also is not proposed that a price-setter
should build his price primarily on costs. Rather, it is argued that the
price-setter must employ a view of costs that will not place an inordi-
nate burden on the new item and cause it to be stillborn. Management
must separate the costs of the decision to enter the TV set business from
the costs of making TV sets after it is already in the business, and on a
scale roughly in line with what is expected in the near future.

Let us make these vital notions more concrete. The three-price analysis described above, plus other estimates, would lead management to an
estimate of the size that its enterprise would attain in a few years. For
example, top management might estimate sales at an annual rate of
150,000 within 9 months, 250,000 within 15 months, 400,000 within 36
months, and then an increase of 10 percent or more annually for at least
several more years.

We will assume that the firm has established production capacity of
approximately 400,000 units. Management will have estimated its costs
over the next three years while taking account of technological change,
which usually is rapid under such circumstances, and changes in level of
output. Let us further assume that management believes that it can get
the production costs of its main model—a medium-size-screen table
model—down in cost from approximately $525 in the first year to
roughly $260 in the third. It anticipates further cost reductions in sub-
sequent years of the order of 10 or 12 percent. What is being proposed
here is that management regard the cost of a TV set to be in the vicinity
of $250 *even during the first year*, although it is considerably higher than
that. In other words, management should reason that although it costs
about $250 to make a TV set, getting established in the television in-
dustry costs a lot of money. At the sales level it can output during the
first year, if it knows what it is about and is established to produce on an
efficient scale, to spend about $200 above costs to get a customer. But it
will get those heavy launch costs back after the product has proved itself
and won general acceptance.

If management cannot foresee that it will recover those initial costs
of entering the television business, it should not begin to make TV sets
in the first place. But after it has entered the business, those entry costs

should be considered sunk—irrelevant to the cost of making TV sets. The firm presumably would recover its high launch costs because the strong demand for TV sets would permit it to charge substantially more than costs.

So much, then, for locating the floor under the price of TV sets. How could the price-setter find the ceiling? Earlier the ceiling for a price was identified with the prices charged by very close rivals. Producers of a completely new product have no rivals; the ceilings for their prices reflect the evaluations of customers. It would have been obvious in 1946 that none but a tiny group of fanatics would pay above, say, $1,000 for a TV set and that only a very small group would pay $500. And given such a small number of TV set owners, the cost of advertising on TV would be so high that the number and quality of programs would be low, which would further reduce customer willingness to pay a high price for TV sets.

Estimating the ceiling for a new product is probably more difficult than estimating the floor, but for similar reasons. A price-setter must expect customer valuations of his product to change markedly over product life, and particularly during the early years, as people learn about the properties of the product through observation, trial, and hearsay. The main task of the marketing efforts associated with launching a new product is to raise that ceiling and do it quickly. Management must not be strongly influenced by the valuations that prospective customers place on the product before the product is in use for some time. It is very difficult to learn reliable customer valuations of an unfamiliar product.

Despite the difficulties of estimating the ceiling for his price, the price-setter and other marketing executives must make such an estimate if they are to do their jobs well. They will be able to make it better if they are clear about their goal, which is to estimate the highest amount that *particular kinds of people* would be willing to pay for the product *after* they had been exposed to the firm's efforts to create a desire for the product, retail salesman efforts to persuade them to buy it, the reports of people who own it, and the social pressure to possess it and after producers of competitive products or services have made adjustments that might affect the value of the item. In the case of TV sets, the actions of the telecasting industry had a strong effect on customer valuation of TV sets, and the response of advertisers was crucial to the telecasting industry. In turn, the responsiveness of people to TV commercials would determine how much advertising would be diverted from radio and print media to TV and, later, whether total advertising expenditures would rise because TV would prove to be an unusually effective medium. In other words, to forecast in 1946 the ceiling price for TV sets, a price-setter would have had to forecast the quality of TV programs in the years ahead. And even more important, he would want to forecast the expectations of various groups that represent the strongest prospective markets with respect to future programming, while again taking account of seller efforts to create favorable expectations.

The foregoing is a sketch of the more important elements related to the ultimate customer that should have been considered by a price-setter for TV sets before his firm decided to enter the business and after it did so. He would have been estimating a series of ceilings; for the ceiling would change fairly rapidly. He would have needed to know the current ceiling to establish price for the immediate future and would also have wanted to influence the subsequent ceilings in his firm's favor.

The ceiling price for most products, as has been indicated, is determined by the prices charged by rival firms. If our TV set producer had started to operate after one or two large producers were already in production and offering sets for sale, it would have been severely constrained by their actions. Of course, it would not have been compelled to match their prices, but it would have recognized that most customers would consider other brands very real alternatives and, furthermore, would probably have examined them very closely. Hopefully, the price decisions by the other manufacturers would have been based on an intelligent appraisal of existing limits to what customers would pay. If they had had actual market exposure with their sets, their appraisal would have received a partial reality test.

The price-setter would have been given to understand that the firm planned to distribute its TV sets through its present resellers of household and auto radios. He would know the traditional markups, and he probably would want to explore the possibility of persuading the retailers to accept lower ones. Inasmuch as the demand for and sale of TV sets was high and it turned out that many buyers were among low-income groups, resellers would have been eager to obtain the right to sell the manufacturer's TV sets. Very early, it was quite apparent that television and TV set manufacturing would become major industries, and distributors of major appliances would have been deeply resentful if a manufacturer whose radios they distributed had not permitted them to handle his line of TV sets.

Given the apparent strong demand for TV sets, a manufacturer would not have felt obliged to offer resellers larger than usual margins in order to persuade them to give strong sales support to his line of sets. In the first place, the resellers would have been expected to recognize that

TV sets were a major source of future income and they would
be well-advised to cultivate that market. In the second place, th\
fear that the manufacturer would be able to find other resell\
would be eager to represent them now that TV sets were to be a\ _.. to
his line. On the other hand, manufacturers had to recognize that increased sales of TV sets would come partly at the expense of radio sales,
so that resellers did need some help to cover their expenses and TV set
sales could serve that function.

Accordingly, the price-setter would presumably adopt a strategy
that relied little on the sales efforts of his resellers. And consequently he
could bring downward pressure on reseller margins despite the fact that
the TV set was a new, unfamiliar, complex, and costly product—characteristics that ordinarily would lead manufacturers to offer their resellers
high margins.

The key questions that the price-setter had to face were these: How
much can and should I vary from the prices charged by other TV set
producers? How soon will other producers enter the market and what, if
anything, could I do to forestall them? Is there a particular part of the
TV set market that my firm should try to cultivate? Should we apply the
same marketing/pricing approach to TV sets that we employ in radios to
maintain a consistent brand image?

In answering these last questions, the price-setter would be directed
by the objectives, strategies, and philosophy of top management and the
company's owners. He would be expected to price TV sets to meet the
goals and values of his management and in ways that contributed to a
coordination of success of TV sets and the firm's other product lines.

SUMMARY

New product pricing is largely from-scratch pricing. Accordingly, it is
strongly affected by the whole superstructure of directives and constraints that governs a firm's actions. Also, the pricing of a new product
necessarily revolves around two key strategic choices: (1) between a pull-
through and push-through strategy and (2) between a penetration (stay-
out) and a skimming policy.

The essential characteristics that distinguish new product pricing
from other kinds derive from the greater uncertainty that sellers have
with respect to conditions of cost and demand. They have little experience to draw on, and what they can learn from market tests and interview studies, although vastly better than pure guesswork, is subject to

great error. They must expect their initial price decisions to be erroneous, often badly so; they accordingly must monitor what is happening and be quick to make changes when their assumptions and expectations prove to be mistaken.

Even if a price-setter can find a reasonable cost floor and price ceiling for a new product, he is likely to find a big gap between the two; usually any estimated cost floor and ceiling price must be shaky and unreliable. He will, moreover, distinguish between price and reseller margins before and after the introductory period. Basically, a price-setter for a new product, as against one pricing products in their prime, will be required to forecast the tangible and intangible responses of different parties to the business process to the most attractive feasible price-marketing programs that he can devise. Perhaps more than in the case of products in their prime, it is essential to fashion a mix of marketing instruments that creates a favorable, consistent, and believable image. No new product can succeed by price alone.

9

Pricing
Declining Products

MOST FIRMS THAT SELL MANY PRODUCTS offer some whose sales are already declining. Products in decline are the opposite side of the shield to new ones. The introduction of new products now takes place on such a broad scale that many items face a drop in sales and may be largely superseded before long. A price-setter will usually be wise to accord products in decline very special treatment. He will want to identify them early and consider the advisability of dropping them. While they are continued in the line, the fact that their sales are declining must be taken into account when price is set.

It is not easy to identify products whose sales are about to decline. Hope springs eternal in the hearts of businessmen also, and most drops in sales can be viewed as temporary even when the products affected show many signs of being superseded. Products that are in decline for the purposes of pricing are those whose sales future is perceived to be bleak; thus the number and identity of such products depends on the astuteness of those who produce them. Economic history tells of many industries that refused to recognize the emergence of competitors that would supersede them, as in the case of railroads by buses, trucks, and planes, department stores by discount houses, and motion pictures by television.

LIFE STAGES OF A DECLINING PRODUCT

A declining product usually passes through fairly distinct stages that a price-setter should take into account in making his marketing decisions. The stages are the reciprocal of those through which most new products pass. For example, consider the new product still in its developmental stage, when it seems to be a marketable item but there is some doubt about the level of performance it can reach. During that stage, the product it might supersede also enters a new stage: its future has become questionable in the view of ultimate customers and resellers. If the product is costly, ultimate consumers may withhold purchase to await further development of the new product. Some resellers who had considered adding the old product to their lines may now delay decision.

The second stage through which a new product passes is the introduction, during which the product is offered for the first time and begins to make sales but slowly. During this stage, consumers and resellers in increasing numbers become informed about the existence of the product. Producers of both the old and new products form fairly strong convictions about the futures of both. During the third stage, the new product usually takes off; its sales spurt and, concurrently, the sales of the old product ordinarily slump. Sales of the old item experience their sharpest decline in this period.

During the fourth stage the item has reached its prime. Its sales are now high and may continue to grow in absolute terms, but the rate of growth has declined substantially. During this period, the old product will have approached a new lower sales level from which it might subsequently achieve steady modest increases. During this period, both old and new items are sold in fairly stable proportions.

During the final stage, the new product itself faces an immediate decline of sales because another new product that has come on the scene will replace it wholly or in part. The product it superseded upon its advent now also faces the prospect of another sudden decline, although not necessarily total extinction. We might identify a sixth stage during which some products are no longer manufactured commercially but some individuals continue to want them enough to arrange to have them produced on special order.

CLASSIFICATION OF PRODUCTS IN DECLINE

A price-setter would be wise to classify declining products into similar groups; for they vary in important respects that are relevant to price decisions. Before we discuss problems of classification, we should define declining products more precisely. Many products experience a sharp decline in sales for a while and then stabilize at levels from which no further decline occurs. Indeed, their sales may increase subsequently. For example, the total demand for freight service from railroads has risen, yet railroads experienced a steady decline in demand for a long period. The same pattern has been exhibited by many products that have lost popular favor but have not been wholly superseded—motion pictures, radios, razor blades. Accordingly, we will not limit declining products solely to those that are pointed to total oblivion. As defined here, declining products include those whose sales by all sellers are perceived to be falling and are expected to fall further. If their sales are believed to have stabilized, they no longer are products in decline even if their sales had declined for a substantial period.

A classification system for products in decline might be developed around the following dimensions: (1) the speed of the expected sales decline, (2) the level at which sales are likely to stabilize, (3) the speed of decline in individual brand sales, (4) the number of firms dropping the product or leaving the business, (5) the strength of the commitment to the product of consumers who continue to use it, (6) the age of the continued users, that is, whether they are going to remain in the market a long time, (7) the number of distributors and retailers that continue to carry the product in stock, (8) factors that affect distribution and production costs of the product, including durability, physical bulk, and economies of large-scale production.

A classification system incorporating only a fraction of those dimensions would produce far too many classes for discussion here. Rather than attempt to discuss each such class from the standpoint of its pricing problems and possible solutions, we will discuss the relevance of the dimensions simply to price decisions. (Their significance in combination with the other dimensions might be different, but it will not be considered here.) After that we will explore the classes of declining products that are most numerous and that embody the major problems faced in pricing most classes of declining products.

The speed of the expected sales decline

Products that gradually fade away over decades pose different pricing problems than do those that experience a sharp decline. The significant differences are to be seen in the responses of the key parties to the pricing process. First, how will ultimate customers for the product respond to a decline in sales and what will be their reactions to a very gradual decline rather than a precipitous one? Second, what will be the responses of manufacturers of products that are in decline, recognizing that they too probably will differ according to whether the fall in sales is sharp or gradual? Third, what will be the reactions of those who resell declining products and how will they differ according to whether the decline is rapid or slow? Let us examine these questions individually.

The response of ultimate customers to a decline in demand. A decline in the demand for a product signifies a shift in ultimate-customer preference. When customers stop buying a product, they are telling those who sell it that they value it less or that they value some alternative more. In short, a decline in sales is associated with a decline in the value that customers place on the product. Accordingly, ultimate customers could be expected to be willing to pay less for a product, and the sharper the drop in sales the less they should be willing to pay.

That analysis may hold as far as it goes, but it probably describes the wrong customers. Rather than be concerned with ultimate customers who have forsaken the product for something new or have changed their life styles in such a way as to leave no room for the product, a price-setter should be concerned with customers who do continue to buy it. Stated differently, if customers give up one product for another, it is doubtful that they can be won back. The valuations that matter most to the seller or producer of a product in decline are those of customers who continue to buy. If we speak only of that group, it often turns out that products are valued more when they are in decline than when they were more popular.

That generalization surely does not hold in *all* cases. An executive must be very alert, even when it does hold, to determine when many customers do place a higher value on the product. Persons who continue to use a declining product may, after a time, come to question its value, especially since other customers are shifting away from it. Apparently, when a declining product becomes difficult to obtain, many customers who prefer it to the new product place a higher value on it.

The valuation of manufacturers. When a manufacturer finds that one of his products is steadily declining in sales, several things ordinarily happen. First, those responsible for assessing the profitability of individual products in the company's line inform management that the product profitability is declining. Also, an effort will ordinarily have been made to reduce costs and stimulate demand for the product. But as the sales continue to drop, management ordinarily considers dropping the product or adjusting in other ways to the sales decline.

Often management must decide whether to replace or modernize equipment used to make a product in decline. The need for a sizable investment in a declining product will lead many managements to drop the product even before it has become unprofitable. That is to say, some products whose sales are declining are dropped, even though they may be moderately profitable, because their continued production calls for increased investment. Other still profitable declining products are dropped because new products could make better use of the productive capacity that they require.

Manufacturers clearly place a lower value on declining products than on expanding products and even less on products whose sales are declining rapidly. They tend to assign the least promising of their executives to the divisions that make such products. The products usually receive little attention from top management and even less of the available investment funds.

Evaluation of resellers. Ordinarily a declining product will occupy the same amount of limited space but give a reseller smaller sales volume than his usual wares, or at least smaller than it did before. Thus it becomes one of the least attractive and less profitable items he carries. Most resellers are constantly deluged by requests of manufacturers to take on new items. As a result, resellers will usually drop items whose sales are declining rapidly to make room for new items unless they have a special reason, such as long margins, that justifies continued stocking of the declining items.

Product stabilization

The level at which sales are likely to stabilize. As indicated, some products experience a sharp decline in sales but stabilize at a lower level; others decline to oblivion. (Note, however, that even today some companies manufacture buggy whips.) Clearly, the actions of a company depend heavily on whether a declining product is expected to disappear from the market entirely or to stabilize at a level of sales that permits profitable operations for one or more manufacturers. If a product is expected to vanish from the scene, its producers will often price it in a manner that permits them to exit from that business quickly, leaving them with no inventory. Ordinarily, the situation calls for a sharp cut in price. That need not be true of a product that is expected to enjoy substantial sales into the indefinite future, albeit at a lower level.

The speed of decline in individual brand sales. Not infrequently, the supply of declining products falls more rapidly than the demand for them. That occurs when the producers of other brands withdraw from the market, presumably because of a drop in sales and profitability. The companies that remain in the business might indeed even find their sales rising sharply even though the total market is declining. What matters most to a price-setter is not the change in total sales of the product but the expected change in the sales of his own brand, and the two need not move in the same direction.

If an individual brand suffers a sharp decline in sales, presumably the company making it will want to consider dropping it. The company will nevertheless want to set a price for the product in a way that will minimize the losses that will occur when the product is dropped. Many sellers—resellers as well as manufacturers—can be expected to cut prices when the drop in demand for a product becomes generally recognized. No single brand price could be maintained under those circumstances. However, the price decline would ordinarily end after some time and might be followed by a price increase.

The number of firms dropping the product or leaving the business. When firms drop a declining product, they raise the sales of companies that remain, or at least slow the decline of sales. Another factor that has a similar effect is the curtailment of output and productive capacity by the firms that remain in the business. Both factors that curtail supply have a strong supportive effect on price.

The strength of the commitment to the product of consumers who continue to use it. Ordinarily customers who continue to use a product that most other customers are forgoing have a strong preference for it—whether out of habit, taste, loyalty, or special need. It may be that the new product is not truly available to them; they may have a strong aesthetic, moral, or ecological prejudice against its use; or they may not be able to get as much advantage from the new product as the people who have made the shift.

Such people may come to fear that the popularity of the new product threatens the very existence of the old one. They sometimes become grateful to those who make the old product available rather than regard them as merely pursuing their self-interest. In time, consumers of declining products cease to take availability for granted. Among them will be some whose commitment to a declining product is very strong and who would be willing to pay far more for it than they had realized. Presumably they would pay a higher price than before without much complaint.

The age of the continued users. Consumers who continue to use a declining product often are rather advanced in years and are reluctant to make changes. Just as they are reluctant to shift to new products, so they may be very resistant to paying higher prices for familiar ones. Also, if they are elderly, they will not be in the market for long. When they have passed on, the market for that product will have disappeared altogether. Thus, the age of the consumer may have greater relevance to whether the manufacturer will continue to offer the product than to the price he charges. Nevertheless, some knowledge of the age and socioeconomic status of the consumers who remain committed to a declining product would help to forecast the effect of a price change on sales.

The number of distributors and retailers that continue to carry the product in stock. Numerous opportunities are offered to retailers and distributors to take on promising new items; they therefore feel a constant pressure to clean out slow movers. Manufacturers of a declining product find that many distributors and retailers will not carry it. As a result, declining products frequently become growth items for a few resellers even while they are being dropped by most others.

A manufacturer is strongly affected by whether his limited sales of a product are widely spread among many distributors and retailers or among a relative few who sell large quantities of it. In the second case the manufacturer could usually lower the reseller's price and profit margin.

The durability and bulk of the product and economies of large-scale production. The ability of resellers to keep a declining product in stock for a long time without deterioration and the use of valuable space are very relevant to pricing decisions. The two factors influence the cost of handling a product whose sales are low. All things considered, the more durable the product the lower the costs of storage and the lower the price that need be charged for it. Similarly, physical bulk affects storage costs and therefore is relevant to the price that would make the continued offering of a product profitable.

If a product must be produced in very large quantities to achieve low production costs, then a sharp decline in its sales may greatly raise its cost. If that happens, the price charged for the product must surely be adjusted; if a rise in price cannot be sustained, then some producers, and possibly all, will be forced to drop the product.

Any particular declining product is likely to represent a unique combination of the foregoing characteristics plus some that are related to special attributes of the product itself. A price-setter cannot hope to derive effective rules for pricing a declining product simply by classifying it properly. Still, the foregoing characteristics, along with others, do deserve his careful consideration.

A DECLINING PRODUCT FROM THE STANDPOINT
OF ONE FIRM

When it is viewed from the industry or economy standpoint, a declining product may be a growing product for some producers, as we have seen. The pricing problem depends upon the importance of the product to each firm. Let us first list important dimensions by which the position of the product within a firm's total offerings could be characterized:

Contribution to the firm's gross revenues.
Contribution to the firm's total employment.
Contribution to the firm's net profits.
Importance to the sale of other products in the firm's line. (Is the product complementary to another product in the line? Is it a repair part or a supply item?)
Specialized facilities that are used in product production.
(Have they virtually no value in another use or could they readily be shifted to some important application?)

Other questions that might be asked about declining products are these:

Does the firm offer the product that is superseding the declining product?
Does the firm prefer to eliminate the product from its line, or would it be equally desirous of continuing to offer the product if it were profitable?
Has the firm been strongly identified with the old product in the mind of many consumers?
Do individual resellers do a large business in the product, possibly because many resellers have dropped it?

By taking several of the foregoing possibilities into account, one can distinguish many types of declining products, each posing different pricing problems. Table 9-1 presents a classification structure that suggests the wide variety of circumstances that may surround declining products. At one extreme (X) the old product makes a small contribution to the profits of the firm that produces the new item. In this case, the old item makes no contribution to the sale of the firm's other items, and the firm can use the facilities that produce the old item for other purposes. A firm could easily walk away from such a declining item. At the other extreme (Y) are old products that still account for much of the firm's profits, contribute to the sale of other items, and use facilities that could not be sold or devoted to some other use. Furthermore, the firm is not producing the new item. In this second case, the producer of the declining item faces two unpleasant alternatives: liquidate or sell the business (or that part of the operation devoted to the declining product) or stick with the declining product while maximizing rewards from its sale and concurrently searching for other products with which to replace it.

Firms differ greatly in the proportion of their net income that they derive from declining products. A firm that is heavily dependent on a declining product for income will be mainly concerned with long-run returns from effective marketing. A firm that is not so heavily dependent on the declining product may have other uses for the facilities that would be released by dropping the product and would presumably be motivated by a desire to disengage from the old business at minimum cost and bother.

The matrix (Table 9-1) directs attention to situations between the two hypothetical extremes that possess interesting pricing implications. For example, a firm whose present profits are mainly obtained from the declining product might also be doing well with the new product, and so

Table 9-1. A classification of declining items.

Contribution of old item to firm's profits		Firm offers new item		Firm does not offer new item	
		Facilities mobile	Facilities immobile	Facilities mobile	Facilities immobile
Large	No contribution to sale of other items				
Large	Some contribution to sale of other items				Y
Medium	No contribution to sale of other items				
Medium	Some contribution to sale of other items				
Small	No contribution to sale of other items	X			
Small	Some contribution to sale of other items				

it might be able to put the facilities needed by the declining product to other good use. Such a firm will try to shift from the declining product to the growing product at the most profitable pace. It can usually influence the speed of the shift by the price that it charges. If it maintains its price for the declining product, it can speed its exit from the declining business. A low price for the declining product would tend to discourage some customers from trying the new one. Presumably the firm would pick the rate at which it felt the shift to the new product and its eventual exit from the declining one would best serve its goals of taking account of the effect of the shift on stockholder evaluations, the reactions of the senior executives affected, and employee morale, as well as maximizing long-run profits.

PRICING SELECTED TYPES OF DECLINING PRODUCTS

In setting the price of a declining product, no matter of what kind, a price-setter faces at least the following problems: (1) identifying the onset of a sales decline, (2) timing the price change, (3) selecting the amount of the price change, and making changes in sales and marketing arrangements.

Identifying the onset of a sales decline. A decline in sales may go unobserved for a long time. Long-term sales declines are visible only when the reason for a drop in sales can be perceived. One factor making for difficulty in identifying a long-term sales decline is that sales in certain markets may actually increase while total sales are already declining. Similarly, some brands may be rising in sales while total sales are falling, even without an exit of some producers from the business.

Timing the price change. Discovery that a product is likely to decline in sales over the long run should alert a price-setter that it may require special price treatment. A decline in sales is, however, not a sure signal that a price should be changed. What, then, is the signal? Most of the factors that were mentioned earlier are relevant here: changes in customers' valuation, the fact that other firms are leaving the business or liquidating their inventories, and, of course, major changes in a firm's costs.

Prices sometimes are badly shaken by a sales decline, and customers expect and readily find bargains. In such an environment, no seller can raise price. Indeed he is almost certainly going to be forced to join the parade downward. Thus, recognition that a product is in decline does not itself call for a price change. What might occasion a change in price is a shift in market circumstances as a result of drop in demand, whether it be in higher inventories, more severe competition, or the attitude of customers toward the product. It is in the effects of the particular sales decline on other market circumstances that the price-setter must look for his clues to whether price should be changed.

Selecting the amount of price change. Is the magnitude of price changes suitable for declining products different from that suitable for products in their prime? More specifically, should a price-setter raise prices by large amounts or reduce them by large amounts simply because a product's sales have changed downward over some period? The answer would seem to be affirmative, as a general rule. If consumers generally are aware of the decline in sales, they may recognize the probable increase in the producer's costs and expect a rise in price. Others will view the increased supply relative to demand as an occasion for a major price reduction; they will expect price reductions and bring strong pressure on sellers to offer them.

Making changes in sales and marketing arrangements. As indicated earlier, a good marketing executive rarely changes a single marketing instrument; instead, he makes combinations of changes. Accordingly, when the sales of a product begin to slacken, a marketing executive generally finds that it would be appropriate to change more than price. In particular, changes in one or more of the following might be expected: (1) the number and nature of resellers who carry the product, (2) the quantity of the product offered (that is, the weight, volume, or number of items included in the package), (3) the delivery arrangements for the product, (4) the number and nature of promotions.

ALTERNATIVE MARKETING STRATEGIES

Marketing executives and price-setters could deal with each declining product on an ad hoc basis and make changes in price as and if they appeared to be indicated by prevailing conditions. They would, however, ordinarily fare much better if they adopted a long-range strategy for the product that was suited to it and the firm's situation and allow that strategy to inform and constrain individual actions. Without such a strategy, the firm would often make moves to achieve some short-run advantage at the sacrifice of a long-range gain.

Suitable marketing strategies for a declining product

There are relatively few logics that a price-setter might adopt to guide his operating decisions regarding declining products. The more impor-

tant of these and their implications and underlying rationale will be
sketched briefly. No effort will be made to relate each strategy to the
particular circumstances for which it is best suited.

Revive the old item. Here the strategy is to learn whatever lessons are
taught by the new product about features lacking in the old one, about
customer valuations, and so on and stem the drop in sales and possibly
regain the ground that was lost. A threat by another product should
challenge management to reevaluate its performance in all phases of the
business. Under severe competitive pressure from a new item, management might be able to effect substantial improvements and occasionally
even innovations that would completely recoup the ground that the
product had lost.

Mine the product. Drain out of the product, as it is, what is left in it
of value. When the product no longer yields benefits commensurate with
its costs, abandon it. Do not invest in further development of it; its day
has past.

Join the new wave rather than fight it. A marketing manager must not
regard the fact that his product is being superseded as a personal and
emotional matter. Generally, the new product is available to him for
production and sale. He should not be led by a false loyalty to the old
product to be tardy in taking on the new one.

Go the new product one better. Do not adopt the new product but make
special efforts to take the product into its next phase.

Recognize when a product has had its day and don't waste time on losers.
Acknowledge that the superseded product will never contribute much
profit and close that chapter expeditiously. Recognize the danger of remaining attached to an old product. Recognize too that many individuals
in the organization may have vested interest in retaining it long after it
ceases to offer benefits. Take the position that it is best to make a clean
break.

Try to turn a product's weakness into a strength. Capitalize on the product's growing unavailability and the lack of attention it receives from
other manufacturers and their resellers. Remain in the business in the
hope that the product will become hard to get and some sizable amount
of demand will endure. Recognize that old items can be profitable, especially if their profitability is computed as the difference between what
the firm would have made if it had dropped the product and what it
could make by exploiting the product cleverly.

The preceding strategies are only a few of a potentially large number. To identify others, we can build a classification system on the important dimensions incorporated in the four listed. Each offers several
choices.

1. Amount of effort devoted to improvement of the existing item: massive, major, modest, slight, none.
2. Company position on the new product: adopt it, don't adopt it.
3. Company attitude toward the old product: hold onto it until it becomes scarce, hold onto it until something better comes along, phase it out gradually, phase it out as quickly as possible, drop it immediately.
4. Attitude toward investment in the old product: reinvest, don't reinvest.

Selecting one of each of the sets of mutually exclusive possibilities produces about eighty strategies, each of which represents a long-range policy that would guide and constrain individual actions. Regrettably, several optimal pricing actions are compatible with each strategy; still, the adoption of a particular strategy rules out certain options with respect to price. For example, the strategy of improving the declining product would usually rule out pricing actions that would depress product price.

ALTERNATIVE PRICING POLICIES FOR DECLINING PRODUCTS

Even as a firm has many choices of strategy with respect to a declining product, so it can select among alternative pricing policies that are subordinate to and derive from its marketing strategy choices. Interestingly, the number of strategies that a management might adopt for declining products is far greater than the number of distinct pricing policies. Apparently price actions are not usually the primary means by which a firm adjusts to a long-run decline in the sale of a product. The following represent the chief pricing policies that a price-setter would have at his disposal:

1. Resist all pressures to lower price, because price reductions will not turn the tide in that situation. Don't raise price if it is feared that customers would resent it.
2. Seize all opportunities to raise price.
3. Lower price sharply to slow the shift of sales to a new product, especially if incrementalist thinking about costs would permit a sharp price cut and if there are major economies from higher levels of operations.
4. Reduce price gradually in proportion to drop in demand or costs. Reduce advertising and research and development, drop extra service, and simplify or cheapen the product to lower costs.

5. Run a special field promotion to stem the sales decline; initiate production of the new item and try to lead its price up; price solely with the goal of injuring the new product and discouraging potential customers from buying it. If the firm is producing the new product also, set price in a way that delays the demise of the declining product until the firm has the capacity to fill the demand for the new one.

Pricing a product whose sales are declining fairly rapidly

When a product is declining in sales fairly rapidly but is expected to stabilize at a level that would support several enterprises and at least several current producers are expected to drop it, it is probably the most common of all products in decline. In this category we find important differences of the kind suggested earlier. We could use as our prototype a pharmaceutical that has been superseded by new improved medication but nevertheless continues to be prescribed by many physicians. Railroads, urban transportation systems, propeller-driven aircraft, motion-picture theaters, window shades, automobile radios, and soap powder might also serve as examples—each poses unique problems. But, in general, how should a price-setter proceed in such cases?

First he will want to forecast carefully the rate of sales decline, the number of firms that will drop the item, when the other firms will drop the item, and the level at which sales will stabilize. We will assume that he has concluded that sales in, say, five years will still be large enough to support several firms. Second, he must assess—and possibly do some research into—the strength of customer commitment to the product in the face of forces that are causing the general sales decline. Third, he will want to forecast the demand for his own brand while taking account of the market developments that are expected.

He will then elect a price strategy that is suited to his firm under the conditions he has forecast. If his management is determined to remain in the business and hopes to make attractive profits as other firms withdraw from it, he will try to maintain price during the early stage of fairly rapid decline and try to raise it thereafter. However, he will usually try to postpone any price increase until other firms leave the market lest they delay their exit. A price increase must therefore be carefully timed. The price-setter might encourage some resellers who carry his product to drop it and thus concentrate resale of the item in a few reseller hands. By designating certain wholesalers as sources of hard-to-get items, he could spare other wholesalers the need to carry them and also generate demand enough that the remaining wholesalers would find it worth their while to carry and even promote the declining product.

Ordinarily, a price-setter will settle for avoiding any price reduction for this type of product in decline. However, he may be able to bring about a price increase. Ordinarily the opportunity to do so arises only when the decline in sales continues for a substantial period after many manufacturers have stopped producing the product and most distributors are complaining about low profits and volume. Under such circumstances the distributors may be able to get general agreement for and cooperation from all members of the trade in a price increase. When that has been done, consumers have little recourse and, in time, they come to accept the higher price.

When the sale of a product is declining rapidly and is expected to drop too low to sustain an economically viable enterprise, the product has actually been superseded by products that are clearly superior. The declining product is bought only by persons who don't know better but are certain to find out before long. When the declining product is bought by firms for their own use, the amount of time that will elapse before orders for the old product virtually disappear will be very short. If the customers are individuals, the disappearance of a superseded product usually is slow but is greatly accelerated by the actions of resellers, who generally do not see why they should carry an inferior product when they can carry its successor. They welcome an opportunity to release space and capital for new products and are reluctant to have their customers accept a now-inferior product when they can supply a better one.

How should a price-setter handle a product whose sales are rapidly declining? He finds distributors and retailers in large numbers dropping the product, a few manufacturers who have stopped making it, and some executives in his own firm who are proposing that it be dropped, especially if the firm already offers the product that supersedes it. Some general principles and questions apply to such products and firms.

☐ The firm may have strong reasons for giving up production of the old product at some particular time. If so, the pricing decision will usually be considered subordinate to the decision about when to stop production.

Reasons for producing a declining product that yields little or no profit for a fairly long time could include (1) fear that a decision to drop a product would upset stockholders, resellers, and so on, (2) desire to avoid labor difficulties in already sensitive plants, (3) the belief that a hard core of users of the product will remain and can be served for a long time at a profit.

Possible reasons for wishing to terminate a declining product even faster than the decline in sales would suggest are that (1) the company can make excellent use of the resources that would be released by dropping the product and (2) management wants to create a showing of strong action to allay stockholder fear of complacency.

☐ After the decision has been made to drop a product—a decision that should usually not be publicized—the firm must calculate the tangible and intangible costs of continuing to handle the product. It could possibly drag out the sale of the product for a long time by building sizable inventories before stopping production altogether if that should seem advantageous. It could also wash its hands of the product by offering dramatic price reductions on it while its sales are still fairly high but declining. It could pursue a middle course and continue to handle the product for some time but set a fairly early termination date for sale of the product, as well as a termination date for production.

☐ The price set on the declining product is likely to influence sales of the replacement product. The price-setter should recognize that interrelation as well as the fact that his price for the old product will affect the price that rival firms charge for it.

☐ Underlying a price decision on a declining product is a forecast of sales and the attitudes and actions of the many parties involved. One scenario has the producers and resellers who have dropped the old product in favor of the new one taking strong action to divert sales from the old product for the customer's own benefit. Since, as we are assuming, the facts are very much on their side, they are likely to be quite successful.

THE TV SET ILLUSTRATION: A HYPOTHETICAL DECLINE

Clearly, TV sets are currently products in their prime. Still, we can imagine many circumstances in which they would be partly or wholly superseded and become products in decline. Accordingly, we will assume one such set of circumstances: specifically that both visual images and sound can be produced in the home from tape cartridges. The cartridges, which are obtainable on either a rental or a sale basis, make available all kinds of entertainment—motion pictures, plays, past sporting events, and documentaries. A great many are already on the market and more are being added rapidly. The cartridges can produce large visual images, far larger than those on a TV screen if desired (they are adjustable), and they are free of distortion. They can also produce sound of high quality. Of course, they do not offer current news or sporting events; those remain the province of televison. However, the entertainment side of the TV business is shifting quite quickly to the new device and to the cartridges it uses.

Producers of TV sets, telecasters, producers of TV programs, advertisers, and others have put up a strong fight against the new entertainment system but have not prevented a continued and rapid shift to it. The use of TV sets by households (that is, hours of TV viewed) and sales of sets have fallen substantially in two successive years, and a further substantial decline has been almost universally predicted. Along with the reduced sale of TV sets, motion-picture attendance has fallen sharply.

Now let us place ourselves in the position of a price-setter for one of the major producers of TV sets and explore how and whether to adjust the prices of our sets to take account of the market developments. We will assume that our firm has already entered upon the production of the new device and is even considering the production of cartridges on selected subjects for educational purposes. We will not discuss the pricing problems associated with the new item but will consider only the price decisions related to TV sets, although the two are somewhat interrelated. We will further assume that the firm expects to remain in the TV set business, because TV, in some form, will continue to be the chief medium for visual news and sports. Also, TV sets will continue to be owned and viewed by almost every family, and the company cannot leave the TV business and hope to remain among the big names in major appliances.

A second strategic decision that might be required of top management is whether it wishes to speed a shake-out of the TV set industry or avoid any general market disruption. A convincing case could be made for either strategy; we will assume that the second is adopted because the pricing problems it creates are more complex. As already indicated, a two-year substantial drop in sales combined with the general expectation of a continued decline is generally associated with price weakness. What can a large producer do to combat the downward pressures on price in the face of declining demand and poor future prospects?

Most importantly, the firm should avoid contributing to the price decline because, except in highly unusual circumstances, lowering the price will not spur added sales. In all its actions and in the statements of its executives and salesmen, the firm must show a determination to resist price reductions. Even when that policy imposes painful short-term costs—as it almost certainly will from time to time—it should be followed. It could also help those firms that have been injured most by the sales decline to avoid such pressures so severe that they are forced to cut price. Thus a rapid spread of price-cutting may be forestalled.

A sales decline rarely affects all sellers equally, and the financial resources to withstand a drop in sales—and revenues—also vary from firm to firm. Part of such diversity reflects differences in financial resources, which are often associated with the size of the firm. Differences in ability to withstand a sales decline partly depend on the adaptability of the firm's production facilities and the dollar sales volume that the brand can provide for distributors. With a decline in sales, some brands may not provide enough business to induce the better distributors to carry the line, given the alternatives available to them. To return to the central point, a large firm that wishes to prevent a sharp decline in prices often must take measures to protect the weak links in the market—the most vulnerable firms. Its means for helping them are limited, however. Mainly, it must not conduct promotions or take other actions to build its sales by winning business away from such firms. Again, this behavior requires restraint and financial sacrifice, and the large firm would adopt it only in the conviction that it would otherwise suffer even greater injury.

In addition, top management could, in its public and private statements to the top executives of its strong rivals, stress the danger of a sharp break in price that would result from injury to weaker firms. Its purpose would be to discourage other TV producers from pushing vulnerable firms to join in the price cutting out of ignorance. Such statements usually are not effective, however, because they call for financial sacrifice at a time when the firms' profitability has fallen sharply.

A policy of resisting downward pressure on price cannot prevent a decline in profits when sales volume is falling; at best it can reduce the severity of the profit decline. Ordinarily a substantial decline in sales would force some readjustment of the industry in the form of reduced production facilities, lowered employment, and fewer distributors, retailers, and possibly manufacturers.

A manufacturer who adopts the policy of avoiding extreme disruption is trying to slow the adjustment process so that whatever TV sets he sells will bring relatively high rather than low prices. He hopes, of course, that the flow of resources from the TV set industry will be speedy and orderly. That result is most likely to be achieved if the firms that give up the production of TV sets (who are both the most vulnerable and those with the most adaptable facilities and management) are able to move into other fields. Perhaps they will move into the production of the product that has depressed sales of TV sets, but they might enter a quite unrelated field. The firms that intend to remain in the TV industry could minimize downward price pressure by assisting the others to identify and shift into another field, but not by pushing them out of the industry by price cutting.

Once those shifts have brought about a rough equivalence of productive capacity and TV set sales, our hypothetical price-setter presumably will pursue the goal of raising price. His ability to achieve that result will depend partly on his behavior during the period of downward price pressure and outflow of resources from the industry. If he exhibits statesmanship and restraint, he may earn the respect and trust of rivals, who, like himself, probably would welcome a rise in prices.

To bring about a price increase, especially in an industry whose sales have fallen and from which some firms have departed, poses the usual difficulties that occur in getting firms to resist the temptation to profit by picking up customers when their competitors raise price. The temptation is greatest for firms that are feeling strong financial pressure. However, knowledge that a firm that tried to bring about a rise in price would withdraw the price increase speedily, unless it were followed by all rivals, would go far to discourage a yielding to that temptation.

SUMMARY AND CONCLUSIONS

Declining products are of many different kinds and pose very different marketing and pricing problems. Numerous characteristics of such products should govern the choice of marketing strategy and pricing policy. The most important of these are the speed of the expected decline, the level at which sales are likely to stabilize, the number of firms leaving the business, the decline in sales of individual brands, and the strength of customer commitment to the product. The most important decisions involving declining products concern marketing strategy, rather than price; price is one tool, and usually the most effective tool, that firms use to implement their marketing strategy for declining products.

The decision whether to continue to offer the product is crucial. If the decision is to remain in the declining business, the firm has a choice among several marketing strategies: It can seek to revive the old product and build up its sales or simply mine it; it can adopt the new product or even try to develop a substantially improved product that would supersede it. It also has a choice among many pricing policies ranging from a sharp price reduction to slow the decline in sales to a seizing of all opportunities to raise price.

10

Price-Cutting

A PRICE-SETTER'S NIGHTMARE

EARLIER CHAPTERS PRESENTED a structured approach to the pricing of a product line. This chapter applies that approach to the most painful and persistently threatening problem faced by price-setters: price-cutting. An industry that avoids price-cutting is likely to be far more profitable than one that is afflicted with it much of the time. Interestingly, it is not usually clear why one industry has constant price-cutting and another has none; in other words, price-cutting does not appear to be the inevitable result of an industry's structure or circumstances. Rather, it appears to be a behavior of persons that, like others, can be encouraged, suppressed, and perhaps even extinguished.

The following discussion of price-cutting adopts the viewpoint of firms that are threatened by it. It does not consider whether and when a firm should become a price-cutter. Also, it does not consider the social implications of price-cutting.

Price-cutting must be distinguished from price reduction although both look the same to an outsider. The first is intended to draw customers away from rivals, whereas the second is undertaken in the conviction that the entire industry might fare better at lower prices over an extended and indefinite period. Price-cutting is undertaken as a competitive action, whereas price reduction is intended to gain benefits from a favorable customer response.

PRICE-CUTTING AND HOW TO MEET IT

Once price-cutting starts, many firms usually get hurt and few firms, if any, benefit. The moral that emerges is that marketing managers should try to forestall price-cutting by others whenever possible. Often the best way to do so is to treat each case of price-cutting in a way that discourages others from electing that course of action in the future. Here we will discuss situations in which efforts to forestall price-cutting have failed.

A program to cope with a price-cutter includes at least the following elements: detection of price-cutting, a description of the timing, form, magnitude, and locus of the price-cutting, an explanation of the reasons for the price-cutting, the adoption of a basic strategy, and the selection of the initial countermove, if any.

Detection of price-cutting

Whatever the reason for a decline in a firm's sales, the damage suffered usually depends importantly on the speed with which the decline is detected and appropriate action is taken. A firm facing open price-cutting usually knows its sales have declined and why. Secret price-cutting, on the other hand, often escapes detection for some time. Because space is limited, our discussion is confined to open price-cutting.

We start, then, with a firm that unexpectedly and unhappily finds its sales reduced or threatened because a rival firm has reduced its price sharply. Here the detection of open price-cutting poses no difficulties, so the first step that needs discussion is the description of the price-cutting.

Description of price-cutting

Diagnosis rests on full knowledge of the disorder, but what constitutes full knowledge? With respect to price-cutting, the following questions are usually pertinent:

When did the price-cutting start?
In what markets did it begin?
Are the timing and location of the inception of price-cutting associated with particular developments in the market?
How large is the price reduction in each market?
Are there any places where price-cutting has not occurred?
Did secret price-cutting precede open price-cutting? If so, what customers received the secret price cuts?

The description of price-cutting should include a description of the behavior of rivals and customers. Such questions as the following usually should be answered:

How do different types of customers interpret the price cuts?
Which rivals have responded, in what sequence, to the price-cutter's prime move?

Diagnosis of price-cutting

A price-setter's main purpose in diagnosing price-cutting is to determine whether the action is likely to be of limited duration or might continue indefinitely if unchecked. The reduction may originally have been planned as temporary in the expectation that rivals would retaliate sooner or later. In the absence of some response from rivals, the price reduction might become permanent. If the price cut were to last only a short time, any counteraction to it would probably make things worse for all sellers; otherwise, counteraction would probably be needed to bring a difficult situation to an end.

The reasons for price-cutting are of two major types: push and pull. Firms are *pushed* to cut prices by such considerations as these:

1. They need to raise cash.
2. Senior executives must make a showing to top management.
3. The firm's sales are so low that the company must do anything that might help.

Price-cutting in response to such pressures is likely to end as soon as the pressures are gone. That is not true of price reductions to which a firm is drawn in the belief that it will increase its profitability if it lowers price indefinitely or if it adopts the price strategy of undercutting its rivals. The retailer who goes discount is an example of *pull* price-cutting, and the lowering of price by a retailer to raise cash represents price-cutting under pressure.

A seller facing a price cutter who is clearly seeking to meet a short term financial difficulty might be well advised to facilitate the price-cutter's attainment of his goal. "Let him get out of trouble and get his price back up as soon as possible." A price-cutter who apparently has adopted price-cutting as a long-range strategy can—and usually will—injure most or all of his rivals whether he succeeds or fails. His rivals can best end the injury that the price-cutter is inflicting on them by refusing to accept it. They will try to make price-cutting an unprofitable price strategy.

Thus, whereas push-based price-cutting usually calls for no counter-measures at all from rivals, price-cutting in response to pulls usually requires rapid, resolute counteractions.

Chief reasons for price-cutting

The following reasons for price-cutting are of the push type:

1. The firm urgently needs to raise cash because its sales have been disappointingly low, it has suffered reverses on some other products, its investments have been unprofitable, it has overextended itself or taken on too many new activities, or it has been cut off from some usual sources of borrowing.
2. The firm's sales of the product have fallen and thereby caused layoffs and losses because customers don't like the product, a competitor has introduced a more attractive version of the product, or the firm has alienated and lost some of its best distributors.
3. The firm's costs have risen unexpectedly.
4. The firm has sustained extraordinary reverses of some kind; perhaps, some of its equipment has broken down and caused great waste and heavy repair costs.

The following reasons for price-cutting are of the pull type:

1. An unexploited price segment of the market has been discovered.
2. Management has decided to drive out marginal producers.
3. The price-cutter has achieved a substantial reduction in costs of production.
4. Management expects to achieve major production economies by expanding sales.
5. Management believes that larger sales at lower prices would enable the firm to attract higher quality distributors and retailers.

DIFFERING EFFECTS OF PRICE-CUTTING

Price-cutting affects the various parties involved in a business enterprise differently according to the circumstances under which it occurs. If, for example, it is a hasty and ill-advised move taken in desperation, its effects will be quite different from those of a carefully considered and skillfully executed program. Similarly, if it is carried out at a time when most affected parties regard it as timely and appropriate and in their interest, the responses will be greatly different than when it is widely believed to be ill advised and exploitative. Nevertheless, some rough generalizations can be made about the reactions to price-cutting of different parties to the pricing process. Even more important, we can raise some important questions that generally go unasked. Once they are asked, they suggest lines of thinking and actions that should lead to better price decisions.

Responses of ultimate customers

Price-cutting almost always is initiated in an effort to win customers away from rivals. When a manufacturer cuts prices with the intent that the price reduction will reach the ultimate customer, he seeks to make his brand relatively more attractive than before and thus draw customers away from other brands. Presumably the customers he will attract are those who are somewhat dissatisfied with their present supplier, and those who are particularly responsive to price appeals because they are temporarily or chronically short of funds, buy at lowest prices as a matter of principle, put a symbolic value on getting a bargain, or actually could not buy the product otherwise.

Of course, the number of customers who would shift to the price-cutter depends on (1) the frequency with which the product is purchased, (2) the timing of the reduction, and (3) whether the product can be easily stored if it is purchased well in advance of use.

Now, the price-cutter would normally attract some new customers through brand-switching and what is called attrition. We could assume that group to be, say, 5 to 10 percent of all the price-cutter's customers during any period. The price-cutter would want to ask how that group would be affected by a price reduction on the assumption that it would react differently than other customers. In addition, he would get some proportion of completely new customers, people who were purchasing the product for the first time.

The price-cutter must take special account of the effect of his price action on his present customers. He should usually distinguish between those who feel a fairly strong tie to his brand and those who have no strong desire to own his brand rather than another and could easily be drawn away. How would these two extreme types of customer react to price-cutting?

Persons who are going to patronize a firm anyway can be expected to be delighted when that firm cuts its price sharply. And it appears that they usually are. Several possible negative reactions should be recognized, however, and special efforts should be made to avoid them. Some customers may be afraid that the price-cutter may be about to leave the business and would therefore not be available to service the product, or that the merchandise sold is not of the usual quality.

One of the effects of a sizable price cut—an intended effect—is to attract the attention of potential customers and get them to change their attitudes and behavior. But although it is designed to alter the behavior of persons who patronize other firms, a price cut is likely to cause the usual patrons of a firm to ask questions and make interpretations about matters that they would usually settle by habit. The price-cutter must expect some of the hypotheses considered by his usual customers to be adverse to the making of a purchase.

Effects on resellers

When the price of a brand has been cut—and particularly when a brand has evidently become one that stresses the appeal of low price—resellers are likely to have conflicting reactions. Many will expect to increase their sales volume and profitability. Underlying that expectation will be the conviction that price appeals are very effective with their customers. Others may be reluctant to be associated with a brand that features price appeals because of the likelihood that many of their customers will regard the brand as low in quality. In particular, they may fear that their own company image will be adversely affected—that is, customers will view them as specialists in low-priced mediocre merchandise. One consequence to be feared is that they will begin to attract a different and less desirable type of clientele—people who are mainly concerned with low price and who have little concern with good quality or service.

Other aspects of price-cutting must be considered in assessing the effect on resellers. Typically, price-cutting means a reduction in reseller margin. Some resellers are required to accept a reduction in reseller margin. Some resellers are required to accept a reduction in percent margin (which means a still lower dollar margin) on the ground that the manufacturer is accepting an even greater reduction and they will be more than compensated by increased sales volume. Even when his percent margin is unchanged, however, a reseller obtains a smaller dollar margin on each price-cut item he sells. Any reseller who views his market as essentially fixed in total size views a change in margins as extremely adverse to his interests.

Another very sensitive issue is the loss in value of reseller inventory.

Price reductions ordinarily are made when reseller inventories are heavy. If the manufacturer does not share in the inventory loss—which resellers would ordinarily view as having been inflicted on them arbitrarily by him—their response to a substantial cut in prices is likely to be negative and hostile.

Resellers have other typical reactions to price-cutting. They are apt to feel threatened by the inception of price-cutting because it may spread and deepen, and reduce profits in all branches of the industry. All experienced resellers have seen one price cut provoke retaliation until the price-cutting grew in scale and spread to other firms. Most resellers welcome stability, or at least fear the consequences of a major change.

Effects on rivals

As indicated earlier, a firm almost never welcomes price-cutting by its rivals. At a minimum, price-cutting reduces either sales or profit margins. It creates considerable uncertainty; at least it threatens a steady loss of business, and it may even threaten survival. It strongly discourages investors and lenders from becoming involved with the industry. It discourages resellers who had considered taking on the product whatever the brand. Now they will question the profitability in general: some who would have entered the business if price-cutting had not occurred may now decide against it.

Another effect of price-cutting is often overlooked. A price-cutter ordinarily prods rival managements to reassess their policies and procedures. As a result, the rivals often make substantial changes in their mode of operation that result in increased efficiency. The net consequence is to increase the vulnerability of the price-cutter.

STRATEGIES FOR VICTIMS OF PRICE-CUTTING

Price-cutting does not have equal or even proportional effects on other firms. Therefore, the strategies appropriate for different firms facing a price-cutter vary mainly with the impact of the price-cutting on sales, but other factors must be considered as well. Some firms possess financial resources sufficient to withstand a decline in revenues for a considerable period. Others are cash-short; a reduction in their income due to price-cutting by a rival can put them in a serious financial difficulty. A strategy suitable for such a firm must somehow include a way of meeting the pressing needs for cash flow.

Some top managements and boards of directors strictly limit countermeasures to price-cutting. They fear that executives will react emotionally, and that is why they will not permit a speedy retaliation. Other firms place no such constraints on the responses of their management to price-cutting. Thus no single strategy would be suitable for all firms confronting a price-cutter. What alternative price/marketing strategies are available? It will be useful to sort them out by whether they are suitable to combat push-based or pull-based price-cutting.

Push-based price-cutting

The main strategy choice for a firm whose sales have been reduced or threatened by price-cutting is between seizing the opportunity to eliminate a rival in distress and helping him to overcome his present difficulties with minimum disturbance and cost to the industry. The first strategy almost certainly does mean disruption of the industry, with consequences that are highly uncertain; the second may avoid serious upset to established relations and industry practice—though that usually is far from certain—but obliges the firm to accept a decline in sales for an indefinite period. Neither alternative is alluring, but a firm confronted by price-cutting would do well to face the unhappy alternatives and adhere to its choice consistently. Either strategy depends for its effectiveness on the price-cutter's understanding it and also on the firm's determination to follow it despite costs and difficulties.

The wisdom of bailing out a rival who frequently gets into financial difficulties because of faulty management can certainly be questioned. And the choice of strategy to eliminate a price-cutter or aid him to survive often revolves around his survival capacity. A rival who is very weak usually will eliminate himself by his own shortcomings unless he receives help, as by his rivals adopting the second reaction to his price-cutting. But he will barely survive for a time and will ultimately expire.

A third possible strategy choice is to act as if nothing had changed, even though a significant rival is actually making a serious bid to win away a sizable number of customers. It is difficult, however, to view that as a strategy; for the logic behind it is apparently that it obviates the need to deviate from a chosen course, and not that it might achieve some particular benefit for either the firm or the industry. The most important benefit to be sought in a push-based price-cutting situation is either the elimination of a rival who is disruptive to the trade and an added source of competition or the avoidance (or at least a minimization) of disturbance and unrest.

Pull-based price-cutting

Firms facing rivals who select price-cutting as a long-range marketing strategy also enjoy a choice of strategies. Again the intent is mainly to minimize injury rather than augment sales and profits. In selecting one of the possible strategies, a marketing executive must rely heavily on his diagnosis of the situation and, especially, the capabilities and resources of the price-cutter. By his choice, the price-cutter is a large potential threat, especially to the firms he may decide to attack. Not frequently a price-cutter will pick his victims. He will concentrate on attracting the customers of vulnerable rivals, to whom he could represent a threat to survival.

The choices in strategy range from "concede nothing and prove that the policy won't work" to "you can't stop success." Those strategy choices, like the alternatives for firms facing push-based price-cutting, essentially represent choices of objectives. They should be based on an assessment of the resources, weaknesses, and capabilities of the contending parties. In other words, they represent substrategies—subgoals combined with an underlying logic for achieving them.

THE TV SET ILLUSTRATION

Now let us apply some of the notions discussed in the preceding pages to the TV industry. Assume that a small manufacturer of TV sets, Company A, unexpectedly reduces prices of all of its models by 12 percent and advertises that general reduction to the retail trade. We will adopt the position of the price-setter for a medium-size producer of TV sets who also manufactures other major appliances.

He first received word that his competitor was about to cut prices from one of his distributors, who was told by the distributor for Company A in his area, or from a reporter for the newspaper in which the price cut was about to be advertised to the retail trade, or possibly from a friend who works for Company A. His most urgent aim was to find out what Company A was up to and why. He therefore asked his regional salesmen and distributors in all areas where Company A operates to get all possible information about the imminent price cuts; when, on what items, on what quantities, and how long. They are expected to exploit all potentially useful sources of information available to them, but the two most likely to be useful are personal acquaintances who work for Company A or for resellers of its products and important customers who also carry A's products. As a rough generalization, once a manufacturer informs his own sales force of a significant market move, the move will quite quickly become known to most of the trade.

So now he has clear evidence that Company A is going to reduce its prices by 12 percent on all its TV items and that the action is to become effective in 10 days. As a price-setter for a rival manufacturer, how should he react to that finding?

First, he would consider the possibility that he could discourage Company A from carrying out its price reduction. Second, he would try to understand the reasons for Company A's action. Let us assume that he quickly informs top management about the impending price cut. He assumes that any effort to forestall Company A's move must take place at the very top level. One possibility would be the issuance of a public statement to the trade press that any price cut would be especially ill-advised at this time accompanied by a commitment to distributors to match any competitor's price reduction. Next he has this problem: How can he uncover the reason for Company A's decision to reduce prices across the board by 12 percent? (He does not ask why the reduction was 12 percent instead of 10 or 15, he asks why it was so large and so general. He assembles the following kinds of information.

> Company A's recent sales experience in TV sets.
> Company A's recent sales of other significant items in its line.
> Recent management or ownership changes.
> Public statements by high-level executives.
> Recent borrowings by the company.
> Recent gains or losses of distribution.

Much information is fairly readily available from published sources, for trade publications try to keep abreast of such developments. Also, the company ordinarily conducts formal market research studies and receives reports from its field salesmen, regional sales managers, and distributors, who in turn obtain information from their own salesmen, retailers, and retail salesmen about significant shifts in sales by brands. If our price-setter were efficiently organized to perform his function, he would already have in hand and would have partly distilled most of the information he required to make a diagnosis of Company A's projected price cut. Indeed, he might have assembled enough evidence to have anticipated a price move from Company A.

A price-setter usually will know whether a rival is hurting and is taking drastic action to combat a painful market situation, is being pushed by its board of directors or top management to get added volume, increase market share, and achieve growth, or has—possibly under the influence of managerial shift—adopted a new low-profit-margin, high-volume marketing strategy. We have already discussed the kinds of things that the price-setter would consider in reaching a conclusion on those points. Hopefully, he would recognize the possibility that he has misjudged the situation and will remain receptive to additional evidence that might alter his diagnosis.

Again let us assume the most usual situation: The price-setter and his colleagues have concluded that Company A is hurting for cash to finance its operations because of an unexpected difficulty in borrowing funds for working capital. A general tightness of credit has curtailed the availability of funds to small and medium-size firms most. Company A's TV business has not shown particular weakness, and sales of its other major product lines have been holding up pretty well. In short, it appears that Company A would not have cut its TV set prices if its usual borrowing ability had not been impaired. It also appears that the company will restore its prices once it has met its working capital needs, which it seeks to do by inducing its distributors—and they in turn the retailers—to build up their inventories of sets.

Given that diagnosis, the price-setter is likely to yield to the near-inevitable; that is, he will accept the fact that Company A will do whatever is required to raise the capital it needs and will probably do so by loading up its distributors. Also, he might conclude that the added volume that Company A must have to meet its capital needs is too small to affect his company's sales significantly. Finally, he might conclude that his main rivals will reason as he does and will not fight Company A in this price move. He might also reason that the price cut will not be passed along to many ultimate customers; for the relatively strong demand for TV sets in retail markets makes a price reduction unnecessary.

The preceding assumptions are highly simplified, suggesting that the price-setter should refrain from changing price. Now let us complicate matters a little. The price-setter is convinced that one large manufacturer, Company B, is likely to overreact to the price-cutting—that is, he will expect a large shift of business from *his* firm to Company A and therefore will decide to match the price cut. As a result of this move by Company B, our price-setter expects a chain reaction of Companies C, D, and E responding much as Company B responded. He believes that the combined effects of a 12 percent reduction in price by Companies A, B, C, D, and E will substantially reduce his sales unless he also lowers price. Further, he doubts that those companies will be able to raise prices when one of them tries to do so. More important, he wonders whether Company A will be able to meet its needs for working capital if Companies B, C, D, and E match its initial price reduction. He may therefore see it as vital to discourage Companies C, D, E, and especially B from matching Company A's 12 percent price reduction.

Pull-based price-cutting

The hypothetical example just discussed assumes a push-based case of price-cutting. It does not raise the many difficult if not insoluble issues that firms confront when a rival, especially a very efficient producer and marketer, starts to cut price—possibly in the expectation that it will prove to be a profitable long-range strategy.

Accordingly, let us assume that the chief executive of a medium-size producer of TV sets, Company R, has concluded that his firm produces at lower cost than the major companies and that its marketing costs are as low or lower than all but possibly one of the largest producers. In the past, Company R has charged prices just about equal to those charged by the largest firms in the belief that the latter would contest any serious effort that it would make to grow at their expense. With its new conviction that it enjoys an enduring cost advantage over all other TV producers, based on superior methods and better management, its top executive has decided to launch a concerted program to become one of the three largest TV set producers within four years. He believes that substantial economies in both production and marketing would be achieved at a larger volume of sales and that the firm would also enjoy greater security if its market were broader. Also, as one of the few largest TV set producers, Company R could hope to add other product lines that would benefit from its strong position in the TV set industry. Top management of Company R is willing to sustain a sizable drop in profits to achieve its sales goal, but it does not expect its profits to disappear altogether as a result of its price-cutting program.

Part of Company R's program calls for an expansion of productive facilities, including the production of some components that the firm is currently purchasing. The expansion is to be started some time after the company cuts prices. The reasons for the price-cutting and the firm's intentions to enter other parts of the major appliance business and to expand its production facilities were all announced in the trade press and were the subject of interviews with Company R's top executives and editorial comment.

What would the price-setter for a large and profitable TV set producer do in the face of such a move by Company R? We will assume that his firm, Company T, is fairly profitable because it enjoys a good reputation with both ultimate customers and resellers; it has a strong body of distributors who are quite loyal. Its production costs have, for a long time, been no lower than average and usually above average. Also, its marketing outlays, aimed at sustaining the firm's strong brand image, are about average for the industry on a per unit basis. (They would be above average were it not for the firm's large sales volume.)

Company T's top management is prepared to concede that Company R is a very effective producer and enjoys significantly lower unit production costs on the order of 10 percent and marketing costs that are slightly lower than Company T's. In discussions among themselves following Company R's price announcement and the surrounding discussions in the press, Company T's top executives agree that Company R is a very effective organization that will inevitably grow substantially unless its managerial strength is somehow dissipated. Several executives think that Company R would have been wise to maintain prices and enjoy very high per unit profits while growing slowly. Most, however, think that they would do just what Company R is doing; they would try to turn their lower-cost advantage into a basis for rapid growth in both TV sets and other major appliances. They say that Company R cannot be prevented from becoming one of the largest factors in the TV set industry and that Company T's aims should be as follows:

☐ Company R should take no more business from Company T than Company T's proportion of the total TV set business; that is, all companies should share proportionately in the loss of business to Company R. At least, Company T should not lose more ground than other firms.

☐ The reduction in the price of TV sets should be held to a minimum. That would mean that Company T would surely not lower its own price and would try to discourage other TV set producers from lowering their prices.

☐ Company R would not expand its production facilities at a very rapid rate.

☐ Company R would be encouraged to raise its prices and temper its striving for growth with concern for profitability to the extent that it could be done legally.

Several executives emphasize the need to discourage Company R from expanding its productive capacity. They say that ideally it should be encouraged to purchase existing facilities, perhaps by acquiring an established company. Otherwise, the industry might be burdened with overcapacity for a long time. They point out that Company R also would gain by limiting the industry's production capacity. They hope mainly to prevent Company R from expanding its production facilities, and they call for the development of a market strategy designed to achieve that end.

What should the marketing vice president for Company T do under those circumstances? To answer that question it would help to ask what he would say to the top executive of Company R if he could converse with him freely and frankly and legally, although he might be able to find legal and indirect ways to achieve the same results. These are among the things he would presumably want to say:

☐ Company R should not add to the productive capacity of the industry.

☐ Company R will be allowed to grow, but only at a reasonable pace.

☐ You must not attach our best distributors and markets.

☐ Your being allowed to grow is contingent on your behaving responsibly and showing concern for the long-run health of the industry.

☐ You have the power and the willingness to use it to protect the long-run health of the industry from disruption, and you could enlist support from other firms in the industry toward that end. If you do not accept the first four conditions, you will not be allowed to offer a significant price incentive to customers. That is, we will match your low price.

A price-cutter's success is highly dependent on his rivals' allowing him to pursue his chosen strategy. If his rivals are prepared to pay the price, they can even make it impossible for him to offer customers a price advantage. For example, they could announce their readiness to match any price that he offers or to sell for slightly less than his price. Thus, they are not without options.

Firms that confront a low-cost rival who has adopted a long-run strategy of price-cutting must compare the costs they will incur if the price-cutter carries out his program without opposition with the costs of opposing him. To do so they must identify courses of action that might frustrate him and then assess the effect and cost of each course. Again, the price-setter faces extremely difficult forecasting tasks and cannot escape them except by default.

What alternative courses of action are open to firms that oppose a rival who elects a price-cutting strategy based on superior production

listed several: (1) offer to match the price-cutter's price,
or less than the price-cutter, (3) inform the price-cutter of
prevent him from growing by all possible means, (4) in-
-cutter that he will be limited in his rate of growth, (5)
devo.. ces that might be consumed in matching the price cuts to
superior service, product improvements, and additional advertising, (6)
provide special services to resellers, (7) increase the firm's own reseller
margins. In general the strategy is to counter with benefits for customers
and resellers that cannot be readily matched.

SUMMARY

Most products ultimately are outmoded by others or decline as customer
tastes change. When they fall into decline, they pose pricing problems
that are markedly different from those posed by either products in their
prime or new products. The pricing problems usually become closely involved with a decision to retain or drop the products. Often a firm is
well advised to offer a declining product at a loss for a period of time in
the expectation that its sales will rise as other firms leave the business. (It
can, by its actions, speed the departure of other firms from the business.)
Very few products disappear altogether in a short period; declining
products can offer attractive profit opportunities for a few firms.

One form of decline of a product occurs when a rival tries to increase its sales sharply by price-cutting, whether under the pressure of
financial necessity or in the belief that price-cutting represents a profitable long-run marketing strategy. When price-cutting occurs, other firms
will almost invariably be injured. Their actions should be aimed at mini-
mizing the injury and reducing the probability of recurrences.

No firm can insulate itself from damage if a sizable rival makes a determined effort to increase its share of the market. Recognition that some
injury is inevitable will help a price-setter adopt an effective policy to
combat a price-cutter. His belief that he can somehow avoid injury, or
that it just isn't fair that his firm should be damaged because of the price-
cutter's stupidity or avarice, can delay effective counteraction. Counteraction usually requires communication with the price-cutter, customers,
and rival sellers through price offers and statements to the press. Those
messages must signify a determination to limit the growth of the price-
cutter, to equalize his impact on various firms in the industry, and to
prevent a major expansion in the productive capacity of the industry.
The effectiveness of counteractions varies and depends on the apparent

readiness of those injured by price-cutting to limit the price-cutter's inroads. Some price-cutters are quick to learn; others take a long time to understand the signals that are sent to them.

Price-cutting often proves to be highly expensive and unsuccessful to price-cutters. When some firms in a market have had a painful experience with price-cutting, other are reluctant to try that pricing strategy. But it is only when some firms have been willing to oppose price-cutters at cost and risk to themselves that price-cutting usually fails. When firms just wait for others to do the opposing, the price-cutter will usually have made significant and irreversible inroads before effective counteraction can take place.

The Pricing Process

A SUMMARY

IN THE PRECEDING CHAPTERS an executive's approach to the setting of price was said to depend on where the product is in its life cycle. New products, especially those that embody a new concept and do not draw their customers from other products, entail so much uncertainty that their pricing problems are almost different in kind. Products in decline pose strategic problems very different from those posed by either new products or products in their prime. Despite those differences, and they are major, fundamental similarities are present in the pricing of all three types of product. In all cases a price-setter will generally seek a reasonable starting point—a provisional price—for his deliberations. He will then conduct an incremental analysis the chief elements of which are:

1. An identification of the firm's marketing and pricing objectives.
2. An identification of the key parties to the firm's pricing process.
3. The identificaton of alternative pricing substrategies.
4. An identification of the significant effects of price changes on each party, including tangible and intangible and present and future consequences.
5. A forecast of the consequences of each attractive and feasible price move together with its associated changes in other marketing instruments.

6. An evaluation of all the consequences—favorable and unfavorable—to determine whether the net effect of the price move would be in the firm's interest.

A price-setter's success with incremental analysis depends upon his knowing how price can and does affect the different parties to the business process and how those effects relate to the attainment of the firm's objectives. Almost as difficult and quite as important as the forecasting of the diverse consequences of price change is an evaluation of net impact on the firm—that is, a cost-benefit analysis.

A price analysis can be deficient because the full effects of price changes are not understood or because specific price substrategies have not been developed. At present, most price-setters appear to take account of the short-run tangible (mainly financial) effects of price changes. Also, some price-setters appear to be more concerned with the responses of ultimate customers than with those of resellers and rivals, even when the latter should be given major weight.

As explained in Chapter 7, the incremental approach to setting price should be governed by a set of interrelated ideas that give direction to marketing and pricing executives and that represent the directives and constraints of owners and directors. Those that affect the price-setter and other functional specialists in the marketing department are: (1) the firm's objectives, (2) the line of business in which the owners, top management, or both wish to engage, (3) top management's philosophy and credo, (4) the firm's basic marketing strategy for the product, (5) the firm's target brand image, and (6) pricing substrategies. The absence of the last of these explains much defective price-setting. These ideas both limit the options that the price-setter will consider and direct his thinking to particular options. They also determine the value he will place on each of the consequences of his price decisions, for the valuation of consequences is possible only in terms of objectives.

This brief description of the pricing process might appear to contradict the thesis presented in the opening chapter that no formula will grind out a correct price. True, we have described a *process* that would apply to virtually all goods and services; but it is not a *formula*, and it will not produce a single result. It certainly is not argued here that all price-setters can apply this form of incremental analysis and arrive at the same price. Far from it. Major differences in price conclusions can be expected from price-setters who vary in skills and experience. Another thesis presented in the first chapter is that a price-setter needs to be skilled in many business disciplines—particularly finance, economics,

marketing, and statistics—and would benefit greatly from long experience with his markets. There is much that price-setters can learn—
beyond incremental analysis—and many ways in which they can distinguish themselves from those with lesser skills. Thus persons who master
everything contained in the preceding chapters can still perform very
poorly as pricers of their product.

One of the skills and abilities that price-setters certainly need is the
ability to understand and forecast the effects of price changes. In addition, they need to know how price and other marketing actions interact—that is, whether they combine synergistically or are redundant or
self-canceling. One other requirement for success deserves particular emphasis: Price-setters should quickly recognize unusual developments in
their market. Normality is perhaps the rarest of market conditions.

In what ways do the tasks faced by individual price-setters differ
most? Do individuals facing particular pricing tasks need special skills
and aptitudes? What do some price-setters need to know that others can
do without? Three possible answers deserve consideration: (1) differences in the key parties to the business process, (2) special market arrangements, and (3) product differences.

The pricing of certain products or by certain firms requires attention to special parties to the pricing process. For example, in the pricing
of some items, government figures prominently as a customer or a regu-
lator. During periods of price controls, of course, almost all firms are
concerned with government to some degree. The price-setter's colleagues
can also represent key considerations in price decisions. Customers and
rival producers are other occasionally important parties. As was said in
the discussion of consequence nets, a price-setter must be quite explicit
about his firm's objectives. As to these special parties, he must identify
the things he can do with price that will influence them in ways that help
to achieve his firm's objectives. More specifically, he must ask what he
could accomplish by altering price or price arrangements that would influence the regulatory authorities in ways favorable to his firm's attainment of its objectives of long-run profits, survival, and growth. What
consequences of price and price arrangements are in conflict with the attainment of those objectives?

Many price-setters must take special account of unique market circumstances: price-leadership patterns, personal ties between members of
buying and selling firms, reciprocity relations with major customers, a
limited number of huge customers, and government ownership of large
supplies. Price decisions must then rest on a thorough understanding of
the circumstances.

One question discussed briefly in an earlier chapter requires further discussion in this connection: Do price-setters need to know different and special things if their products are consumer goods rather than industrial products? Are the required skills, aptitudes, and experiences different for persons responsible for, say, pricing durable products than for persons pricing perishable products? Every product and every brand faces pricing problems that are unique to some degree, even as the process by which an executive would reason about price is much the same regardless of the product or service. Many intelligent and well-informed persons maintain that price-setters need to know very different kinds of things and should behave quite differently according to the type of product for which they are responsible. Let us take a close look at this line of argument.

Do, and should, special features of products affect decisions about price? The answer surely is affirmative. But do the special product features require significant changes in the process by which an executive should arrive at price? The answer to that question is not so clear. Every executive believes that his product and his particular situation are different and special; most executives also believe that generalizations that apply to, say, a pricing decision for packaged goods would not be valid for a major appliance or for a consumer service. And they certainly doubt that the same principles apply to the pricing of a large industrial product. Indeed, executives who would travel far to hear a discussion of the pricing of consumer goods would not walk across the street to hear a learned discussion of the pricing of industrial products.

The purpose here is not to demonstrate that the approach to pricing developed in the preceding chapters applies to all products. Instead, it is to examine and appraise the importance of product characteristics that are widely believed to make a difference in how a price-setter should approach his price decisions. Although the following discussion is confined to products in their prime, it probably applies almost as well to both new products and products in decline.

Several classifications of products were presented in earlier chapters. They differed because the characteristics selected as the basis for classification were related to different kinds of pricing problems. Here we will discuss product differences that many marketing specialists believe to be crucial in pricing and see whether they might make a difference to price-setters. What, then, are the main distinctions made among products by persons interested in pricing?

The chief distinction found among products in pricing discussions is that between consumer and industrial products. The distinction is based

on the economic role of the customer; it distinguishes household consumers from industrial buyers. Other classes of buyer could be distinguished for pricing purposes on the basis of economic role: institutional
buyers, middlemen, and manufacturers of original equipment might also
be treated separately. Let us consider why the role of the buyer is considered so important for pricing purposes.

Household buyers are widely believed to differ from industrial
buyers in the following respects: They possess far less information, devote less time and attention to making a selection among alternatives, are
less intelligent and professional in making buyer decisions, are under
weaker pressure to buy economically, and are more emotional in appraising alternatives. In addition, industrial buyers are believed to know *why*
they are buying—it is directly or indirectly for resale at a profit—
whereas ultimate customers buy to satisfy some desire that may be fleet-
ing, if not frivolous. Those characteristics lead many people to the conclusion that you may be able to overcharge housewives, but you cannot
fool purchasing agents.

Many exceptions can be found to the preceding generalizations.
Some industrial products are very simple, whereas certain consumer
products are highly complex; some household buyers devote a great deal
of time and attention to particular purchases, whereas purchasing agents
responsible for buying thousands of items often rely on near-mechanical
means of supplier selection. Sometimes ultimate customers are far better
informed than industrial buyers and are under terrific pressure from
their families to be economical and efficient. In other words, none of the
listed differences between industrial and consumer goods buyers holds
for all products.

The preceding discussion has not exhausted all of the alleged differences between industrial and consumers' goods as pricing problems.
We have, however, carried the comparison far enough to support several
conclusions:

☐ Whatever the differences that may exist in general between
household and industrial products, they do not exist in many
specific cases.
☐ Differences among products in respect to the kinds of persons
who buy them are so numerous that each product represents a
unique pricing problem. That it is an industrial or consumer
product gives the price-setter little guidance.
☐ The differences among products that matter most to marketing

and pricing executives include a substantial number of characteristics that have no relation to whether the product is a consumer or an industrial product: durable versus nondurable, product versus service, a big ticket versus small ticket, convenience versus specialty. These characteristics are relevant only to the extent that they are somehow associated with the market behavior of parties to the business process.

The product characteristics that have marketing and pricing significance are those that affect the actions of ultimate customers, rivals, resellers, colleagues, suppliers, government, and possibly other parties to the business process. In other words, it is not the product characteristics themselves that are important; instead it is the fact that the product characteristics affect the parties involved in the production, sale, purchase, and logistics of the product. The factors that matter most to price-setters may be related to product characteristics, but certainly not directly or in any simple way. Among the market circumstances that are of particular importance to a price-setter are those that help him to develop consequence nets for the various parties that are deeply involved in his firm's marketing efforts. They include the items listed below and many others. An inspection of those listed indicates that few are directly related to product characteristics—they are about as likely to be present if the product is industrial or consumer. As a result, the price-setter must concern himself with the circumstances in his specific situation.

1. The ultimate customer's desire for the product, and especially his preference for the brand.
2. The ability of target customers to pay for the product.
3. Similarities and differences among ultimate customers in their valuations of the product.
4. Knowledge, bargaining skills, and effort devoted to purchase by ultimate customers.
5. Bargaining power of ultimate customers and the alternatives available to them.
6. The number of rival producers of the item.
7. Rival producer resources and capabilities and willingness to use them aggressively.
8. Rival seller motives and the strategies employed to implement them.
9. The behavior patterns of rival producers singly and as a group.
10. The bargaining power of resellers.

11. The similarity in the skills and resources of available resellers.
12. The aggressiveness of resellers in their dealings with manufac-
    turers.
13. The readiness of resellers to integrate backward or to develop
    private brands.
14. The involvement of governmental agencies in the regulation and
    control of the industry.

To extend the list and group these market circumstances would
carry us far afield from our interest in price-setting. Furthermore, it is
not clear that a catalog of such market circumstances and a discussion of
their potential relevance to pricing decisions would help particularly.
The price-setter's task remains primarily that of identifying parties relevant to the pricing process, understanding his firm's objectives and especially the subobjectives related to price, forecasting the relevant effects of
price changes on those various parties, and evaluating the effects of price
changes on the firm's attainment of its objectives. A catalog of market
characteristics potentially relevant to pricing decisions could suggest considerations that he might otherwise overlook, but ordinarily a price-setter
would know all that would appear on a general-purpose list and many
others besides.

We thus conclude that price-setters need not know different things
according to whether they are responsible for pricing industrial rather
than consumer products. They must familiarize themselves with all of
the parties to the business process and not simply their customers. They
must give equal attention to the nature of their rivals and resellers, possibly to their suppliers and colleagues, and sometimes to government. Any
classification of products that takes account of only one of the affected
parties can be more misleading than helpful. Furthermore, as indicated,
the industrial-consumer distinction does not separate products cleanly on
the basis of the behavior of customers.

One last question that might be raised is related to the special things
that some price-setters may need to know and others do not need to
know: Do price-setters for the same product—but different brands—
need to know the same things? Do price-setters for all brands of toothpaste, autos, shirts, paint, TV sets, and so on need to know essentially
the same things to arrive at price? To make the question more specific,
would the price-setter for a price-leader firm, if there were one, have the
same needs as the price-setter for a small firm in the same market? The
needs of the two surely differ greatly. The price-setter for the leader
firm would essentially set prices on behalf of the industry, whereas the

other would simply follow his lead. The latter essentially delegates his pricing responsibilities to the former.

In the absence of a price leadership situation, the difficulties of arriving at price might move in the opposite direction; that is, the price-setter for a small firm might have a more complicated task than the price-setter for a large one. Ordinarily, smallness of size is highly associated with instability of market; small firms usually find it more difficult to forecast their sales and costs because their past has been more erratic than that of their larger rivals. Also, they are more affected by shifts in the actions and strategies of their large rivals than their large rivals are affected by their own actions. And price-setters for small firms usually have little opportunity to gather data to help with their price decisions. As has been stressed, the price-setter is mainly a forecaster of the consequences of price changes as they occur with respect to all parties to the business process. The firms whose actions have the most unclear effects confront their price-setters with the most difficult tasks. Similarities between price-setting for new products and for small-firm brands can be seen.

In summary, then, we observe that price-setters have responsibilities that vary greatly in complexity and importance. The biggest differences in what they need to know relate to the number of parties to the business process with whom they are concerned. Those who must predict the responses of more parties ordinarily have the more complex task, though some parties are harder to understand than others. The need for special knowledge by a price-setter may also arise from the existence of unusual market arrangements.

Nevertheless, one conclusion that emerges from this analysis of the pricing function is that two approaches are suitable, and perhaps required, for successful price-setting. The first has been termed an incremental analysis of changes from the prevailing price and the second pricing from scratch. The first has a rationale that is quite simple, but its execution is extremely difficult and depends upon a thorough understanding by the price-setter of the behavior and responses of the important parties to the business process. The second is more complex; it requires an implementation of top management directives, constraints, marketing strategy, and policy. But a price-setter need only price from scratch for new products and from time to time for others. The kind of thinking and data underlying the incremental approach outlined here is also at the base of the second approach. Consequently, that is the approach to pricing that can best meet the needs of a large majority of price-setters.

INDEX